MW01293149

RELIGIONLESS SPIRITUALITY

RELIGIONLESS SPIRITUALITY

Paradigm for a Global Spirituality

PATRICK MOONEY

authorHOUSE®

AuthorHouse™ UK Ltd.
1663 Liberty Drive
Bloomington, IN 47403 USA
www.authorhouse.co.uk
Phone: 0800.197.4150

© 2013 by Patrick Mooney. All rights reserved.

Front Cover image by Patrick Mooney

No part of this book may be reproduced, stored in a retrieval system, or transmitted by any means without the written permission of the author.

Published by AuthorHouse   10/08/2013

ISBN: 978-1-4817-9716-0 (sc)
ISBN: 978-1-4817-9715-3 (hc)
ISBN: 978-1-4817-9717-7 (e)

Any people depicted in stock imagery provided by Thinkstock are models, and such images are being used for illustrative purposes only.
Certain stock imagery © Thinkstock.

Because of the dynamic nature of the Internet, any web addresses or links contained in this book may have changed since publication and may no longer be valid. The views expressed in this work are solely those of the author and do not necessarily reflect the views of the publisher, and the publisher hereby disclaims any responsibility for them.

"A God who doesn't fart isn't very interesting," Fr Pat said.

At this point in his lecture, his great nemesis, Miss Prado, a stalwart member of the parish, scraped her chair on the auditorium floor, stood up and walked toward the priest brandishing her ubiquitous small tape recorder. All eyes were fixated on her.

The parishioners had become used to her intrusions. Fr Pat allowed her disruptions to add a spark of excitement and colour to the relevant topic of discussion.

Fr Pat had lived in the parish of St Jude for eleven years. In retrospect it seemed like a life sentence to him Many of his fellow clergy considered his parish the Siberia of the diocese where newly ordained priests were sent to be tested and supervised by the watchful eye of the Pastor. At times he felt that he also had been appointed to test his orthodoxy, as almost immediately upon his appointment, he discovered that the Pastor's beliefs were tinged with Jansenism. He had heard the Pastor preach on numerous occasions that the flesh and the body were evil and should be considered a millstone round the neck of humanity. To give strength to his authoritative preaching, he resorted to quotes from St Augustine, including "Mankind's concupiscence is the cause of all the evil in this world." Besides Augustine, the Pastor often quoted verses from *The Imitation of Christ* by Thomas A. Kempis, such as "Every time I go out into the world and return to the monastery, I come back less a man."

Fr Pat considered it rather ironic that the Pastor, while hating the world, loved every dollar the faithful placed on the offertory plates in the parish. It had taken Fr Pat years to realize that the church, like all corporations, was in the business of making money, and even more excruciatingly, they did so in the name of a man who had no place to lay his head. With Roman approval, the Pastor had been elevated to the rank of Monsignor. The Bishop had nominated him in appreciation for his faithful witness to the diocese and his monetary support for his bishopric.

Miss Prado had become an extension of the Pastor's stewardship. Everywhere she went Fr Pat could smell, see, and hear the Monsignor. She was his watchdog, omnipresent not only in the church but also in the rectory, where he had met her at ungodly hours, even in the upstairs hallway. Once at about three o'clock in the morning, she had called him on the rectory intercom: "Prompto, emergency in the hospital. Prompto, emergency." As Fr Pat dressed himself, he wondered why it was she and not the telephone operator who called him. How or why did she have access to the rectory's internal intercom?

"She didn't even have the courtesy to call me by my name, and what the hell is she doing in the rectory at this hour of the morning?" he said to himself. He put the holy oils in his coat pocket almost mechanically, and his mind wandered. "Could it be?" he mumbled to himself. "Oh, God, no, it couldn't be. He's too much a bloody *Jansenist* for that. She wouldn't; so she wouldn't. Yuck! How could she, with that prune-faced old devil? He's all shrivelled up. At his age it's easy to preach about celibacy. No, he wouldn't. The courage of celibacy is only for those who find it hard. But he never finds it hard; he's a *Jansenist*. It's easy for him. She was probably just bringing him cough medicine. Baloney! He fakes a cough just to get her attention.

He stopped when he reached the emergency quarters in the hospital. He was already too late. A sheet had been placed over the corpse's face. He pulled the covering back and anointed the corpse anyway. He had been told that the spirit stays with the body for an hour after the person had passed away. How would the Church know that?

"I anoint you with the chrism of salvation. May God forgive you for whatever sins you may have committed through your sense of sight. May God forgive you for whatever sins you may have committed through your sense of smell. May God forgive you for whatever sins you may have committed through your sense of hearing . . ." He was called out to the hospital three times that same night, and he repeated the same ritual each time.

"The Catholic Church is not a democracy!" The Monsignor pounded the table as he shouted to the assembled parish council. Miss Prado was, of course, present. Fr Pat saw her look over at him as Monsignor raged on in his shrivelling Jansenistic voice.

She was a civil lawyer and had qualified as a Church canonist. Often she would quote some innocuous canon law which Fr Pat had never heard of. Of course, she used this knowledge whenever possible to put an end to Fr Pat's argument. *Roma locuta est. Causa finita est.*

He tried his best to be obedient to the teachings of the Church, but as he grew older, having lived longer with the moral dilemmas of struggling honest people, he had begun to see that there was often little compassion evident in the magisterium's pronouncements, especially in the arena of human sexuality. The Church continued to brand homosexuals as intrinsically disordered and homosexuality as intrinsically evil. Once, with sweat pouring out of him, he had refused to read a letter from the Bishop's office on homosexuality. He was totally opposed to the Church's stance on this subject. He had argued with one of his Bishops that the expression of human sexuality depends on the person. Black is black. Gay is gay. There is no possibility of one becoming the other. There is no choice. If one has blue eyes then one lives with blue eyes.

Homosexuality is. and in no way can that 'is' be altered. It is part of the human spectrum and endemic to the experiment of the evolutionary process., What man made religion demands is like compelling an elephant to grow a beard instead of a trunk. If the Church condemns homosexuality because it is unnatural, then by extension the virgin birth should also be condemned as unnatural. Bishop Tutu of South Africa reportedly said: "If gays are not allowed into heaven then I would prefer to go to hell".

Miss Prado of course reported him to the Pastor For refusing to read the letter. She had already known that Fr Pat's views on homosexuality were at variance with the teachings of the Church. This was not an unusual event, and she had always tried to intimidate him by taping his Sunday sermons, not, indeed, for their inspiration but to report the heresy contained within them. Neither he nor any of the other priest assistants had ever been invited to her home for evening tea. That privilege was reserved for the Pastor alone.

St Jude Church ministered to various institutions within the confines of the parish boundary which included a centre for the treatment of alcoholics, a nursing home, and a general hospital. Every day Fr Pat was on duty, his ministry obliged him to bring Holy Communion to and hear the confession of every patient in the general hospital who requested it, and he visited the alcoholic centre and nursing home once a week. Each day, immediately after morning mass, he filled a small ciborium with consecrated Hosts and proceeded to the general hospital to accomplish his rounds. Inevitably afterwards, as he rushed home to the rectory for breakfast, the sight of Monsignor and Miss Prado walking up and down the church property awaited him, as she always attended Monsignor's morning mass, he dressed in his purple robe with a red sash,. She dressed professionally in her lawyer's grey suit. Even though Fr Pat had to brush by them in order to reach the rectory door, they never as much as raised their heads to acknowledge him. When he had been first assigned to the parish, he used to say good morning, but he gave up the practice when they gave him no recognition. "Good Christians," he thought.

Now, yet again, she had invaded his territory.

"May I speak?" she asked as she pointed towards the microphone on the podium.

"Of course . . . by all means," Fr Pat said, handing it to her.

"I apologize for my disruption," Miss Prado said, "but as a devout parishioner, to be quite honest, I feel the time has come when we Catholics must stand up and support one another, united in our faith. The time has come for us to take a courageous stance against this new malevolence which is corroding the very doctrine and foundation of our Church. This priest speaking to us tonight preaches modernism, condemned by Pius X in his encyclical '*Pascendi Dominici Gregis*'. Jesus himself forewarned us, 'The day will come when they will persecute you and utter every kind of slander against you because of me.' People of the parish, that day which Jesus warned us of is already upon us. It has crept in among us like a thief in the night, like a wolf in sheep's clothing. And most terrifying of all, the enemy is already here among us, as I am speaking to you." She was furious. Her hostility towards Fr Pat increased daily as she listened to what she called "his Sunday crap."

If Fr Pat could be described as a thorn in Miss Prado's side, then she could be considered a whole briar of thorns in his. She shared the tapes of his recorded sermons and lectures with her Opus Dei group, including, of course, the Pastor. The more material she gathered, the more evidence she possessed to condemn him. She had built up quite an exhaustive file, and soon she would make her final bounce to entrap him.

She prayed for the trap to spring. She had already succeeded in having Fr Pat hauled before the inquisition board of the previous Bishop. She had not been as successful with the present one, but not from lack of trying. In her view, the present Bishop was much too lenient with men like Fr Pat.

"These new, faddish priests are destroying the very fabric of Catholicism. Why does the Bishop seem so indifferent? He never answers any of my letters, although he does talk to me on the phone," she said to herself.

"Gather the evidence first," the Bishop had told her. "Then we'll see what we can do."

Miss Prado was on a mission. She detested Fr Pat's language and the topics he preached about.

"What does cosmology have to do with holy mass?" she once asked him. "Don' t you get the message? Haven't you noticed that parishioners walk out on your sermons? The Cosmic Christ? Who ever heard of him?"

But no matter how severely Miss Prado attacked him, Fr Pat remained true to his convictions. "The cosmos is one" was a common theme. He preached that sin and virtue are the same reality, that the devil and the saint both exist inside each of us, ready to appear at any given moment. He believed that there can be no light without dark, no faith without doubt, and no everlasting life without the present one—forget about the next life if you have no reverence or respect for this one. The dualism of the Church was an anathema to Fr Pat. Platonic rather than Aristotlian philosophy appealed to him. The anathemas of the Church were often intellectually insulting to him

He agreed that myth like a mask hides a hidden truth. It has wondrous appeal but myth must be living and not dead.!

The mega myths of the Church no longer appealed to his imagination. He felt they insulted his intelligence. In light of the findings from scientific cosmology they had become more and more incredulous.

He believed that the need for transformation was the primary urge in the evolutionary process and that there could be no genesis apart from it. "Our future lies nascent in our present," he preached. "We notice it in the biosphere. We are forever on the road to somewhere. The unquenchable longing is written on our psyche; it is the greatest proof that we are not a complete entity yet. Some great unquiet is pulling us, although we may be unwilling to go, into an Eden pregnant with new possibilities. If we listen intently enough, we will hear a whisper in the forest of our being. If we bow low enough in reverence, we will find the beauty of heaven transferred to earth."

Miss Prado despised his theology, accusing him of pantheism.

"You make God too common," she said. "I've heard you preach many times that 'nature is my primary scripture.' I heard you say it, and I recorded those words. Please don't deny it. You belittle Jesus and rob him of his power to perform miracles. You are more impressed, it seems to me, with the birth of an ordinary baby than with the virgin birth of Christ. You're more impressed with the chemical make-up of water than you are by the miracle of Jesus walking on it. These wonders have sustained the Christian West for two thousand years. What the Church has always declared as the truth is good enough for me but it seems not to be for you."

Miss Prado paused and continued her rant. "You preach destination without the need for salvation. And without actually saying it, you imply that the whole story of Jesus our Saviour must itself be rescued and retold within the framework of evolution. What nonsense. You forget this Darwin thing is but a mere theory. No missing link has been found yet, and furthermore, you indirectly, promote atheism, which preaches that natural selection is the final chapter in our human story. But what about the Cambrian explosion? How do you explain that, Father? Darwin's theory of evolution is an insult to God, who the Bible tells us created heaven and earth and everyone and everything in it in six days. I'd prefer to follow God's word than the findings of some silly scientist."

Miss Prado certainly was articulate and very passionate. In many respects, Fr Pat admired her, as just like him, she had convictions, and in no way would she prostitute them.

Some of those who attended his adult education class were titillated by Miss Prado's confrontational ways as much as they were interested in the content of the lecture, and many of the traditional Catholics attending his talks were delighted when Miss Prado defended the doctrine of the one true Church established by Jesus Christ. "She has been so brainwashed" Fr Pat thought, "that even now, in a more ecumenical and tolerant world, she still believes that there is no salvation outside the Catholic Church and that only through the kindness and goodness of God could non-Catholics go to heaven."

Miss Prado although a member of Opus Dei, a very conservative Catholic group determined to defend the papacy, seldom broached the topic of Protestants entering heaven. On this matter she seemed neutral, perhaps because quite a few of her clients were not Catholic, and she would only upset them by calling them heretics. Besides, she reserved that title for Fr Pat.

Like her, many of the older parishioners thought that Fr Pat came from another planet, religiously speaking, but nevertheless, they held him in high esteem.

Grabbing the microphone Miss Prado invited the assembly to express their opinions on Fr Pat's Theological presentation. She was rather sure there would be a public outcry against what she considered his heresy and blasphemy.

Instead rather than reacting to his theology in an in depth way, the elderly parishioners turned the challenge around and almost unanimously defended Fr Pat as a good priest.

Most of them did not understand his talk on Dualism. All that mattered to them was that he was a kind and caring man.

"Unlike a lot of priests and ministers he cares more than he damns" a middle aged man said.

To most of the assembly God remained God and the rest just human squabbling.

Although many of the Catholic adults attending his lecture series were well educated, sophisticated and professional, they still maintained about a sixth grade mentality concerning God. Their preoccupation concerning the Divine centred on salvation and damnation. Their prayers were far more petition formed than laudatory.

"He's very kind, you know, and that means everything," an old woman said "He's not like the Pastor," another woman declared. "Monsignor preaches hell and damnation even at funerals, when maybe, just maybe, the departed soul may have reached purgatory with God's gracious mercy. I remember Monsignor actually preaching at my friend's funeral. Well, how would he know whether a soul is damned? Has he been to hell? God surely didn't make us to damn us; that cannot be right. Who needs to hear that, especially at a funeral? That's no way to bring comfort to someone who's grieving. That fear stuff is not what Jesus taught. If Monsignor isn't preaching about hell and damnation, then it's money, money, money, always damn money. I'm sick of it."

"That is not what we're here to talk about," Miss Prado responded. "The Pastor is not here to defend himself. And may

I remind you of all the good the Pastor has done with your money. He runs your primary school and pays the teachers' salaries. Furthermore, let me remind you, Mrs Gorman, that he built us that grotto in honour of our Blessed Lady. Have you failed to look at the beautiful grounds of our church with all the statues of the saints? And most of all, remember that it was our Pastor who installed the Chapel of Perpetual Adoration so that people can pray perpetually for the sick of the parish and the sins of the world. Don't you think, Mrs Gorman, that Jesus appreciates the constant attention our Pastor pays our Blessed Lord through the constant adoration going up to God From our own little parish centre?"

"Ah, yes," Mrs Gorman answered. "But I never notice him in there praying. He spends more of his time on the golf course than he does in church, as far as I can see."

"Well, we would have to say that Fr Pat thinks differently," another woman said. "He never talks about money except in reference to the Bishop's annual collection fund, and then only because he has to do. No question about it, I've seen the discomfort in his eyes."

"God, you must have been sitting very close to him to notice that," another old parishioner said gleefully.

"You know what I mean," the woman said in defence. "He gives off an energy. There's an aura about him. You can sense it in his animation."

"You sound very uppity," a fourth old woman joked. "Energy and aura and animation, I must look up those words in the dictionary."

"Well, that's precisely what Fr Pat does to me," still another woman remarked. "When I get home after mass I often look his words up in the dictionary, and to be quite frank, he often sounds a bit uppity to me. He talks a lot about science and things like that. You know, atoms and cells. He loses me. I don't understand what cells and atoms have to do with religion! And the genome project. I've never heard of it, and I don't think Jesus ever mentioned it. But in spite of all that, love is what matters most, and I've never heard Fr Pat Say a bad word to anyone."

9

"Well, yes, he is a little uppity at times," the woman's husband said. "And he's a bit strange, maybe. He thinks he's a poet, you know. Personally, poetry helps me. And I love those shows he puts on with his photography. Such beautiful pictures. I've never seen the likes of them. He'd make anyone believe in God. Since he's come to our parish, I now look at a tree and say a prayer.

In a way, he's taught us how to see differently. I'm not educated enough to know what he's talking about all the time, but in the end, it really doesn't matter. Once you begin to see differently, words become less important."

Miss Prado did not like what these parishioners were saying or that they addressed all their remarks to her as if Fr Pat wasn't present. They were also overlooking the fact that she had invited them to address the questions which Fr Pat's talk had raised. Their comments were much more personal than theological.

Fr Pat generally received the same reaction when he presented his audiovisual meditations. Most parishioners posed questions concerning the beautiful photography and very few discussed their theological message.

Miss Prado called all this "faddist theology". She considered Fr Pat to be the main agent of this dreadful disease in the parish. Not only did she think that his thinking was heretical, but worse still, she considered it to be a contributing factor to the mounting decadence and immorality in modern society. To her view, traditional Catholicism was the only antidote to modernism. She believed that society behaved in a more civilized way when governed by strict and unbending theological legislation, and although she adhered to the strict principle of the separation of Church and State, as if through osmosis, she brought her Catholic upbringing to bear on her considerations of secular law.

"I believe in justice at all costs," she had said on the matter. "Criminals must be punished for their offenses. Modern society's soft attitude towards criminality only promotes dishonesty and a lack of accountability. Our country has arrived at a juncture where rehabilitation has replaced incarceration. As a committed Christian, my attitude on punishing criminals is the same as Christ's—he whipped the moneylenders and chased them from the temple."

Miss Prado listened as a few more parishioners had their say about Fr Pat's use of uppity language, but their condemnation of him was too tempered and unconcerned with theological discourse.

"Father," she then said determinedly, "we all have had enough of your blasphemy." She was tough. There was no hesitancy in her criticism, she spoke like a prosecutor, as usual.

Even though such confrontations were growing more frequent, the old tug of insecurity still reared its ugly head inside of Fr Pat. He felt queasy when she confronted him, especially in public like this.

Miss Prado dressed impeccably and had a refined air about her. She looked scholarly. Her obvious confidence and transport of carriage added to Fr Pat's nervousness. He, from the other side of the track,. was born in poverty achieving no degree. She was a very wealthy woman with degrees dripping from her like diamond jewellery.

He looked upon her as someone attempting to box in eternity. She was truly a Church submissive, unquestioning and obedient. She behaved like a trained monkey or perhaps a dancing marionette pulled by the strings of a hidden puppeteer. To Miss Prado, God was an all-seeing watchdog up in the sky.

"It's human arrogance, especially the sin of heresy, which makes God cry," she said to Fr Pat. "The truth is as simple as one, two, three. The Church, under the inspiration of the Holy Ghost, guides humankind. It alone holds the key to salvation. Without the dispensation of God's grace through the Church, there is no redemption or salvation. Christ said so himself 'I give to you the keys of the kingdom. Whose sins you shall forgive, they are forgiven them, and whose sins you shall retain, they are retained.'

"Miss Prado, you are very selective in the material you quote," Fr Pat answered. "Did not Jesus also say, 'the kingdom of God is within you'?" He wondered how a woman of such intelligence could be so tenacious and uncritical about her religion, especially since the discoveries of modern science demanded that we look at life more objectively. He valued the empiricism which scientific materialism demanded and disavowed the obnoxious uncritical depth into which fundamentalism, whether material or religious, had fallen. Along with Religious fundamentalists he equally abhorred the triumphalism of materialistic scientists, not because of their discoveries but because of their arrogance in thinking that such findings presented the whole truth.

"There are two types of fundamentalism which scourge the human prospect," he had once said to a group of businessmen. "One comes from mechanistic science and the other from religion. The miracles which science report are reasonable and amazing, but arrogant scientists must learn that miracles, when uncovered, present a million others of a much more complex and mysterious nature. Scientists and corporations need to practice reverence. Equally, the miracles which the church proposes are unnatural. They violate reasonable intelligence. The imposition of the supernatural on the natural is contrary to the law of God.

Sensational miracles which the Church supports destroy God's ongoing evolutionary plan. The meta-myth which the Church imposes is as vicious as the myth mechanistic science offers in promoting matter. One system proposes Christ as our Saviour and the other matter as our redeemer. The great fallacy of our time is that neither system offers a complete solution to our quest for meaning. If we are to be saved, we start by saving ourselves. God intended it to be this way from start to finish. We must integrate the God of the within with the God of the outside mechanistic world. We will have no future without this integration."

The Church would, of course, dismiss Fr Pat's discourse and uphold Miss Prado as a faithful ambassador of the truth. In time, she would be crowned with a papal honour, from that point to be addressed as Dame Prado.

MELANCHOLY

As usual, it was Fr Pat's duty to lock up the auditorium after his lecture. He said goodnight to the audience and then proceeded to lock the doors of the hall. He switched on a torch before turning off the last light, leaving only the torch and the green exit signs over each door lighted. Now he felt all alone. A nagging sense of hopelessness and lack of purpose swept over him once again. Was it depression? He had walked the dark tunnels of this mental room many times before, and he knew from experience that the fires of hell would seem more lenient and less torturous. Such was the depth of his recurring bouts of melancholy. But through the firestorm, he had learned that only people who have been to hell could speak about heaven.

After previous bouts, he had emerged into daylight and thanked God for that light which showed the promise of life. He promised God that should he ever embrace the full gracious serenity, he would never again feel entitled to natural blessings and would respect and treasure them more than gold.

But in the darkness of the auditorium, the depression terrified Fr Pat. These intermittent stabs of hopelessness had begun to grip his psyche more frequently of late. Was he regressing? Oh, God, no. He would never go back to the hell he knew before.

A wrenching weariness and loneliness manacled him. The darkness in the hall matched his mood. But why did the exit signs seem so luminous? Were they beaming a deeper meaning? Was their brightness a sign of things to come? He wondered as he walked from one sign to another.

As he trudged home to the rectory, the hall's darkness gave way to the night's serenity. A full moon shone through the half-naked trees, the fallen autumn leaves having left their bones poking through in the mystery of unveiling. "Beautiful," he said to himself.

He thought of how nature teaches the enthronement of true ethical behaviour. Clarity and truth are found only by denuding, never by cover. The initial is the cradle for infinity. The small is the begetter of the all. The micro is a baby macro.

Reality is often the exact opposite of what we think it to be. The leaves must leave before we notice the ghost-limbed tree. To be bear is the greatest wisdom of all. Man is foolish to stockpile materially for security. Moneyed wealth is a monstrosity. Through dress and camouflage, we steal the truth. It is wiser to learn from the trees and announce to a world corrupted by deceit the purity we find in nakedness.

The leaves touched him as they tumbled down. He thought about them for a minute longer and sensed their courage in surrendering to insecurity. One by one, they just let go, and then in an avalanche accepted the flow of the inevitable and the ordinary.

He knew what the leaves were teaching him. *But, oh, God, not yet. I want to live before I die.* He began to cry. When he returned to the rectory, he wrote a meditation on the leaves.

A HYMN TO AUTUMN

God speaks to us through each falling leaf. The magnificent reds and yellows and browns of the changing leaves fulfil a deep-felt ontological need for beauty. When we fully appreciate the autumn leaves, we recognize that all life is fragile and transitory. We experience in their passing our own passage. We also change. Nothing in life is permanent. Nothing remains. Autumn teaches us the wisdom of insecurity. We cannot fix flux; we all pass from spring to winter, compelled to let go of our youth. To live is to change.

Mechanistic materialism hates the messages which the natural world declares. Change, old age, death, and pain are our strongest taboos. We refuse to see that the full glory of the river lies not at its source but at its estuary. Ads tell us to be young is beautiful and to be old is ugly. If we were more attuned to nature, we would know that youth does not tell the full story. The harvest time of life is replete with seed for spring, and autumn brings to a life a splendid colouring. So soon, so very soon, the green leaves of spring turn into the yellow and red leaves of autumn, ready to drop to the earth and enrich the soil for growth in the next year.

So soon, so very soon, our black hair turns to grey and our voices fade to a faint echo in the voices of our children. The Autumn leaves remind us of our own mortality. Not one of us can cling to a limb of security. The call reminds us that, as the leaves depart, we too must go in obedience to the law of infinite departure. We too must drop from the material tree, leave what is familiar, and be swept by the torrents and winds of time through the door of death into another realm. As awakened humans, we feast in a sumptuous banquet where all the good wine of life is kept until last.

We wonder how will we pass. Will we leave all that is familiar with the same flare and colour as the autumn leaves? Will we do what the leaves do and proclaim the beauty of life, or will we display the anguish and torment, the pain and the loneliness of death? Will we trust that a great Intelligence will turn our chaos into harmony? When confronted by the strangling demands of life, will we really understand that, just like the choking off of chlorophyll in the Autumn leaves, we too are provided with our best opportunity to display our most resplendent colours?

Gold is tried by fire; we are tried by suffering. The colours of autumn appear only through strangulation. Possibilities appear from lacking. Contrasts are complementary The autumn leaves teach us that without departure, there can be no return. They cry out to us, "Let go! Surrender!" We must leave as leaves leave. Our ultimate address is elsewhere.

Was Fr Pat lonely because the nights were becoming longer? The autumn handed him dishfuls of beauty, yet it coupled its gift of colour with melancholy. Had he taken his medicine? He couldn't remember.

"No, I cannot ever let this depression get the better of me again," he mused. He remembered the awful nights when he could think of nothing but suicide, and the overdose of pills he had held in his hand. Then he had said, "No! I must stop this, for it is pure selfishness. But no one will miss me. Except . . . except . . . Oh, God, Susie, sweet Susie. She has been like God to me. I cannot hurt her. I owe it to her to stay alive. She has always said that I have much to give."

"If you give, you have a reason to carry on," Susie, his eldest sister, had said. "You're not mad, you're different, and that's good. Jesus himself was different, and he certainly didn't allow anyone to box him in. I don't understand what ails you. Have you ever talked to another priest about it? You need to open yourself up emotionally Don't take life so seriously. Get going with your photography again. You've shown a lot of people how to see God in the ordinary. Now that is a gift from God, and you're only slapping him in the face by not using it." Susie was the most significant woman in Fr Pat's world.

He had heard throughout his life that reality is all in the mind. He had never realized the veracity of such a pithy statement until his depression taught him the depth of its truth. He had awakened to the fact that as individuals, we are masters of our own machine. The world is according to our outlook. We have the capacity within us to use tragedy as a stepping stone to a higher reality, or we can allow it to destroy us.

Suddenly Fr Pat brightened. He thought of the leaves hauntingly passing and passing hauntingly. The natural passage of their going spoke of courage more than failure. Their message brought peace and serenity to his troubled mind. The world of nature was far more salutary and honest to him than all the convoluted messages of an over testosteroned Wall Street and Madison Avenue.

The crushing and the crunching of the frosted dying leaves underfoot had their own way of talking. His daddy had once taught him how to listen to the sound of God running through the trees, and now, once more, nature spoke to him. He found it strange that seemingly inconsequential things reminded him of deeper and more significant happenings. Leaves in reds and gold fell from the trees only to fertilize the land for a new, green beginning.

But many people didn't get the message, it seemed. There was no way of hearing or seeing the truth for shopped-out souls. Commercial landlords and greedy bankers already have monopolized even the territory of our departure.

They have exploited even the arena of death and departure with their own insidious lies. They have plastered the human mind with hideous cosmetics. People have become so deadened to the real that they no longer recognized it. The madness goes on. Economic gurus stock their shelves with burdensome things and bottles of nothing only to restock them for repeated purchases. The sunlight is going out, and the young land, once gorgeous in green curls, dressed in fertility, is dying, leaving us to inject it with unnatural growth hormones to satisfy our grasping greed. We have been programmed to posses far more than we ever need. The trees are dying. Soon there will be no leaves to renew and replenish us.

† † †

Priests walk to their rectories alone from halls emptied of men and women who had gone home to socialize around their kitchen tables. Then they go to bed and make love. Fr Pat often wished he could do that. He loved women. He loved their feminine gentleness and their intuitive ability to drive to the heart of the matter without undue discourse. It was far easier for him to talk with women than with men. Perhaps it was because their bodies were predisposed to nurturing life. Masculine feminists wouldn't agree, of course, but to him, it seemed women were disposed to spirituality, making matters of consequence significant to them, whereas men talked mostly of superficial concerns such as sports and money. Fr Pat marvelled at their passion for such tedious preoccupations. Cynically, he called their interests unimportant nothings. We would have a better world, he thought, if instead of wizened and emotionally depleted old patriarchs, women rocked the cradle of the world.

Fr Pat had seven sisters. He had never seen them undressed, and even now, he felt too ashamed to allow a woman see him naked. He had never known a woman in the biblical sense, his seminary training having programmed him to stay away from women, and now, in his later years, he still viewed them with a Madonna complex. Somewhere in a shadowy corner of his mind, he reserved the idea that sex with a woman was a violation of her essential purity. He could never accept that perhaps women loved sex as much as men.

He had spent his adolescent years in the exclusive company of boys, first in a seminary for minors beginning at the age of eleven. All through his young manhood when his hormones were raging, he remained physically incarcerated with other boys and, even more psychologically detrimental, removed from any association with girls. He had spent six years in a minor seminary in County Cavan.

BROTHER LARRY AND THE MAJOR SEMINARY

Upon graduation, even though the experience in the minor seminary was cruel and harsh, he still was determined to continue his studies for the priesthood. His father could not afford to pay the fee which the Major Seminary expected.

He had seven siblings, younger than himself still to be housed clothed and fed. His eldest sister had emigrated to America and was a nurse at the Presbyterian Hospital in New York City.

Arrangements were made that he would study at a major seminary in the United States.

He was twenty one by then. If his experience in the minor seminary was hell, then his experience in the major seminary was heaven.

During his second year at the major seminary he fell in love with Larry, a fellow seminarian, but was too terrified to ever tell him. He had never felt like this before and his emotional state became unbearably confusing and burdensome. He thought he was the only person in the universe with feelings such as his. He scarcely understood his emotions and felt lonely and bottled up within himself. Sometimes he felt he could no longer keep the lid on all the psychological pain and confusion welling up within him. Even in the ecstasy of Larry's company he felt an aching sadness. He knew he must never be alone with him.

Through tremendous discipline, Pat remained chaste, receiving relief only from wet dreams, and even then he scrupulously confessed them to be absolved of even a tinge of mortal sin resulting from these eruptions.

Pat adored Larry and thought he was the most beautiful young man in the world. He loved Larry's blue eyes and golden hair, his gentle voice, and the way he spoke English with a French cadence thanks to his Quebecker mother. Pat wanted desperately to touch Larry, but he knew he could not. Larry always used Aqua Velva aftershave, and Although it was cheaply concocted, it smelled to Pat like the most expensive French eau de toilet. Although he himself never smoked, Salem cigarettes took on a mythic glow because Larry smoked them, and Pat transfigured him into the handsome man sitting beside the pure waterfall of the advertisement.

Larry became Pat's world, haunting his studies and his prayers. He could not keep his eyes off his Adonis and noticed him on the ball field and in the classroom and, most alarming, in the common shower room.

Pat couldn't figure out what was wrong. "Could I be queer?" he had asked himself. "Oh God, no, not that. I can't be a priest and a queer. Queers are strange. They have men's bodies but act like women. I'm not like that. I am sensitive, but men can be sensitive too. Gentlemanly behaviour is the essence of masculine civility. No, I can't be queer. I'm manly and masculine and women always tell me I'm handsome. That beautiful woman in the subway was keen to make a date with me, and when I told her I was a seminarian, she looked so disappointed and said, 'What a waste.'"

Each seminarian had received an official guidebook when they entered the major seminary that warned against "special friendships". In the beginning, Pat hadn't realized what the term meant. Slowly, he came to understand its implications with respect to Larry. Pat had wanted to walk with him, talk with him, and live every intense experience of life with him. He cried in Larry's absence and became overjoyed in his presence. Larry had become his reason for living. Eventually, the ache in his heart became unbearable.

Larry had been in the Marines before entering the seminary. He had a lot of worldly experience. It that respect, he could teach Pat a lot. Circuitously, Pat asked Larry questions about Larry's sexuality only to find out that he had a girlfriend in the outside world and had intercourse with her very often. Pat felt insecure. Why couldn't he be like Larry? The pain worsened until Pat thought he would go mad. Was he the only one in this world who could feel this way? He wanted with all his heart to become a priest, but he knew that homosexuality and the priesthood were incompatible.

Pat decided to speak to the Rector of the seminary in general terms about his feelings without discussing Larry in particular. In a desperate state, he knocked on the Rector's door but got no answer. He knocked again and again. Still no answer. As he walked away, tears welled up in his eyes, and when he reached his room, he cried uncontrollably.

Now there truly was no one he could talk to, except, perhaps, Larry. Pat determined he would speak with him because he must. Of course he would not tell Larry how much he loved him. He was too terrified that Larry would reject him, as he felt sure straight men hated gay men and looked on them as an abomination. Somehow, though, on a deeper level, he recognized that Larry would not hate him. He had always been kind and gentle, especially when they had discussed human sexuality.

Pat was shaking when he tried to broach the subject. His mouth was left with not even a sliver of spittle anywhere. Finally, his voice quivered, "I think I may be a homo . . . sexual."

Larry laughed. "Oh, for God's sake, is that all that's troubling you? No, you're certainly not a homosexual."

But he had to ask, "Why do you say that, Larry?" Larry looked at him with his gentle blue eyes, took him in his arms and hugged him.

"Because I've lived with you here in this seminary for the past seven years and I've never noticed an iota of sexual behaviour which would indicate that to me," Larry responded.

"Thanks. I would hate myself if I was gay. But maybe you don't understand. Maybe what I think inside is different from the way I act outside. It seems straight men can't possibly know how gay men feel."

"Look," Larry said, "I spent four years in the Marines, so I know how gay men act, and anyway, there's a little bit of it in every man. Human sexuality rests along a continuum, and most of us fall somewhere in the middle. You have no say about it. You cant get it like a disease and neither can you choose your sexuality. You're born with it and that's it. You can't change it. The people who shout the loudest against it are merely afraid of their own sexuality."

"You talk like Christ, to me Larry,. I know that if he were around today that is precisely what he would say. But . . ." Like a leaping gazelle escaping the claws of a lion his words ran in a gasp. "What about this avalanche of feelings erupting inside of me? I want to touch, I want to smell, I want to kiss another man. Is there something really wrong with me?"

"A seminary is like a prison in many respects," Larry responded. "Put men together and take away women, and the men turn to each other. Just because a man experiences sex with another man doesn't mean he's homosexual."

Pat felt a million years of pain go out of his head and off shoulders. He could fly again like an unshackled lark into the highest heaven, and from now on, he would spend his time sending down songs like rain blessing the green grass. That was the most liberating news Pat ever heard in his seminary days. Afterwards, he began to hate himself less. In order to overcome his obsession with Larry, he devised a plan to disentangle himself emotionally. He went cold turkey.

One day Larry bumped into him on the seminary stairs and said, "Why are you avoiding me? You know I love you like a brother."

No one had ever said that to him during all his adolescent years in the seminary,. The words scorched his heart., He would carry them with him for the rest of his life.

In time, Pat managed to get over his crush, and he and Larry were ordained together.

Tony, a seminarian with a magnificent singing voice was thrown out of the seminary for homosexuality, for "that", as they had called it. He just disappeared, and no explanation was given to the other seminarians. It was as though he had been murdered and buried without a trace. God, that was awful. Pat hadn't even had opportunity to say goodbye, and he had been friends with Tony for seven years.

"You are entwined in the fabric of my life," Pat had wished he could say to Tony. "Not even Harry Belafonte could sing 'Mary's Boy Child' like you. How could I forsake you? You trusted me. The night before you disappeared, you opened up to me about your struggle with homosexuality, although you changed around the details and didn't speak of it directly. You didn't speak of the full depth of your misery, but I knew. I knew you trusted me; you had no one else you could talk to. You were courageous and manly enough to uncover your true emotions. Why did it have to end as it did? The seminarian you loved was not gay, he made that clear, but he could have treated you more respectfully. Why did he have to bash your face in, leaving you pouring blood on the pillow, when you tried to get into bed with him? Which was the greater sin?" The incident had taught Fr Pat that men would go to extreme lengths just to prove their masculinity.

ST JUDE RECTORY

Fr Pat opened the rectory door and turned on the corridor light. The doors along the hallway were all closed tightly, and the sound of television filtered out of the rooms. He knew all of his fellow assistant priests, but only superficially. Theologically, they were miles apart from him and frowned on his liberal thinking. Naturally, they interacted every day and their duties in the running of the parish overlapped. In the beginning, Fr Pat knew little of their personal stories. In time, though, he learned a lot, not because they uncovered any personal truths to him but because Fr Pat interacted with the same parishioners as they, and the parishioners shared stories of the other priests. Besides, he found clues all around which gave him a greater understanding of what was really occurring in his fellow priests' lives. Once he came home very late to find on the windscreen of the priest's car parked next to his, a piece of cardboard on which someone had scrawled, "Why have you forsaken me? Is it because my hair is growing grey?"

A huge picture hung in the rectory corridor that resembled a Monopoly board depicting all the houses the Pastor had purchased to rent to various parishioner who could not afford to buy their own homes. It seemed that he had been rewarded for his shrewdness in business in addition to his elevation to monsignor. All under the guise of holiness, of course. Priestly success seemed to go along with moneymaking, although this hadn't been written into canon law for obvious reasons.

Fr Pat entered his room. The walls of his little compartment were covered with his photographs. Although he had never received formal training in photography, he had achieved dramatic results from mixing uncomplicated technology with imagination and wonder. The way light touched an object engaged him passionately. Investigation prompted him to traverse into a new land beyond measurement. Birds flying from roosts in trees suffused with light from a young sun had prompted him to say, "Not a bird sings that does not echo God's voice, and not a tree lifts up its branches that does not do so in imitation of Divinity's outstretched arms." If people could really see the exquisite brushstrokes of design on a pansy or a varigated tulip they would nevermore question the genius of the great non-local Artist. A drop of rain on a reed pierced by an alert sun became like fleeting flickering diamonds to Fr Pat. Ah yes, God hangs gems on the faces of seemingly inconsequential things. Heaven is here but for our seeing.

The Church had no appreciation for Fr Pat's applied theology. The Pastor had many times walked in front of the projectors during Fr Pat's photography shows, casting the Pastor's image instead of the pictures on the screen.

"Give up your fucking poetry!" the Pastor had once shouted at him.

Fr Pat had wanted to shout back "When you give up your fucking Jansenism. and money grabbing" But he remained quiet.

He especially loved the world of nature. He was blessed with an sharp eye to see a different perspective in everything. Everything was sacred to him.

Tonight, Fr Pat had been tense and weary leaving the hall in which he had delivered his lecture. Miss Prado had surely kept him on his toes. He knew she would report his heresy and what she called his "coarseness" to the Pastor, who would most likely threaten to report him to the Bishop once again. The trudge home had renewed him, however. In some ways such a walk was far more healing and reassuring than a thousand hours in a psychiatrist's office. The generosity and solace of nature offered gifts not yet understood by neuroscientists. Plants give medicine, but even more importantly, they offer spirituality too.

His spirit lifted. Fr Pat thought about his kinship with nature a blessing. Sunshine and rain, leaves and trees, the comings and goings of the natural order resonated with his own inner personal journey He felt in harmony with the cycle and went to sleep in atonement.

The next day he rose and said his usual morning mass. A handful of parishioners faithfully attended. Many of them had privately asked him to pray for special intentions, and as always, he took a few silent moments during the Prayers of the Faithful to remember them. Words came easily to him, and after the New Testament reading, instead of delivering a short homily, he spontaneously said a prayer that applied the Gospel reading of the day to communal anxieties or world politics.

Each day of his priesthood brought with it a coterie of duties: hospital visitation, funerals, baptisms, and weddings. Sometimes life seemed to be a roller coaster, as often, a wedding was preceded by a funeral. He had to adjust emotionally to each event and deliver the appropriate content with intense personal interest. He took his vocation very seriously and had no time for the politics or the management of the parish, which was often to his detriment. It seemed to him that the Church authorities had no interest in the artistic endeavours of visionary clergy. They tolerated it at best but never supported it.

"What a tragedy," he had said. "Art is the only expression capable of drawing the human mind into transcendence. But inspiration and motivation have long since been forsaken in the interest of more profane organizational skills."

Men like the Pastor who excelled in money management, canon law, or dogma had the Church's full support instead. A chosen few were proselytized in Rome for four years and were later treated as elites when they returned to their home diocese, putting them on a higher rung of the ladder to a bishopric. Fr Pat abhorred the whole system. In his view, the scandal of paedophilia and its consequent cover-up would be the final nail in the coffin of a Church alienated from its people. But in the meantime, he had to carry on although he felt embarrassed to wear the Roman collar. He wanted to fling it aside.

He knew that, like himself, there were still some dedicated, unselfish men in the Church who exercised compassion in their ministry, but many still challenged him with their submission and unquestioning obedience, which they saw as God's will. "Submit as Jesus did to the will of the Father."

They challenged him in these awkward, awful times to be courageous enough to still wear the collar. "Witness is best served when it is most rejected," they argued. But he could not do it. He would not do it—that would be a violation of his own integrity.

"The greatest sign of all is never seen," he maintained. "It is invisible. Where there is love, it hangs on the coat stand of the heart and mind." Although he did not say it to his marvellously submissive obedient and slave conditioned priest friends, in case he might scandalize them, he no longer believed that submission and obedience was necessary at all. He often thought that the story of Jacob and Isaac was more about paedophilia, than submission and obedience. What father in his right mind, no matter the circumstances, would want to murder his own son? If a God that required such obedience were to exist, then Fr Pat would prefer to side with the devil. Why must the Church go on valuing uncritical thinking and obedience rather than constructive challenge and intelligence?

The Gospel for the following Sunday told the story in which Jesus was tested about the great divide between Mammon and God. A clever scribe tried to trick him. "Come on, Jesus. Tell me, on which side of the great divide do you really stand?"

Jesus took the coin in his hand and looked at it. Then he answered cleverly, "Render to Caesar the things that are Caesar's and to God the things that are God's."

Fr Pat thought carefully about the story and asked himself, could this be interpreted as a warning from the mouth of God? Our materialistic secular culture demanded that people render to Caesar but never mentioned that we do so to God. Fr Pat pondered that at this tumultuous moment when economics had become the content of our lives, such a small statement forewarned those in our culture to straighten out their accounts. By refusing to balance them, they would experience terror and turbulence. Like Samuel Becket, we also say, "If I go out into the world it is suicide, but if I stay at home it is slow dissolution."

Had Westerners weighted the coin in the interest of profit? Two thousand years ago, a man told us, "A coin is not complete until we turn it over and look at its reverse side. A coin split down in its middle is a useless thing. Better to keep shadow and substance together."

Fr Pat considered the preparation of his Sunday homily to be the most important duty of his whole week. Hundreds of tired and weary souls still trudged their way to mass for the Sabbath. Like trained seals they came to satisfy their obligation. He knew they were worn out from work and domestic pressure, so he believed they deserved an encouraging and affirming word.

He marvelled at how good and honest most people were, observing that kindness and gratitude usually arise in an individual when that person is treated with respect and care. Motivation is born of inspiration. Therefore, he always tried to inspire the congregation, even if his words had controversial implications. In dealing with troubled souls, he remembered that God loved the little people of the earth prodigiously. It is corporations, organized institutions, and governments who are the true corruptors and sinners. Drug companies which put profit ahead of people's health and the whole machinery of warfare are the sins which most concerned the mind of God. Sin is far more plural than individual. Sin, in reality comes through accumulated diminishments rather than one personal immoral act.

Corporate sin is commited by the rich and the few.

Most of us, despite our struggles stand pure before the face of God. Corporate sin destroys body and soul. It is the cause of real sin in this world. The more we as individuals submit to its dictation, the more we lose our soul. If ever our planet is to heal Corporations must learn to nurture the earth more than their pockets. For the sake of humanity they must reach more than grasp. The life blood of the Corporate World receives its oxygen through consumerism. The more society consumes the more Corporations supply and stockpile profit. In the contemporary process of demand and supply the natural world is literally becoming more and more tortured and exhausted. Cracks in the system are appearing everywhere. The natural world can no longer sustain our inflated needs. There seems to be little recognition in the Corporate world that all life is interconnected and interrelated. Destroy the forests through the supply of timbre and we thereby destroy ourselves because human beings need oxygen to live. Right now there are lakes of garbage floating about in the mid Pacific, most of it in the form of throw away plastic. Birds and fish ingest it but cannot digest it because it is non biodegradable. The invention of plastic while of tremendous benefit to the human race, especially in the field of medicine, concomitantly becomes a hazard when it is used irresponsibly. Corporations, for the sake of greater profit, torture substances into serving consumerism without considering the ultimate consequences.

We need to remember that human beings are but stewards and not masters of the natural world. Corporations need to learn that in respect to the natural world, they do not have the final say. Balance is needed at all times.

Nature demands that we give to God what belongs to God.

Little does the Corporate world, be it Capitalistic or Religious, consider the ethical or moral implications involved in their respective agendas. Their implicit vision concerns itself with power and control, more than the welfare of the human race.

. The Religious Corporate world, for the sake of its own self interest, legislates dogmatically, thereby destroying the human person's capacity and right, to ask serious intelligent questions. The Corporate Church is destructive of spiritual entrepreneurship. It is terrified about any conclusion for the human dilemma which may be at variance with its own. It is paranoid of a liberating good news story. A church that is not open to expanding newness is a dead Church. It has forgotten that all the data about God has not come in yet. This is an inexhaustible journey into newness. There is still an awful lot of room for curiosity and wonder. We are still much more ignorant than we are knowledgeable. The most intelligent human being is the person who realizes he or she knows very little. Miracles uncovered expose a million more of a much more complex and mysterious nature. A hubristic Church which declares it possesses all the answers, is a dangerous and sinful corporation. It destroys the human spirit's capacity for imagination and enquiry. The Church must begin to admit that the journey is the mystery, the answer is the doubt and the question is the answer. The whole planetary journey brings no closure to the human story.

Likewise any Materialistic Capitalistic Corporation, for the sake of profit and money, destroys the capacity of human spirit to rise beyond egotistical selfishness Our sense of entitlement is bogus at best. We are all indebted to gifts much more than we have earned. Indebtness and entitlement never meet.

A Corporation which promotes greed and grasping is ultimately unsustainable. The comforts which Corporations offer may be of immediate satisfaction but are like a sheep in a wolf's clothing. They only mask and camouflage the truth. Who wants to plant a forest where there is no undercurrent of water flow to sustain it? We need the undercurrent of spirituality to bring vitality to the forest of our lives. Otherwise we thirst and die.

Huge corporations who now control the economics of the world are becoming more and more greedy for money and profit. The more these Corporations succeed in their grasping the more they torture the earth and most of the creatures on it. Their profit is a stolen profit and impacts most of all on the poor of the planet. Their large endowments to Ivy League Schools, which incidentally they themselves control to tailor fit their propaganda machine, are a huge lie. Their shadow is their substance. Their masterpiece is their betrayal. It is so convincing that they even use its deceit to salve their own conscience. Their alibi is philanthropy.

When it comes to the natural resources of the earth, which in themselves are non renewable and finite, such as the gift of pure drinkable water, one huge Global Corporation, has moved into some of the poorest countries of the world, draining their aquifers, to fill bottles, offering them at such exorbitant prices that the poor cannot afford them. Their aquifers have become so depleted that the poor can no longer reach them through their ancient methods of extraction. Consequently impoverished people are left with only polluted water to drink, which in turn makes their children vulnerable and full of disease. The gurus of the Corporate world preach that the poor must boil their water before drinking it. But how can they do this without money to buy firewood. All the while the wealthy few drink contentedly and serenely in their mansions of thievery, while their counterpart, the deprive poor sleep squeamishly on dirt floors.

Does not water belong to nature? Is it not a human right. Are not such Corporate monopolies the real devils in our midst. Yet the controllers of these Corporations along with indifferent humanity never once consider the interconnection and interrelationship of all being. Corporations never learn the wisdom of a spirituality which teaches 'THOU ARE THAT" Meanwhile, the poor children of the so called third world with huge innocent eyes, while shivering and quivering in awful stomach pain, seem to ask all of us, Corporations and individuals alike 'WHY'?

We hear a lot contemporarily about the disappearance of the honey bee.
This news is alarming because pollination of vegetable, fruit and berry trees depend almost exclusively on the bee. Science is in a quandary in respect to the insect's disappearance. Though still not proven, anecdotal evidence seems to indicate it is due to the spraying of insecticides.

The producers of these awful arms against the insect world, motivated by the profit motif, are indiscriminate in aim, killing friend and foe alike. While it is true the wind is mostly the spreader of pollination to the cereal crops, yet the humble bee often sets its focus on these genetically modified plants. There seems to be a definite connection between the death of the honey bee and insecticides.

One corporation in particular, acting as though it were God, claims the life of the genetically modified seed which it has copyrighted as its own!. We now have arrived at a stage where hubristic Corporations tell us that they can decide what lives and what dies. The copyright of this seed gives them the exclusive discriminatory policy to operated like an army. Paradoxically this Corporatioin kills and maims without physical gun or bullet. Theirs is an operation of legalism and mind control. This corporation is so diabolic that it now claims not only the creation of its modified seed but far more insidiously the potential LIFE of the seed.

> Now this is not the claim of some old shrivelled Religious Quack.
> It is the talk of a Corporation gone fanatical.
> It is the talk of a Corporate world gone totally mad.
> For all of mechanistic science's insistence on reason
> This is truly irrational.
> It is the chatter of an atheistic materialist world
> Much more fundamentally intolerant and terroristic
> Than all of the religious fanatics put together.
> Truly some Corporations have gone Satanic.
> If they continue to pursue science without the balance of spirituality
> Then only Armageddon awaits the human race.

Evil, Sin, war, mayhem and murder erupt in our midst precisely because Corporations, in the name of glamour offer fanciful consumer objects proclaiming the to be eternal, but in essence they are but a fake and a placebo. Every Corporation, beyond its own self interest, must take responsibility to

31

connect the spiritual with the temporal and the temporal with the spiritual. Quantum physics teaches us this. The whole is greater than the sum of its parts. Everything is interconnected and interrelated. Science is finally teaching us this. Consciousness goes on after the material vanishes. Corporations must embrace this huge discovery and respect it in their deliberations.

The same process must be embraced by each individual on his or her own personal inward journey of responsibility. Analogously, which man or woman working on the production line of our arms factories realizes the exponential horror and mayhem which the production of these arms of destruction cause.

Does any mother or father, grandmother or grandfather who work on these production lines ever pause to think that the last single bullet they packed in a crate for export may be the very one that shattered the mind and scattered the brains of an innocent little child. Is not the beautiful little mind and brain of an innocent foreign child as equally important and significant as their own children and grandchildren. Do they not all pump red blood?

RENDER TO GOD THE THINGS THAT ARE GOD'S

By Saturday, the day before Fr Pat would have to preach at three Sunday masses, he had already read the Gospel in his room and had been ruminating on it, living with it until an applied theology could be developed. He found his simile and ran with it. What a connection: Caesar and God, immanence and transcendence, incarnation and eschatology, dark and light, body and soul, sin and virtue, scientific materialism and spirituality, all found in the unity of the coin. There must be balance In life. We cannot have one without its opposite. Contraries are complementary. The coin which Jesus held in his hand symbolically summated all the struggles of humankind. The next day, he delivered his homily:

"We are living in disturbing times. Everything which once offered sustenance, comfort, and security is crumbling.

The moral compass quivers; we have lost direction. What should be primary is now secondary. Shadow has become substance. And we have given our souls away. Through manipulative advertising and crude commercialism, we have been drugged and duped into thinking that final satisfaction comes through immediate acquisition. There is disorder everywhere; just turn on the television or look at the newspaper.

"'Render to Caesar the things that are Caesar's and to God the things that are God's" To which side of the coin do we pay most attention? And in what order do we view the sides? We've kicked God to the tail side of our interests. We've drained our spirits in the name of our checking accounts. And in doing so, we have violated the most basic insight of quantum physics, which states that the whole is greater than the sum of its parts. We have thereby disturbed the most fundamental law of all by making the one great All less than the sum of its parts. This is the fundamental flaw underpinning all our eruptions of mayhem and anxiety.

"It is we who make the choice about the planet's destiny. Awesome is the power that has been given to us. God is so provident and generous that through free will, we can wantonly kill not only ourselves but the God within us. Materialistic science and the greed of global corporations are doing precisely that. They are destroying the planet. They look only to the Caesar side of the coin.

"Without the reverse side, there is no balance. If the heart or the kidney of our own body became so arrogant as to walk away and say, 'I no longer need you,' soon the body itself would atrophy. There is no longer balance on our planet. This, precisely, is the main problem in our world today.

"We set a birthday table laden with a sweet cake of the choicest cream and honey; we scatter around the sideboards boxes of gifts purchased for outrageous sums of money; we sit at the table and call our friends to partake in the feast. But we forget to invite the honoured guest to take a seat. We have kicked God out. Do we not believe that we should uplift the whole above the sum of its parts? The truth is, a Godless world

33

is an oxymoron. The magnificent insight from quantum physics opens the door for immanence to move into transcendence. When atheistic materialistic science learns to embrace this truth from its own discipline, then balance will begin to be restored and humankind will have climbed up one more step on the evolutionary ladder.

"'Render to Caesar the things that are Caesar's and to God the things that are God's.' Parents, feed and clothe your children, yes! But also teach them how to pray. Jesus said as much when he held the coin in his hand. The language of God and the fierce uneasiness and the unquenchable yearning of the human spirit for something more has been usurped by reverse psychology, by greedy moguls whose only passion is the profit motive.

A SPIRITUAL REALITY

An energy with fierce Intelligence, the All of its parts is wiser and wilder than we humans can comprehend. The immortal God will not be mocked. A bucket of water thrown wantonly away by a stuffed and spoilt materialist through his front door will return like a tsunami through his back door. If Jesus were here today, he would surely say, 'Oh, ye kings of capitalism and commercialism, beware! If ye continue with your greedy exploitation and disrespect for the birds of the air and the lilies of the fields, your pampered ways will end apocalyptically.'

The tortured planet which did without our species for 95 per cent of its existence has the awesome capability to end human existence at any given moment. If the oxygen in the air or the water in the river were to become depleted, what then, ye master builders on Wall Street? Your selling and buying for profit is as sinful and corrupt as a church which sells indulgences. You criminalize innocence and incarcerate trust while you yourselves, fattened by your thievery, walk around arrogant and free! However, your bulging checking accounts will be your undoing.

The person who refuses to grow in consciousness will forever remain in mediocrity. The mediocre are the listless and the listless are the damned. Unlike the prodigal son, they never return home,.

They wander as cosmic orphans in the dark. More dreadful still, they do not even recognize themselves as lost. Shall we go on polluting and robbing the planet of its spiritual potency, which nurtures and sustains us? If so, our stockpiled bombs will become superfluous. What use are nuclear bombs when no one is left on which to drop them?

We rape our planet through commercial greed. We uphold our profit as our new god, but in doing so, we put the cart before the wheel and the wheel before the horse. We have become terribly confused. We have turned the earth into real estate and spirituality into religion. The greatest problem facing the earth is not the economy but spirituality. As de Chardin said, 'Our future lies either in adoration or annihilation.' We are arrogant to think that we can substitute our temporary acquisitions for the eternal. As Chief Seattle said, 'We did not weave the web of life, we are merely strands in it. Whatever we do to the web, we do it to ourselves.'

The pressure is on to spiritualize, for unless we remember where we came from, we cannot know where we are going. As Yeats said, 'An aged man is but a paltry thing, | a tattered coat upon a stick. unless | soul clap its hands and sing, and louder sing'.

"We are but stardust, each of us but a speck of energy. We behave too arrogantly, claiming ourselves to be the whole instead of the parts. If our species is to survive, we must learn to humbly take our place in the interrelationship of all living things and return to our original ground. It behoves us to re-knit the spiritual into the temporal because that is what we are, an integrated whole of body and soul.

"We are now in our noosphere! The epoch of the human mind is upon us. It is mandatory that we use it intelligently and carefully to grow in consciousness. Evolution has brought us from a lower sphere to our noosphere, but why must our evolution stop here? Materialistic scientists and atheists tell us the brain is the end of our story, but why must the story lead to a dead end? Can there not be more on a higher level? In a totally different realm? Does the longing stamped by nature on the human heart for meaning and purpose not lead us to something greater?

It is this very longing which the advertising world has capitalized on for the sake of commerce, appealing entirely to the ego. It denies the need for any growth in consciousness. This paradigm must change if our planet is to survive. Respect, reverence, and wonder are the ingredients necessary for growth in consciousness and, therefore, for our planet's survival. It is only when the Prodigal Son of Jesus' parable has done his philandering and wasted his inheritance on the selfish obsessions of his ego that he decides to return home. The decision to return was a growth in consciousness, and it finally saved him. We cannot be total human beings if we cater only to our egos. Consciousness is necessary for integration. The ego is not the end of our story. We cannot come home without growth in consciousness."

Fr Pat had been accused many times of being long-winded in his sermons, and in the interest of the flow of traffic through the car park, he realized at this point that he had to hurry it up. Besides, the Monsignor had said, "That's not what you should be talking about anyway. People don't want to hear that stuff when they come to mass on Sunday."

"God," Fr Pat thought. "It's old farts like Monsignor who have gotten us into the mess that we're in."

He remembered quite specifically that just a few weeks earlier, in the same auditorium where Miss Prado had challenged and lectured him, a group of young boys and girls who had been gathered for religious education ran over to him. Fr Pat had been preparing his audiovisual equipment for a later adult education class, and the children were excited to see the pictures and the machinery. They loved his sermons about astronomy! They excitedly explained to him the difference between asteroids and meteorites. They talked of supernovas and the Big Bang theory. Some of them remembered that he had once told them that humans were made of stardust. There was great enthusiasm in their interchange. But all the excitement was interrupted when the religious education teacher clapped her hands.

"Children, I do not want to repeat myself. Get into your religious education classroom immediately!"

Fr Pat went back to preparing for his presentation, but he could clearly hear the rote lesson of the rosary's glorious mysteries wafting on the air. He wondered, "Why must children have all the wonder knocked out of them in religion education class? Why in God's name is it so important to learn by rote the miraculous happenings surrounding the Virgin Mary's body when the astonishing machinery of the human body is scarcely alluded to or discussed? Spirituality cannot be put into us; it must instead be invited out of us."

A PASTORAL MINISTRY THROUGH NEW STAINED GLASS WINDOWS

On that same evening, he presented his audiovisual meditation and talked very sensitively to his audience about parent-child relationships.

"Mothers and fathers," he said, "your child's mind is the most fragile reality in the world. A toddler's view of life is shaped by the images mirrored back. Cradle your offspring compassionately and attentively, Of love and affirmation be most careful. Your child's mind is like a sponge soaking up even the smallest glint in your eye. The first few years of your baby's life are astonishingly fragile.

To the extent that you image love and welcome to that same extent will your child grow up to love and be welcoming of others. To the extent that you image disinterest and rejection, to that same extent will your child seek replacement for your negligence, even to the point of becoming violent.

Family homes are the precursors of heaven or hell. They shape a nation's destiny. Each family home may be but a pebble, but depending on its structure it may end as a support or a collapse to a more expansive structure.

The greatest gift you can give your child is yourself.

Fr Pat peppered his presentation with pictures he had taken of a beautiful little boy and his parents' in the parish. Invariably after such presentations, the lights in the hall would brighten slowly, and after a moment's silence, he would ask, "Are there any questions?"

No one ever responded at first, and this time was no different, but then, rather squeamishly, a little old woman raised her hand and asked, "Who is the beautiful little blond boy in the pictures?"

So much for theology and psychology in his adult class. His worst response of all came on the night when he presented a very sensitive piece on his mother's death. Even the men in the audience were crying privately. When the presentation ended, a woman with blue-rinsed hair put up her hand and asked, "Do you have any comedies?"

In most respects the parishioners were wonderful— joyous, appreciative and generous. Fr Pat loved them, and, for the most part, they loved him. If it wasn't for the support and love Fr Pat received from them, he would long ago have gone insane. They affirmed him. He felt at one with them in their struggles and thanked God for blessing him with the capacity for compassion. In the deepest recesses of his own being, he believed that his own wounds were the very instruments which helped him to bring healing to others. Suffering instructs. Besides, Fr Pat was the middle child of fifteen children, and when one is born into a family like that, there is no room for selfishness.

Because of his background, Fr Pat had become a young man with a very serious outlook on life. He vehemently believed in a spirituality of gentleness.

He ministered well in bringing healing and care to other souls but remained harsh with himself.

He had received much love and understanding from many parishioners and this helped him to love himself a little more.

A gnawing feeling of inferiority and insecurity sometimes made him feel quite inadequate.

He tended to be melancholic about the meaning to human existence. He often wished God had made him differently. Yet he recognized that his own inner turmoil was the very instrument which helped him to be compassionate with others.

Lately though he had begun to feel more sure of himself and despite the debasing attitude of Miss Prado toward him, he felt very affirmed by the gracious attention and affirmation which a great number of parishioners directed towards him.

His stabs of depression had become less frequent of late. He had learned the truth of the Jesus aphorism or paradox-WE FIND BY LOSING, WE RECEIVE BY GIVING. He had truly hammered out on the anvil of his own personality that human beings are best when they give themselves away.

Some of his parishioners were simple people possessing minds washed with traditional respect and love, so the priest was the most important man in the world to them. Fr Pat delighted in calling around to their homes for a cup of tea or coffee. Like the birds in the sky, they allowed the air to fly them here and there and didn't know exactly where their next meal would come from. They ignored convention but said their daily prayers to Mary and Jesus. God was in the sky. Nothing else mattered to them except their families and friends. So long as they remained healthy, they had little need to say any other prayer of petition, except, of course, for our Holy Father the Pope.

Apart from these families, the parishioners were highly educated and sophisticated, but despite their comfort and wealth, they, too, often sought Fr Pat's advice on matters psychological and spiritual. Periodically, these families would join in each other's living rooms to talk about spirituality and its impact on their lives.

Of course, Fr Pat couldn't know what went on behind closed doors in the latter parishioners' lives. Children eloped, children doped. Extramarital affairs, a million inadequacies. But through it all. parishioners expressed a common concern for staying spiritual in a materialistic, un-holistic world. The Church had only alienated them and had become irrelevant, saying nothing in an interpenetrating theological way that applied to their everyday lives. Many of them felt they had lost their moral compass, and in their search for meaning and direction, the only value they could still cling to was the message of Jesus. It reflected the pain of their individual struggles and gave direction to their quest for meaning.

Many of them had suffered immeasurably through struggles such as the premature loss of their children in road accidents. Others walked around like ghosts with cancerous cells demolishing the healthy ones. Some had been hurt by the departure of a spouse who had found a new lover. Sometimes the children of these parents cried for the loss of their daddies, and their mammies could only tell them, "He's gone away."

Such bereaved people joined the discussion group simply because they did not know what to say to their children. Some of them were pacifists and members of Amnesty International. Others belonged to the Society of St Vincent De Paul and sent loads of food and clothing down to the poor in Harlem NYC. every month. They following the wisdom of JD Salinger's *Catcher in the Rye*: "See Christ and you are a Christian, all else is talk."

Even before Fr Pat had become comingled with the fabric of their lives, these soul-searching men and women had already realized that something had gone terribly wrong with both their Church and their secular culture, both of which had alienated them. Once they believed in the American Dream and the comfortable security it brought them, but the more they luxuriated in the illusion, the more dissatisfied and uncomfortable they became. They had abandoned their inbred need for spirituality but lately realized that without it they felt empty.

One member of the group echoed the words of Fr Pat's homily, "When we throw God out through the front door, we invite a tsunami of materialistic distraction through the back door. This in turn swamps our life with trivial pursuits and escapism. Finally we realize that lasting peace is not possible without some spiritual purpose."

"Materialism alone only spells death," a woman in the group said. "The American Dream is based on a very narrow economy."

The group thought and talked about the way of Jesus, but the businesspeople among them thought the approach of Christ was too naïve. Though they continued to go to church, they spurned the Christ which the Church presented. A church which was all head and little heart no longer appealed to them. How ironic that a church which professes itself as philosophically intelligent and enquiring should at the same time be so fundamentally dogmatic.

"Perhaps the economic recession now strangling Western culture initiated a deeper consciousness," Fr Pat thought.
Parishioners had already decided that while their hands had been given over to money and profit, they needed to balance this by giving their minds over to a higher power. The world of the ephemeral had to be reconciled with the eternal.
The on-going recession and, more personally, the tragic display of neurosis through their offspring's behaviour prompted

them to ask basic questions about life's meaning and purpose. Many of them had witnessed their children grow up to be totally narcissistic and selfish, in some cases lacking even basic social graces. They had become so glued to their gadgets that within the space of a few years, the virtual had become actual to them. So accelerated was the pace of contemporary change that social development, which had taken hundreds of years to unfold, was now actually happening before parishioners' eyes. They noticed that their sons and daughters looked more often at their smartphones than at the person standing next to them. They took little time anymore to actually say hello to the human person standing next to them. Now, most people's interactions happen through the mediation of a machine. Something unparalleled was happening to the human mind.

"It's as if we're raising some kind of new species instead of children," one father in the group said.

"Technology is making our lives easy," another man said, "and we have to be grateful for that. But humans have remained the same throughout the ages, no matter our accoutrements. The human heart is the same, and the affairs of the heart remain the same, but we have removed ourselves from what is essential. We have become smothered by our technological wonders, which in turn has engendered our imbalance. Both the body and the spirit have to keep their head above water or else we'll drown. We should praise and acclaim the marvellous achievements of science but our greatest Hosannas should be for the runners who win by cooperating more than by competing. Right now we may be winning the sprint but we are losing the race."

"I was thinking about this the other day," another father said. "Mother Nature still plays a great role in all our decisions. Even though we spend most of our lives in neat little boxes and journey to concrete cities on asphalt roads, we cannot escape the truth of our own minds. Our technology attempts to provide such an escape, but the more successful it becomes, the more it separates us from what we truly are. Far better to realize that we are spiritual beings in human bodies, not the other way around. It's almost like the water we drink.

The further we take it from its source, the more technology has to refine it of pollution so that we can drink it safely in the comfort of our homes. It would be much more healthy if we went back to the original spring to drink pure water. In the same way, our technology interferes, replacing what is primary with something secondary."

Despite all the comforts which technology and materialism had given them, the group decided through their discussion that they were not satisfied with the American Dream. Their children largely didn't appreciate what they as parents had given them, and the more they rescued their children, the more their children demanded from them and felt entitled to. The parents realized they had sheltered their children too much from the natural world, which sometimes dealt hard punches. Worst of all was that through their overprotection, these parents had robbed their children of the values vital for their unfolding futures.

So, they viewed modern technology more as a hindrance than an assistance. All the gadgetry they had bought kept their families apart. Their children had become cybergs, with the machines no longer a mere tools for living humans. Their children had also failed to internalize that when something is given to them, they must give something else in return.

Brought up in a culture of the gorgeous and the visually perfect, these children made little room for the ordinary. Only the extraordinary sufficed. In the culture they were brought up in, a corpse must be painted over, at all costs,. The living used lipstick and rouge as the solution to all irritating occurrences, and death, to this mindset, was nothing more than an inconvenience. In time, science would solve even this problem. Scientists would soon find the gene responsible for ageing. Science would solve all our puzzles. Anything else was superstitious rubbish.

Contemporary young men and women are teaching their parents that if they want to be modern, they, and not their children, will have to do all the listening. Already a machine able to simulate an erotic touch anywhere on the human body was about to come out on the consumer market. What would parents do then? Throw machine lovers out of their daughters' bedrooms? Those possessing the mindset of these children no longer possessed the capacity for suffering or pain.

Parents of such offspring seemed to be reed warblers with cuckoo chicks in their nests, and they wondered where these monster chicks came from. The cuckoo chicks, like their true parents, knew the trick: after feeding and growing, they would fly away fat and happy. These children's selfish behaviour modelled what was taught to them by their parents' behaviour.

The chicks, in their own time, would repeat the same trickery, leaving their parents with an empty nest. To those devoid of spiritual values, no promises are sacred. Such was the scenario which prevailed in many human homes.

Fr Pat learned much from these highly intelligent men and women. He was inspired by the quality of their thinking. To his amazement, many of the men were more interested in talking about spiritual matters than about sports. They even tried to bring ethical and moral concerns into their professional decisions.

The group were very critical not only of the Church but also of the colossus of American culture which was engulfing the world. They even had a problem joining America and culture together.

"We are a young country, and a culture takes thousands of years to build," one woman said. "This country is still in its infancy. So far it is only an experiment. The same tactics of mind control and propaganda used by the Church over the ages are now at work here, but now these manoeuvres are all the more lethal and subtle because of the subversive techniques of the media.

America the Land of the Free is only a myth."

"I used to admire my country," another woman said, "But now I am ashamed of it. The Dream is dead. In the beginning we had a democracy, but now, without even knowing it, we are being led like sheep to slaughter. The noose is tightening ever more, and we scarcely even hear one call for an end to this madness, not just nationally but globally. The imperialism of our media to say nothing of our military's sabre rattling throughout the world imperils us. This whole terrorism thing is nothing more than a ploy to keep us, the natives under control. Just like the Church, governments know that the best form of control is fear."

The discussion went on to cover the immorality of the war machine and the fact that the United States sells more arms than all other countries put together. It recently sold sixty thousand tons of tear gas to Turkey.

"We constantly hear about the horror of the three thousand people murdered in the Twin Towers, and may God bless them, but what about the million and a half innocent people killed in Iraq?" one group member offered. "They're mostly women and children. We have never prayed for them in any church I've ever attended. Are these innocent people not worthy of our remembrance? Are they not as human as the rest of us? This country has lost its innocence., The media discloses what the Government imposes.

It's all propaganda I'm beginning to think that our human rights are little by little being taken away from us all under the guise of security.

"I've been thinking lately," another member chimed in, "about all this talk of the Israelis and the Palestinians. If Jesus were around today, he'd be on the Palestinian side of the wall. Jesus himself said, A prophet is never accepted in his own land.'

"And you know what else angers me? These born-again Christians. I don't understand them. When it comes to Israel, they put all their eggs in the one basket. Even if Israel is the homeland of the Jews and theirs by divine right, as born-again Christians claim, why does this make it right to politicize and compromise the compassionate Nazarene? By politicizing the message of Jesus, these Christians are sinning against the very revolutionary reason for his existence. It is what Jesus stood for and not where he came from that matters. But born-again Christians value his ethnicity more than his message, it seems to me."

THE BASALIANS

The group, which Fr Pat had been gathering with every week, little by little had become a homogenous community. They called themselves the New Basalians. Their meetings renewed Fr Pat's passion and energy. They had appointed him as their leader and were keenly interested in what he had to say about various theological subjects. He had told them at the beginning that he had no credentials except the fact that he had read some good books on allied disciplines and that he had never allowed himself to destroy the wonder of the child within him.

The little community was very pleased with his leadership. When they began meeting, he joked to them, "No Miss Prados need apply." Everyone laughed heartily.

Tonight, he went home energized by his contact with like-minded people. As he walked down the corridor of the rectory, all the doors to the priest's rooms were closed. Perhaps they were in bed already. He saw the lights from a television set flickering under the Pastor's door.

Fr Pat went into his compact compartment, which comprised a small sitting room, a bathroom, and bedroom. It was comfortable, and he looked upon it as his sanctuary.

He frequently stayed up all night trying to tape his audiovisual programmes in the quiet. His approach was primitive. He taped his narration on an old Wollensak reel-to-reel tape recorder. He had already prepared his background music on a smaller tape recorder much like the one Miss Prado used at his sermons. Over and over he recorded his narration, attempting to perfect his dramatic elocution and fervour as he read the script. The difficult part was holding the microphone in one hand while turning the nearly twenty pages of script without a crackle with the other hand, all while the background music played on. It was a monumental endeavour. Inevitably a dog would bark, a plane would fly overhead, or a toilet would flush, and then he would have to start all over again. Sometimes he had to repeat the process nine or ten times. By the end of the night, he had usually become so tired that all his anxiety had left him, and only then could he complete the recording.

Before beginning each session, he had already collated the pictures to match the script. Sometimes he would venture out to take a new picture to complement a particular point in the script, but he mostly selected pictures from his collection of approximately fifty thousand slides of photographs he had already taken. Then, with two Kodak slide projectors, a slide dissolver, and a sound amplifier, he would give his presentation. To the best of his ability, he used his art form to invite people to think more deeply about one's place in the universe and to see with new eyes, usually by discussing matters close to home: such as father and mother, parent and child, love and marriage, life and death. The creative process usually took about six months, after which he felt emotionally drained but gratified that was making the reality of God more available to his parishioners in their ordinary lives.

Tonight, though, Fr Pat was happy not to have to address his creative urge. It was time for relaxation. The hour was late, but he wasn't tired. He still felt the afterglow of belonging from his meeting with the New Basalians, his newfound community. As he often did after an emotional day, he lit a candle, stretched out on the couch, and listen to a Mozart sonata or a Chopin nocturne. He loved Beethoven's sonatas too. He used these masterpieces as background music for his audiovisual meditations. The candlelight flickered and the low sound of Beethoven's *Patheticque* carried him home, to the place he cradled most fondly in his memory. He wondered how Joe Cooney was doing. Pat had not seen him in fifty years. Had he gotten married and finally ceased his erotic talk about parts of women's bodies? Pat was in reality three years younger than Joe Cooney but about fifty years younger when it came to sexual fantasies. He couldn't understand Joe's fascination with women's anatomy. His mother called Joe "an awful little brat".

"If he ever tries that again I'll throw him out of the house and you along with him!" Pat's mother had once said after Joe came to visit.

"Why, Mammy? What did he do? He's my best friend."

"That's enough guff out of you," his mother said sternly. "You know very well what he tried to do."

"No, Mammy, honest to God."

"Well, he tried to pull down your sister's knickers. He's a right little pup. If I caught him in time I would have slapped him across his arse. He acts like a little cock sparrow. He's too old for you. I know he's only your size, but he acts miles bigger than you. Try to hang out with friends your own age."

"But if I do that, I'll lose his older brother Sean too." Pat protested. "I could never do that. I'm telling you, Sean's the best and most kind man in this whole world. I love him as much as Daddy."

"Don't say things like that, son. Your father is the best man in this whole world. There is no dispute about it. You forget all the walks he takes you on up the mountains. How would you know so much about rabbits and hares and hazelnuts and elderberries and cuckoo laurel if it wasn't for him?"

"Yes I do remember our walks. Do you remember the time when I wanted to make a net out of the small bag they came in to catch pinkeens in the river and I mixed the people turnip seed in with the cow turnip seed? Daddy was so mad and ran after me 'cause that small bag cost ten times as much as the big bag of cattle turnip seed. I hid under the kitchen table so he wouldn't catch me. But the next day he had forgotten it all and said nothing about the mess I had caused."

"And what about the time," his mother said, "when you fell out of a tree looking for a bird's nest? Wasn't it your daddy who put a hot poultice on your leg where the barbed wire poisoned you? Oh, you forget all that, don't you? And don't you remember the tracing paper he gave you of the beautiful parrots in Brazil and how you spent hours painting them?"

"Yes, of course I remember that. I'm not saying he's not a good daddy, it's just that Sean Cooney is so holy. When I grow up I want to be exactly like him. You don't know it yet, Mammy, but now I know how to play golf and cricket 'cause Sean taught Joe and me how to do it. And he's teaching us how to do the breaststroke down in the River Brosna."

"You know your poor daddy would teach you those sorts of things too, but he's so busy trying to keep the shop going so he can put food on the table for the lot of you. Don't get me wrong—I know Sean will knit you into a fine man because he's that sort of chap himself. He has the makings of a fine priest in him. I'm grateful to him for opening you up to new ways of doing things. And he's so handsome. God chooses wisely when he selects such good-looking men. He keeps the scent of women far from their nostrils, and that can be a good thing. I wish God'd done the same to Sean's brat brother, though."

The world of nature took on a new meaning to Pat through his friendship with Sean and Joe. They spent delightful times together in summer fields that freely offered adventure. Joe knew better than to ever say a bad word or to talk about women's parts in front of his seminarian brother. Once when the boys were exchanging their pants for swimming trunks behind a hawthorn tree, Pat saw Sean walking towards them and was afraid that Sean might see his penis. It would have been a sin for Pat to let that happen in front of a future priest, so he ran away, naked, with the speed of light to hide behind another hawthorn tree to dress.

Life was a paradise then. "Ye children don't know how well off you are with your pancakes and chips," Pat's mother had said. "And even ketchup to go along with them."

"Mammy, that's disgusting! You don't put ketchup on pancakes," Pat responded.

"Now, son, don't be smart. You know what I mean. It's not nice for a child to contradict his mother, especially not for a boy who's going into a seminary to become a priest."

When he was a little boy of four or five the rituals of the Church calendar fascinated him. He loved the smell of incense and the sight of the priest shaking smoke from the thurable as he walked around the altar.

. He waited from the pew with the rest of the family for the priest to come down from the altar and shake holy water on him Easter Sunday.

He thought the sprinkle was a waterfall. Ciborium's, chalices and monstrance's took on an aura of a precious magnificence to him.

His mother had told him that only the consecrated hands of the priest could directly touch these holy objects. Lay ministers must wear white gloves before carrying or touching them.

Sean Cooney told him many interesting facts also. For instance, he did not realize that chalices and ciborium's were not necessarily made of gold. However the inside of the chalice and ciborium was always gold plated. The reason being that only gold was worthy of touching the body and blood of Christ.

Pat loved best of all the Corpus Christi Procession which wound its way once a year through his village. Since this feast day occurred in June, the little girls who had recently received their first Holy Communion rigged themselves out in their white communion dresses and veils once again.

On this occasion however, even more excitedly they carried little baskets of rose petals which they strew on the ground before the canopy with the priest carrying the monstrance.

Because he was small he could not get a good view of the procession as it passed through his village.

His mother suggested that he go upstairs to one of the bedrooms overlooking the main street. In that way he could see everything.

His mother was wonderful., and even though she often told him that she would need eyes in the back of her head to watch him, she always encouraged him when it came to religious matters.

Ever since Sean Cooney told him about the Cistercian Monks in Roscrea, he always wanted to go to their monastery.

"You call them *Trappists*, not Cistercians," his mother said.

"Ah, Mammy, you know who I mean. They stay silent and only talk when it's necessary," Pat said.

"I wish you would follow them," his mother said. "Sometimes you give me a headache with all your questions. You never shut up."

"Mammy, you just committed a sin yourself! You told us to never say 'shut up' to anyone."

"Well, I didn't mean it that way," Pat's mother said.

"You can go to confession in the monastery when you take us there."

"I didn't agree to take you anywhere yet. I'll have to speak to your daddy first before we go."

"Oh, mammy, thanks! Daddy always agrees with you. If I ask him he tells me to speak to you, and if I ask, you tell me to speak to Daddy. It's like having two mammies and two daddies, and it's hard enough just dealing with one.

You're far better than Joe Cooney's mother. She's always fighting with Mr Cooney She threw a brush at him one day . . . . I saw it with my own two eyes"

"You shouldn't be carrying stories from other peoples' houses" His mother said

"Ah mammy, for God's sake, I'm only trying to illustrate my own point of view to you"

"Illustrate" his mother said, "Where did you learn that big word? Sometimes you make me wonder where you came from"

"I came from God mammy. You know that. I heard you say it. Now all I am asking you is to talk to daddy in your own special way."

"About going to the Trappist monastery in Roscrea?": His mother enquired

"Yes mammy., Mammy I do love you. Let me tell you to your face—you are the best mammy in the whole world. I've met many but you're the best."

"I'll see what I can do. I'm sure your daddy will agree. He loves the monks' wholemeal Bread. We'll bring a loaf or two back for him."

Pat's father did agree, and Pat got his first glimpse of the monks in their white scapulars, their heads covered with black hoods, as they marched in single file with spades and shovels over their shoulders. It was a beautiful evening. The Angelus bell was ringing, and the birds harmonized with its tolling.

When Pat and his mother returned home from the monastery, Pat was filled with questions. "Mammy, why don't they ever speak?"

"I don't know," his mother replied. "You'd better ask Sean Cooney. Maybe it's that when nobody is making noise, they can hear God better."

"But, Mammy, what about all the sounds of the birds' wings and their songs? And what about the lows of cows and the neighs of the donkeys and the guard gaggle of the geese to warn about a stranger's coming? And, oh, Mammy, I love that sound when the sea splashes on the shore and when the fresh water gushes down the mountainside, arguing with the stones."

"Yes, yes, I hear you, but that's not noise, that's music. That's precisely why you have to listen if you want to hear God talking. He doesn't speak just in English, you know. Most of the time he speaks only in whispers. Those Trappist monks know how to listen. They're not always blathering on like some little boy who asks too many questions. You'd think I was a dictionary or something!"

"That's not fair." Pat protested., feeling somewhat aggrieved by the insinuation of his mother. "You know I say my prayers every morning and night. I'm not that bad. Daddy already told me the answer anyway."

"Well, if he told you the answer, why are you asking me? You know I'm not as educated as your daddy. What did he tell you?"

"'It's simple, really,' that's what Daddy said. 'Sing like the birds, low like the cows, gaggle like the geese, and fly as high as the larks. Then you will know the right answers."

"Your daddy's right. You should listen to him. He's a good man. Son, I believe you know how to listen. I don't give you enough credit for the good inside you. I see the makings of a fine priest in you. And won't we laugh long then? We'll even light a bonfire and dance around it in thanksgiving to the Almighty for the glance of favour he sent to you."

"Oh, yes, I do, I really do want to be a priest just like Sean Cooney."

His whole being became animated with a wistful longing when he mentioned the name of his hero Sean,

"But you'll have to go away to a seminary and leave home just like Sean Cooney did." His mother said

"Of course I know that," Pat said.

"And you'll have to listen to the priests and do what they tell you to do. They are the voice of God on earth, and you can never challenge anything they say. What's it the Pope calls it? *Insuitable . . . impalpable*? Something like that. Anyhow, he knows best."

"But, Mammy, that isn't always true. "Remember when Fr Dempsey slapped the little girl right across her face on her first Holy Communion just because she didn't stick her tongue out far enough? She bit him on his finger."

"Oh, that was just a minor mistake," Pat's mother said.

"Ah, it might be for you, but I bet it is something that poor little girl will always remember,. A minor mistake by a priest can be a major happening to a child"

"You sound like an auld fella" His mother said. "Are you mine at all?"

"And here's another story mammy that priests are sometimes devils instead of saints. Do you want to hear it?"

"You should never talk about priests like that." His mother said.

"God has called priests to do his work on earth.
Priests are human like all of us.
Sometimes they can make mistakes
And when they do we have to forgive them.
Maybe at that moment, the priest was in a bad way
To go to the lavatory or something!" his mother said laughing.

"Ah mammy stop making fun of me
You remember the time, don't you . . . ?"

"Go on, tell me." His mother said

"It happened when we visited St Joseph's Abbey in Roscrea. After the monks had served us tea with the delicious brown bread they had baked with the butter dripping off it, I smeared it with the lovely gooseberry jam which they sold in their gift shop, and you said, 'Aren't the monks very good for giving us all that delicious food for nothing?' You didn't have a penny to your name. And I said, 'Mammy, we should come here more often. That way we can bring more wholemeal loaves home to Daddy. And you said, 'Well, how are we going to get there on Shank's mare?' Don't you remember, Mammy? How could you forget that when you're so good at remembering when I do something wrong? The monk who served us tea and the brown bread said that we should go into the chapel and hear the choir chanting . . . what do you call it? Matins? No that, wasn't it either 'cause matins is for the morning. Maybe they called it Tenebrae or something like that. Well, it's whatever the thing is that they sing before they go to bed 'cause the monks get up so early in the morning. They twist everything around, Mammy. They're up to work when you tell me it's time for bed and they're going to bed when you tell me it's time for school. Well, maybe not exactly, but anyhow, you know what I mean, Mammy."

"Oh, for God's sake, son. You murder me with your chatter! Mammy this and Mammy that. If I could write a song about you I'd call it 'Why?'"

"Why, Mammy? "Why would you call it 'Why?'"

"Oh, why can't you tell me a thing in straight English? Why does what you say always have to have so many curvatures? You drive me nearly demented!" Pat's mother took a breath to calm herself. "But I love you anyway. You're so innocent and good."

Pat smiled. "Thank you. But what did you mean by *curvature*?

"*Curvature*? Where'd you hear such a word? You're too young for that. You're far too innocent. Was it that brat Joe Cooney that taught it to you?"

"You're always bringing Joe Cooney into everything, and that's not fair. He doesn't have anything to do with this. You said the word yourself."

"I did?" Pat's mother asked. "I don't remember having said such a thing. If I did, I meant it in a way Joe Cooney wouldn't have said it. So what did I say?"

"Oh, forget all about it, Mammy. It's only a small thing. It's the little problems that often cause the most harm."

"Son, where is this coming from? Your mind is far bigger than your belly. Did I say that something like that also?"

"Yes, you did, Mammy. Remember?"

"Your poor mother is growing old. Don't go on holding me accountable for everything I said or didn't say. I'm not God, you know."

"Please don't get cross with me," Pat said. "I'm telling you a story and you're always interrupting me. It's my turn now. Remember when you read all those bedtime stories to us? The wind was howling outside and rattling the windows, but you were like a warm blanket to us on that cold winter's night, I heard Daddy say that to you! Remember?"

"Where did you come from, son? You're like a lump of blotting paper; you absorb far too much for your years. I must tell your daddy what you said. But please, son, a story must have an ending sometime. I can't spend the whole day just listening to you. I have to make your daddy's tea. He loves a bit of lamb's liver, and I have to warm his slippers by the fire so he can warm his frozen feet after standing all day on the concrete floor in the shop."

"Mammy, I beg you, please let's stay for a little while longer. The longer you stay with me, the better I'll remember you."

"You're getting too smart for your trousers," his mother said. "You send shivers into me. Sometimes you curl your words in such a way that you sound just like your daddy. You're picking up much more than you should at your age. I'll have to be careful what I say to your daddy in front of you. You seem to have an ear for music That's deeper than the bird's song. You're a lot like him. Maybe one day you'll be an actor just like he was in *Juno and the Paycock*. Some of the customers in the shop still call him Joxer after his character. Ah, but your daddy's more than an actor. He's a true poet, and that's far better. You're a beautiful boy and powerfully sensitive. Since you came out of me, you go deeper inside me every day."

"Wait for a minute, Mammy. I have something to show you. I hid it in my money box. I don't fully understand it yet, but I keep reading it and reading it."

"Oh, I know what it is," Pat's mother said. "It's one of those love poems that your father wrote to me. He's always leaving them under my pillow. Where did you find it?"

"It was in your little purse under the mattress."

"And what were you doing looking in there?"

"Well, to tell you the truth," Pat said, now bashful, "I stole twopence from you."

56

"You little scallywag!" Pat's mother said. "But do show me the poem, I don't remember it. I don't always know what it is he means, but there are other ways of knowing. It's a different kind of poetry."

Pat opened his money box and handed a crumpled piece of paper to his mother. She read it silently, caught up in her thinking:

Love means that we will never separate or leave one another. On the bullet train of remembrance, we become transported to life beyond a veil where all shall be one. Of this I am sure: life's true purpose is for us to become one together. Love is intolerant of separateness, and until we understand this, there will be no harmony or peace among us. Love such as ours, my beautiful wife, will forever expand and intensify. It cannot be drained of passion, no, never! No matter the eruptions and earthquakes which uncaring happenstance may send to us, we shall remain two in one together. God has designed within us a paradigm for furtherance. Our love will never die. We already are what was intended from the very beginning. We were destined to meet, to be united in and through each other. You cannot laugh unless I laugh with you; you cannot cry unless I cry with you. The curtain now is but a flutter in the wind. Beyond it we go, you and I together forever. Love is one. It existed before our existence. We were, before our maternity ward cast a shadow, and will go on living together, after our graves have cast a shadow. To love is to have been transmuted from the beginning into a deeper cradle where life is immortal and death an illusion. I love you, dear Julia. You are my wife forever.
Alleluia

Pat's mother cried softly.

"Mammy," Pat said gently, "I must tell you the end of my story "His mother's eyes were brimming over with tears. "Go on son" she said softly. "Go on" "Remember when we all went into the chapel to hear the monks chant Tenebrae?" Pat said "Angela and I stole away into the parlour where the monks were milking the cows, and we watched the monks as they washed the teats and yoked the milking machine onto them. We saw all the milk coming out of their udders and running through plastic tubes into a big steel tank. Then a monk came over to us and told us we would have to leave because females were never allowed within the enclosure. We didn't understand him and we asked the monk what he meant. And he just said that girls weren't allowed in the milking shed, so we had to leave. I could have stayed, but Angela had to go. I didn't think that was fair, so I went with her. When we got outside, Angela was mad, and she said to me, 'Since girls aren't allowed in there, the monks should have kicked the cows out too.'"

"What's the point of this story?" Julia asked.

"Mammy, sometimes I think you only half listen to me!"

"I'm sorry. Go on, tell me the end of your story."

"Well, this just shows that sometimes priests don't speak with the voice of God at all."

"But, son," Julia said, "that monk was probably not a priest. That's why we don't call all monks father. Most likely he was just a brother."

"Ah mammy, are you dense or what? That's not the point of the story at all" Pat said

Life was innocent in those years. Pat and his mother were the best of friends, but things were changing, not only in Pat's body but also in his mind. In some respects he had begun the process of individuation. His mother also had her fifteenth baby around this time, a boy. This made Pat the middle child. His aunt Mary, a midwife, delivered the baby in the same room in which he himself had been born. There was an air of sadness and quiet about his home for this baby, though. His aunt warned the whole family to be quiet because both Pat's mammy and newborn brother were very sick. Later his daddy went down the village to the parish priest's house and asked the priest to baptize the baby in case he died. The thought sent a shiver through Pat. It was the first time he really understood that all people die.

"God, please don't let him die, and please, please save mammy," Pat prayed.

He was allowed into the bedroom just long enough to see the priest baptize his new brother and give the Anointing of the Sick to his mother. Not long afterwards, his daddy saw him crying.

"Don't cry, son," his daddy said. "In a few days' time, when your mother is a little stronger, we'll let you in to see her and your little brother."

Pat waited and prayed. Finally, his daddy allowed him into his mother's bedroom.

OF LOVE AND DEATH

It was freezing outside. The wind was blowing little sprigs against the windowpane. Pat's mother lay wrapped in woolly Foxford blankets and a goose-down quilt. She looked pale in the soft light. He knew she must be warm, and that made him happy. They had had their arguments, but he loved her dearly. The fire in the bedroom grate was bright. The light in his mother's eyes was bright. Sometimes it darkened, though, as she gave brief starts of attention to her new baby.

Still, she looked happy. When she smiled, it made Pat feel happy.

"Don't you want to see your new brother?" she asked.

It was strange how he missed her. He was reluctant to tell her that. He tried a protective grin to hide his emotions. He had felt insecure when he learned about her sickness, but now that he laid eyes on her, he felt reassured, less anxious.

His new brother was remarkably quiet. He wasn't like most babies, who were always crying.

His mother held the baby close. "He's not fully developed. He's premature. You'll have to pray for him."

Pat felt awkward. He had craved seeing his mother, yet now he had little to tell her. He looked at his new brother and thought he was ugly. He saw snowflakes flying past the window and moved across the room to watch them as they chased one another down the long corridor of space. The room was quiet, the stillness only broken by the sound of the burning coal collapsing in the fireplace. The air was as soft as the snow outside.

The whiteness reminded Pat of his new brother. He didn't know why. The baby wasn't sucking. He wasn't crying. He was asleep.

"My little pet . . . oh, Jesus, my little pet!" The anxiety on Pat's mother's face shifted to horror and disbelief. Contortions of sorrow swept over her whole body.

"Daddy! Get Daddy quick!" she said as she squeezed her dead baby. "Go down to shop and get him."

Pat stood still in terror and watched as she became more quiet and calm in her grieving but still rocked her baby senselessly.

"Go down to the shop and ask Daddy to come up," she coaxed.

Pat descended the stairs.

"Stop your crying. You're far too sensitive for your age," Aunt Mary said.

He tried his best, but the terror of death and the feeling of loss overpowered him. Until then he had never entertained the notion that anyone in his family would die.

The little white box his brother was laid out in made Pat feel shivery. He thought of the rabbit Joe Cooney had snared and then killed with a snap of his wrist. He thought of his pet goat. Did the tinkers kill her? Slowly he began to understand that birth and death are very much a part of life.

One by one the whole family kissed the baby goodbye before the man put the lid on the box.

Pat's mother said, "If you kiss him, death will never torment you."

His father held back his tears, but the water of sorrow welled in his eyes.

Aunt Mary said to Pat's mother, "Julia, don't cry so much. If it were you or the daddy, wouldn't that be worse?"

"I know all that," Julia said, "but a child's a child. Even though you might have twenty, you'd love them all as though you had only one."

A DEMENTED HOLIDAY

In the following days, Pat's mother was not getting better. The doctor came and suggested she go into the hospital. Pat was frightened when he saw her being carried down the stairs on a stretcher and into a waiting ambulance.

After Pat's mother was dismissed from the hospital, the doctors determined that she would need some time to recuperate. To facilitate this, Pat's younger brothers and sisters were sent to live with relatives, and Pat was put into the care of his paternal aunt and uncle. They had no children of their own, and his aunt had been always good to him. The arrangement pleased him because he got to live on a farm and be close to animals.

Pat's uncle came to pick him up with a pony and trap, and the pony trotted the whole eight miles home.

As they rode along, Pat's uncle said, "I hope you'll be happy with us, but I want to tell you one thing. I haven't even told your father yet; he has enough on his mind now and doesn't need another worry."

"What is it?" Pat asked.

"It's your aunt. She's getting worse every day. I've noticed it coming on gradually, but now she's impossible. She doesn't even remember you're coming, so don't be surprised . . . I have to take care of the farm. I can't stay inside all day. It will be good to have you there to take care of her while I'm out in the fields."

"What will I have to do?"

"Oh, just stay with her, that's all. You're a fine young chap, and you're big enough now to make her a cup of tea. What age are you, anyway?"

"I'm ten, going on eleven."

"That's a fine age. In a few years' time, the girls will be mad after you."

"Well, they can do what they want for all I care. I've decided already that I'm going to be a priest, just like Sean Cooney."

Pat's uncle chuckled lightly. "You'll change your mind when you grow up a little. Your gollywog will see to that."

"I don't know what you mean." Now Pat was confused.

"You'll learn soon enough. And God help you then. It gets the better of most men."

Pat's uncle didn't even have to pull the reins or guide the pony. It trotted along like a dog keen on the scent of home, and they soon arrived at the front door. Pat's aunt didn't come out to greet them, as was her custom. He missed her warm welcome. When he and his uncle went into the kitchen, Pat hardly recognized her. Usually she was impeccably dressed in an overall bib with her beautiful grey hair spun into a bun, but now she was sitting by the range wearing no shoes, her nylon stockings all full of runs. Her long hair hung in unkempt knots around her face. Her bib was filthy, and her cosy kitchen looked untidy. The floor hadn't been swept in months, it seemed, and dishes lay unwashed in the sink. Worst of all, the sweet scent from her homemade bread and apple tarts did not greet Pat's nostrils. He hadn't seen her in over a year. He missed her cheerfulness already.

"You see what I mean?" his uncle said. "You see the state of the place. A man needs a woman not only for the one thing but also to keep a house clean. She's no good for either one anymore"

"Who is this?" Pat's aunt enquired.

"This is your nephew, Paddy," his uncle answered.

"Oh, yes," his aunt said as she stared into the fire.

"This is your brother's son. He's the child of Sean Malone."

"Oh yes. I remember him. He threw me on a cock of hay one time."

"I think you have the wrong man," Pat's Uncle said. "That was someone from your courting days."

"He had a galvanized bucket and he ladled some milk out for me and the cats. He always gave the cream to me and the milk to the cats," Pat's aunt said.

"But you don't like the cream anymore." Pat's uncle responded.

Pat's aunt got up from the fire as though she were a ballerina, but then she screamed, "Oh, sacred heart of Jesus, have mercy on me! Forgive me all my sins! Oh Jesus of the wounded and most sacred heart, have pity on this house!"

She wafted into her bedroom muttering something illogical and threw herself on the bed. Pat's uncle followed her in and threw a cover over her.

"There, now," he said. "She'll fall asleep. She always does after her tantrums. She's difficult to handle at times, and then she's like a baby. She doesn't let me touch her anymore. I try to wash her, but she screams at me, 'Take your crubeens off my body!' She must think I'm a pig. It's hard to know what's going on in her head. But I'm glad you're here to help me. You can sleep in the room over there," he pointed to a bedroom, "and I'll sleep up in the loft. It's warmer there. But if you ever need me at night, all you have to do is shout up at me and I'll come right down."

At his aunt and uncle's, Pat's young life took on a new pattern. At first he found it lonely and strange. He hoped his mother was recuperating and getting stronger. He missed home, but he realized he would soon have to separate anyhow when he entered the seminary. His application had already been accepted.

As his uncle worked the farm on the outside, Pat spent his days inside cleaning and tidying up the house. He boiled a big pot of potatoes every day and mixed barley with them to feed the chickens and milk with the potatoes to feed the pigs. He then mixed linseed oil with milk to feed the calves. He loved to listen to the two huge pigs, who would soon be slaughtered, eagerly slurp up their evening meal. His uncle was amazed with what he was accomplishing not only in cleaning the house and feeding the animals but also in caring for his aunt. His uncle did the milking, but apart from that, Pat did all other chores around the farmyard.

Somehow he managed to coax his aunt into allowing him to wash her face and hands every day. Finally she tolerated his brushing her hair. Then one day, when she had become a little more coherent, she handed him her overall bib and asked him to wash it. She called him 'doctor'.

"I'm not a doctor, Auntie," he explained. "I'm your nephew, Paddy Malone. Don't you remember? You bought me my Confirmation clothes, and you used to send chickens and eggs up to us to help Mammy and Daddy feed our family. Once you told Mammy not to have any more children, and Mammy said, 'Tell that to your brother. And then you said, 'Take off your apron and go back to school.' Oh, Auntie, can't you remember anything?"

She jumped up from the chair and screamed, "Get away from me, Doctor! I know what you want! You're just like him with your elephant trunk. All you want to do is stick it into me. I don't want it anymore! Stop forcing me! Get off me . . . you're hurting me!"

She rushed into her bedroom. Pat followed her in and covered her. Lately she had fewer tantrums and the house became more serene, although Pat's aunt never made eye contact with her husband, and there was no more conversation between them.

Even though Pat was only ten years old, he had become "a great little manager", according to his uncle. In appreciation for Pat's assistance, his uncle regularly brought him bags of sweets from the grocery shop in the village.

"Since we have no children of our own," his uncle said, "I'm willing to leave my farm to you if you stay with me."

"I can't do that," Pat said. "I told you before, next September I'm going into the seminary."

"That's a lot of codology," his uncle said. "You're much too young for that. Grow up first and then make your decision. Get a taste of the women first. I'm sure they'll change your mind."

"No they won't," Pat repeated. "I've made up my mind. I promised God I would be just like Sean Cooney."

"Who is this Sean Cooney chap?" his uncle asked.

"He's the holiest and most decent man I've ever met in my whole life," Pat said.

His uncle moved closer to him and massaged the back of his neck. "He can't be as good as all that. We're all men. That's what we have it for, isn't it?"

"I don't understand you," Pat said.

"In time you will. In time you will," his uncle said wistfully.

Pat's aunt became less belligerent and easier to mind every day. She spent a lot of time in bed.

Soon, Pat's daddy wrote him a letter to say that his mammy was now hale and hearty again and that s letter had come from the minor seminary listing the clothes he was required to bring with him. His mother had already begun to sew his nametag on each item.

Pat showed the letter to his uncle, who just said, "What a pity."

Pat put on his nightshirt and knelt by the bedside to say his prayers. The bedclothes were usually cold when he first went under them, so he had learned to plan ahead and put a hot-water bottle exactly in the spot where his body would lie. He always performed the same ritual for his aunt before saying goodnight to her.

Already there was a touch of autumn in the air. Soon he would be sleeping in the minor seminary. He was excited with the prospect. Outside the little window in his room, behind the lace curtain, a red geranium bloomed on the sill. Inside, he kept the light in the little Sacred Heart lamp burning to remind him of the good old days when his aunt and uncle's house was more peaceful. Tonight, the chestnut and beech trees which led up to the house were shivering either because of the breeze or the cold. The red geranium didn't obscure the full complement of the silver moonlight from the room. Pat felt heaven must be like this, especially now that the hot-water bottle warmly hummed a lullaby to his cold feet. He fell asleep.

Sometime later, he thought he was dreaming at first, but after a moment, he realized he was awake and that the man standing in the shadow of the doorway was actually his uncle.

"What's a man supposed to do?" his uncle said. He pulled down the bedclothes and snuggled into bed beside his nephew. "She's mad. She's driving me crackers too. I can't find anyone else; none of them want to come to bed with me here in Catholic Holy Ireland."

He put his big hairy arms around his nephew and pulled his body close to his own."

"Before she went mad, she spent hours praying every day" His uncle said.

She'd rather pray than make love. You can thank the Catholic Church for that. Those bloody priests stick their heads too much into the bedroom If they paid more attention to saying their prayers and less guff about sex then this country would be far better off."

Then in a totally different tone of voice his uncle said:

"Long and thin goes too far in. Short and thick does the trick go manifest the baby"

Pat did not understand his uncle.

The phrase, as if branded by a hot iron out of hell scorched his young and tender mind. No matter how he tried to eradicate the phrase it persited to sap and sizzle him.

He would carry the phrase and the memory of what his uncle did to him on that dreadful night into eternity.

Pat was nervous but excited about beginning at the seminary. Along the way, they passed a beautiful little gate house at the entrance with diamond windows and pink roses growing over the front door. It reminded him of the story of Hansel and Gretel. Even if the house didn't look the same, his imagination transformed it until it did.

THE MINOR SEMINARY

It was September and the leaves were already beginning to fall along the avenue leading up to the seminary. There was a horse with a big hanging penis in one of the fields they passed. The sight made him very uneasy. Pat hoped his mammy hadn't seen it. Then, much to his horror, he saw what looked like hundreds of wild hares trapped inside a big cage being released one by one. They ran as fast as hell down the field to another cage at the other end, a pack of greyhounds hard on their heels ready to rip them apart. A huge crowd of onlookers cheered the dogs on. That saddened Pat very much. He remembered hares in his own fields delightfully standing up on their hindquarters and raising their paws for a boxing game. His mother said, "That is cruel. It should be banned, especially on the grounds of a Christian school."

The seminary finally appeared. It looked like a huge castle with blooming gardens and spacious lawns running down from it. Pat thought it might have been an estate where English gentry used to live.

The priest who met Pat and his mother in the front hallway informed them that the castle was not actually the seminary. Instead, the minor seminary was the new building in the opposite field. The priest invited them into another room, the most beautiful one from ceiling to floor Pat had ever seen in his life. A carved mahogany sideboard laden with huge silver pieces reflected light everywhere. The ceiling was exquisitely carved and plastered, the work of a group of Italian artisans, the Priest said.

"The whole character of the building is classical Georgian," he went on, but Pat didn't understand what that meant.

Someone knocked, and when the Priest said, "Come in," a young nun with her habit sleeves rolled up and a grey apron tied around her front, carried in a tray laden with a silver pot of piping hot tea, china saucers and cups, black currant jam, biscuits, butter, sugar, milk and scones all arranged on an immaculate tea cloth. The serviettes were of white linen, which matched the tablecloth. His mother eyed the Carrickmacross lace, made by the nuns in County Mayo, around their borders. "Oh, aren't they just lovely," she said.

"Yes," the Priest said. "We are very conscious of our history in houses like this, and we try to keep alive what is most civilized about our culture. If the Church doesn't do it, then who will? Surely not those bunch of gombeens ruling our country up in Leinster House. All they know is that fingers were made before forks."

The sister laid out the contents of her tray on the huge dining table, which filled the centre of the room. His mother ran her hand along the Irish linen cloth.

"Now that is not what you should be noticing at all," the Priest said. "It's the table on which the cloth is laid that is almost priceless. It's of great historical value. The National Museum wanted it. It's Irish Chippendale. Did you know that Chippendale was originally Irish? With all of our precious furniture being bought by the Americans and taken out of the country, I'm afraid there are very few pieces like this to be found anywhere in Ireland. But then we Irish are an ignorant lot. We burnt most of our great houses down, and the furniture in them, when the English decided to move out."

Pat's eyes lit up at the grand array of scones and biscuits accompanying the tea.

"Thank you, Sister," the priest said to the young nun.

"You're welcome, Father. Will that be all?"

"Yes, Sister, for the moment anyway."

The nun left as quietly as she had entered. Pat wondered why the Priest hadn't introduced her to him or his mother. He loved nuns. They were nicer than priests. He had never seen a priest roll up his sleeves, put on an apron, and serve poor people like his mammy.

How sad that the loss and separation Pat had already experienced were not to be the final chapter in his version of *Paradise Lost*. That very day, another chapter of loneliness and separation began.

His mother hired a car to bring him to the seminary, and before they left, she said, "I couldn't afford to buy all those clothes on your list, so you'll have to do with what's in your trunk. The uniform was dear enough on its own. The seminary required six shirts. I asked your aunt for a loan, but all she could afford to give me only purchased four, so I'll tell you what you can do, just in case. Turn your shirt inside out and pretend it's a clean one."

Pat had never had so many new clothes before. He had gotten used to hand-me-downs or sweaters knitted to fit him from the wool unravelled from older sweaters. He thought that his new overcoat was the swankiest thing he had ever seen, and his mother said he looked adorable in his new schoolboy's cap. The emblem on his blazer said "Amor Totem Est" in gold thread. He didn't know what that meant, so he asked his mother to translate it.

"How would I know?" she answered. "I'm not well educated. I married your daddy when I was only seventeen."

"Where should we leave the trunk, Father?" his mother asked when they had finished their tea.

"Oh, just leave it in the front hallway," the Priest answered. "I'll have two of the senior boys come over later to pick it up. We won't delay you, but before you go, let me show you another beautiful feature of this house. Do you see those shelves over there on that wall? What do you see on them?"

"Books, of course," Pat's mother said.

"Do you know their contents?"

"How would I know, Father? I'm not an educated woman."

"Then come a little closer and maybe we can see what these magnificent leather-bound volumes are all about," the Priest said.

Pat followed his mother to the shelf. Volumes 1 through 9 seemed to all be about how to hammer a nail straight, and the volumes on the next shelf looked the same, except they were about how to successfully abort a sneeze.

"Those are queer subjects, aren't they Father?" Pat's mother said. "They're all about things that really don't matter."

The priest laughed as he pushed the shelves back, revealing them to be a fake door which opened into a huge drawing room full of antique ornaments and furniture. "Well, we'll let you go now," the Priest said as his mother peeked inside. "You have a long drive in front of you. Your son will be as fine as a fiddle by the time we're done with him. We'll turn him into a real man."

Pat was sad as he watched his mother drive away, yet his sadness was tinged with excitement to meet all the other seminarians, who had already started to congregate in the long hallway. A lot of the younger boys, just like him, were still in short pants and wore home-knitted knee-high stockings curled over an elastic band to hold them in place.

The Priest brought Pat from the castle to the actual seminary, and as soon as they entered, the Priest called over two older seminarians wearing long pants who were old enough to shave.

"Maloney and Conlon, this fellow is one of the new lads. You can be his minders for the rest of the day. Show him around the place and give him the lay of the land." With that, the Priest left.

Pat looked around at the clumps of new seminarians surrounded by senior boys in the corridor.

Maloney and Conlon put out their hands to welcome Pat and asked his name.

"Patrick Malone," Pat answered.

"You're never called by your first name here," Maloney said. "They treat us like soldiers. Your Christian name means nothing in this Christian seminary. It's to strip you of your ego. I think that's what they say. He was a stuffy one who brought you over. He has his nose up in the air. You'd better get used to it around here. 'The old man must pass away and a new one put in', or something like that. I don't know why they don't practice what they preach."

"Oh, come on," Conlon said. "They're not all like him. Don't scare the poor little chap before he even begins."

"You would defend them, wouldn't you," Maloney said. "You're carrying on into the major seminary. Thanks be to God, I'm calling it quits after I pass my leaving cert. You have to fit in, Patrick, or else they don't want you."

"Just because you've had your difficulties doesn't mean the boy has to hear about it," Conlon said. "Don't listen to him, Patrick. He's too negative.

"There's an abundance of seminarians around, so they can afford to be choosy," Maloney explained. "We're like thistles among the corn. That's what the retreat master said the last time he spoke to us. Weren't you listening, Conlon? He said, 'Unless you live up to the standard, you'll be expelled for being a weakling.' That's when I decided this would be my last year here. But at least I got a good education out of them."

"Provided you pass the leaving cert," Conlon said.

"What do you mean, expelled?" Pat asked.

"In plain English, it means they throw you out of the seminary. That's it, you're gone, out on your arse. They show no compassion. You have to pass your exams and keep all the stupid rules. Even God himself couldn't obey them all. They're downright stupid."

"They' re there for a purpose," Conlon said. "They strengthen your character."

"How can anything stupid ever produce anything good?" Maloney argued. "In a place like this the words *seminary* and *gulag* amount to the same thing. Soldiers for Christ and all that Ignatius Loyola stuff. It's bloody stupid"

"You'll disillusion the poor chap on his first day," Conlon said. "That's not what we're here for."

Finished with their argument, Pat's minders showed him all the rooms he would frequent as he went about the daily routine of seminary life. The chapel, of course, was the first place they went and then the refectory. Pat had never heard the word *refectory* before, but now he would never forget it. The next place the two minders showed him was the junior dormitory, where he would sleep after long days of work and study. He was assigned a bed right next to the door, so all the seminarians passed by it every time they came in or out.

His horarium was comprised of prayer, class, manual labour, sport, and study, with manual labour and sport alternating each day. Sunday was an exception. Seminarians still had to study, but instead of sport, they would take long crocodile walks in single file through the countryside, always keeping their eyes fixed on the road, neither giving nor acknowledging greetings from anyone they passed. For manual labour, seminarians kept the seminary and its grounds spotless. Each seminarian was required to keep a duster in the pocket of his blazer so he was always ready to clean up any unseemly spot on which he might adventure. House slippers had to be worn inside the seminary at all times to keep noise to a minimum and the parquet floors unscratched. Besides keeping the seminary spotlessly clean, seminarians worked on the farm picking vegetables, fruit, and potatoes.

The beds in the junior dormitory ran along either wall in long rows, and each had a small washstand and a locker for storing personal belongings at the end. The washstand held a white enamel basin and a matching jug. Each night and morning, the jug was filled with cold water for the boy's ablutions before going to bed and rising in the morning.

Pat's mother had packed his towels and soap in his trunk, but she had forgotten the toothpaste. He decided he'd compromise that first night by using soap instead. Then he noticed also that his sports shorts were missing. He wondered how he could manage without them since it was compulsory to play sports. Then, like a thunderbolt, the idea hit him: just as his mother had said to do with his shirts, he would turn his underpants around and pretend they were sports shorts. No one would notice the difference, he thought, but then some of the seminarians did, and they had great fun teasing him about it. He wore them anyway.

Long pipes carrying hot water to keep the dormitory comfortable in winter ringed the dormitory. "You hang your bed clothes over those pipes at the first alarm in the morning," Conlon explained.

"But you must do it quickly because you have only fifteen minutes to get up, strip your bed, wash your face, and get down to the chapel for morning prayer, meditation, and mass," Maloney warned.

Pat was tired already.

"We have a few more details to tell you," Conlon said, and he and Maloney took him downstairs to what they called the sanitation block.

"This is the toilet," Maloney explained. "You're only allowed to use it at designated times, and never otherwise without permission. Along with the dormitory, this is the most dangerous place of all. Don't ever break the rule of silence here. If you're caught speaking to anyone here you'll be expelled instantly." Maloney shot Pat a look of terrible intensity. Again he had used the word *expelled*. It frightened Pat.

Finally the minders showed him a line of shower cubicles and said he had to take a shower at least three times a week. Each class endured them on different days because, at best, the water was merely tepid.

"Is there anything else you'd like to know?" Conlon asked.

"No thanks," Pat responded carefully. "That's a lot already. If I have another question, I can always ask you."

"Oh, but you can't," Maloney said. "That's another mad rule in this place. Starting tomorrow, the juniors and seniors will be segregated."

"What does *segregated* mean?" Pat asked. "You keep using big words that I don't know, like *refectory* and *segregated*."

"Get used to it. In a place like this, everything is surreal," Maloney said. "It's more like an insane asylum than anything else. If God is here, then I think I'd rather be in hell. There's no girls anywhere."

"Stop talking like that," Conlon chastised his friend. "'It's not proper behaviour in a place like this. Patrick is too young to know anything about that sort of thing." Then Conlon cleared his throat and told Pat gently, "Segregation means that juniors and seniors can't mix. After today, we can't talk to you again until Christmas. You'll hardly see us except in the study hall and the chapel. We have our own dormitory, our own sanitation block, our own football field, and our own refectory."

"That's strange," Pat said.

"I know. Didn't I say this is a gulag?" Maloney said.

When Pat was younger, he and a few other lads from his village had searched for babies under the huge rocks which lay in heaps around the ruins of the nearby old castle. He had lost a lot of his innocence since then. The experience with his uncle didn't destroy him. It had seared itself into his memory though. He still could recall most vividly all the details of the experience. He recognized the urge that testosterone brought to his own body, as he struggled to keep himself chaste. The Church promulgated chastity and he was determined to live up to the expectation.

By now, he had progressed from the junior to the senior seminary. Hair grew on his face, legs, and arms, and he had a full complement of it around his private parts. He still found it difficult to say the word *penis*, though. Deep in his psyche, he tied the word to sin. He could never say it to a priest.

He struggled with wet dreams and immediately confessed them. Most recently, the priest asked him if his acts were wilful, and Pat said he didn't really know, but he did remember getting pleasure from them.

"The minute they go from the unknown into the known, they become a mortal sin," the priest said. "You have to be careful of that. If that sort of thing gets a hold on you, then you're crippled for life. You will have an impossible uphill climb to the holy priesthood, and no seminary will want you. Do you understand?"

"Yes, Father," Pat responded.

"And the further you go into knowing," the priest said, "the greater the sin becomes. The more you experience the pleasure of mortal sin, the more it becomes habitual. I hope you can see the distinction. Mortal sin is cumulative. It festers and spreads like a virus until it has you in its full grip. Satan takes us all unawares sometimes, so we must remain on guard against his wiles and snares. Do you understand me?"

"Yes, Father," Pat responded.

"Mortal sin is like a snowball rolling down a hill. As it gathers momentum, it pulls in more snow and soon it becomes an avalanche. You have to be careful that mortal sin does not devour you in that way. This is all the work of the devil. Do you clearly understand me?"

"Yes, Father," Pat said quietly.

"Now, for your penance, say three Our Fathers and three Hail Marys to the Blessed Virgin for the gift of purity."

As the years progressed, Pat felt less and less happy. He now agreed with Maloney that it was a gulag as cold as Siberia. The Master of Discipline, a huge bodyguard of a man from County Kerry with hair sticking out of him everywhere, had a force of spies throughout the seminarian population. Pressure and an atmosphere of fear hung in the air everywhere. Pat's study time at night in the common study hall was often interrupted by a tap on the shoulder and instructions to report to the Master of Discipline for the infraction of some stupid rule such as putting his hands in his pockets or whistling. Pat hated having to join the gang waiting every evening outside the Master of Discipline's door.

Once during a spiritual retreat when Pat was still in short pants, a spy caught him curling up in a curtain in the auditorium where plays were staged. The seminary was as cold as Siberia, and Pat's hands and legs had gone purple numb. The white frost outside had literally tuned his flesh purple. He had tried to be secretive as he warmed himself in the curtain, but the spy caught him and reported the incident to the Master of Discipline.

Packages mailed from home were not allowed to be brought to the dormitory. Instead, seminarians were required to put the contents of any package on the common table so they could be shared by all.

Pat was appointed to work for two months removing used stamps from envelopes by dipping the envelopes into steamy hot basins of water so the stamp could be removed and sold, the money going into the seminary coffers. Letters from family members were delivered to the boys already opened and read, and all letters to the outside world were censored. More than once Pat was called to the Master of Discipline's office to explain what he really meant by a specific word in a letter he had sent home. He received very good marks in English, but time and time again he made spelling mistakes.

Periodically a student was called before the whole community to correct his misspellings. One day, a Dutch priest handed the students their letters from home, calling each seminarian by name. This was the first time in the four years Pat had been in the seminary that someone had called him by his Christian name. On that day he thought that 'Patrick' was the most beautiful name in the whole world. It was the only time at seminary he ever felt affirmed. He felt comfortable with the Dutch priest after that.

Pat's mathematics teacher, a priest from England who lived for football, seemed to hate him and treated him as though he were nothing because he was hopeless on the football field. Pat noticed that the seminarians who were good at football received most attention, and they were always awarded higher grades on their examination papers than other students. Pat customarily re-examined his test papers when classes resumed after the exams. By his own calculation, he should have received a perfect score in algebra, but he only received 53 points out of 100. Joe Dowling, one of the great footballers in the school, on the other hand, received 98 points. The whole class recognized what was going on but dared not complain.

Pat was happy enough with his geometry results, as just to pass was a great accomplishment. He was never taught how the subject applied to life, and it always sounded like a garbled foreign language to his ears. Mention of a hypotenuse brought to his mind a hippopotamus.

His math results were never very good, but he failed his examinations in Irish and Greek. The Master of Discipline told him that he couldn't understand why a student so good in many subjects could fail so miserably in others. He called Pat lazy and as cute as a fox.

His overall grades gave him a low ranking on the student rostrum, which was humiliating since his best friend, Michael Cahill, was a genius in all subjects. Pat felt inferior. The humiliation of his ranking itself was difficult enough, but it was coupled with much more serious consequences. It meant that rather than showering with the first group in the usual warm water, he now had to join the lower ranking group in water which seemed as though it came from a Siberian waterfall. He had to exercise superior will to keep from screaming when it first hit his skin. Worse still, he had to endure it until the priest who controlled the main tap turned it off. His intellectual ranking also determined his place at the refectory table, so Pat had to sit at the end, and there were slim pickings by the time the food came around to him.

Most of the food was home-grown on the seminary farm and organic. Cattle and sheep were regularly slaughtered to provide the necessary protein for a school full of priests and growing young men. Milk came from the seminary's own dairy herd. All the vegetables were grown on the extensive farm. Pat loved to see the beautiful fruit hanging from the trees trained into fans against the stonewalls of the enclosed gardens. He had never seen fruit trees growing like this before or the exotic offerings which they proffered such as peaches and figs. In all his life he had never seen such an abundance of temptation hanging on trees. Rarely were these fruits offered to the seminarians. Instead, Pat surmised, they were reserved for the professor priests, who ate in a dining room removed from the glaring eyes of the students.

Breakfast was served precisely at eight o'clock every morning. It was a welcome relief from the long grand silence overnight and the two hours of meditation cum worship in the seminary chapel. In later years, Pat realized that the meals were probably balanced, except afternoon tea. Breakfast consisted of oatmeal porridge, two slices of wholemeal bread, and tea poured from huge kettles, inconspicuously and silently prepared by the nuns before the students arrived in the refectory. Except on feast days, seminarians were never permitted to talk during meals. Instead they listened to a student read a book of spiritual or philosophical consideration from a podium in the centre of the refectory.

Dinner was the only meal the priests ate with the seminarians. It was usually substantial, with meat from the abattoir, vegetables from the seminary fields, and soup made from vegetables or meat stock. Sometimes students were allowed desserts or cakes, colloquially referred to as *afters*. A priest sat at the head of each table during dinner, and like the seminarians, he listened to the ongoing saga of the Roman martyrology that was read aloud. Sometimes the tales of the blood and gore almost made Pat sick. The stories' severed heads, gouged-out eyes, and pulled-out, pulverized entrails sent shivers through him. He found the recitation very difficult to listen to, especially while he was trying to relish his dessert.

The sweetness of the afters among a menu of blandness tasted like heaven to him. He had been studying Patrick Kavanagh's poetry in English class and knew from experience exactly what the poet meant when he said, "Through a chink too wide there comes in no wonder." He appreciated even the tiniest gift of deliciousness which came with the sugarless tea and stale bread. Deprivation js most often the route or root of true appreciation. And how he appreciated ice cream, a sumptuous offering beyond all compare in the drought-stricken, inhospitable land of the seminary. He learned to appreciate butter as though it were gold. Never before had it seemed so delicate or delicious to him.

Afternoon tea was served at four o'clock every evening, after the students had washed upon the completion of their manual labour. Pat usually felt famished as he walked down the long corridor to the refectory. The menu of tea and bread never varied except for one detail. That was not the type of bread on offer but what was offered on the bread. Most often the two slices presented to each student were covered in dripping or lard and sprinkled with salt. Pat ate it reluctantly. Supper, served two hours later, seemed an eternity away.

Pat craved butter. Every third or fourth day, a thin scraping of butter did appear with tea, and he was delighted with the offering. It became his caviar. Before consuming the bread with its thin sheath of butter, he turned the slices over to check for holes, which often contained immense deposits of the yellow butter. He considered them an undiscovered treasure of sunken gold. When he found them, he could not believe his luck. These were his pearl of great price. The butter spoke to him in what Kavanagh called "the whispered argument of its churning".

By now he was fourteen years old and had spent three years in the junior side of the seminary but still had another year to go before he moved to the senior quarters. A curious and embarrassing thing then started, and it bothered him. He urinated in his bed. It was bad enough that the sisters who did his laundry might see the stain on the sheet. More terrible hoiwever was the fact that, because his bed was next to the exit through which all the junior seminarians passed as they went to the chapel in the morning, might notice his stained bed sheet.t. As soon as the head seminarian rang the first bell of the day, he immediately jumped out of bed, saying his Benidicamus Dominus, and placed the urine-soaked sheet on the warm pipe to dry. He prayed that it would be dry before he had to make the bed after morning prayer. This measure, however, didn't solve the problem of the soaked mattress.

Every night before going to sleep, Pat knelt by his bed and prayed, "Jesus, help me so that I won't pee in my bed tonight. If you do that for me, I'll be the best priest in the world and I'll work always hard for you. Amen."

But Jesus did not hear his prayer, and matters became far worse. Painful spasms which compelled him to urinate racked him during the day, dominating his existence. He had to plan as much as he could to stay near the sanitary block, as seminarians were not allowed to use the urinals in other places. He wriggled, bit his lip, and stamped his feet—anything to dislodge the urgency from his mind, but sometimes the urine still flowed out into his underpants. He didn't mind the hot stream so long as it didn't drip onto the floor beneath him. If it did, he could always mop it up with the duster he was required to carry, but he'd have to do so quickly.

He tried to be long-suffering like Jesus on the cross. "Why should any of you complain about pain?" the spiritual retreat master told him and his classmates. "When you compare your suffering with what Jesus endured in the Garden of Gethsemane—the piercing crown of thorns and the whippings and the pounding of nails into his human flesh—then, my dear boys, it must be clear to you that your sufferings are very small indeed. Furthermore, boys, Jesus never once allowed as much as whimper to cross his lips. No! He never even used a bad word against his executioners. He suffered all this for you and for me to save us from hell and the power of Satan. If the only begotten Son of God could endure such ignominy, then surely we can endure a little pain on behalf of Christ."

Sometimes hot pain poured out of his penis like scalding water. There was no one he could talk to at the seminary, most certainly not a priest. The summer holidays were fast approaching, so he decided to talk to his parents about the pain. He was too old now for his father or mother to examine him, so he would just have to explain in words the excruciating pain he experienced. Until then, he would offer up his suffering on behalf of the poor souls in purgatory. But his suffering overcame him. The pain became so intense that he had to race to the sanitation block to reach the urinal. Sometimes he would arrive only to be confronted with the pain of urine being withheld; other times the urine would spout out of him without warning soaking his pants as he raced along.

The whole experience was overwhelmingly oppressive. Pat had no idea anymore if he could survive until the summer holidays. He had urinated many times on the chapel floor during meditation. He pretended to kneel down in prayer as he secretly mopped up the puddle under the pew.

The worst experience of all happened during his Latin class. He excelled at the subject and was one of the best students in the class, so the professor, Fr Sheridan, a kind, white-haired priest, assigned him to sit in the front row. Pat had taken the precaution of visiting the sanitation block before class began.

He heard Fr Sheridan speaking Arabic or Hebrew, not Latin. Then the piss began to flow down Pat's legs like a mad river arguing with its banks. "I'll show you what a river is!" the piss said. "I'll go on flowing because the minute you try to restrain me, you'll kill me."

"Oh, suffering Jesus, help me!" Pat thought. It was but a small pool of piss, really, but to him it was as big as the sea. Fr Sheridan looked at him up and down, down and up, and Pat felt like the cesspool that had come out of him. He couldn't help it; he began to cry uncontrollably. His mouth said nothing, but his eyes said, "Please, Fr Sheridan. Please help me!"

A RETURN TO REALITY

Fr Pat awakened with sweat pouring out of him. He heard himself shouting, "Please help me!" but he wasn't sure why. All he remembered was shouting and waking himself. The candle had melted into extinction and the CD player had gone mute. He was lying in the same position on the couch as he had been in before falling asleep. He looked at his watch. "Oh, Christ, it can't be that time. I don't believe I've been asleep for four hours." He put on his pyjamas and went to bed.

The next morning, as was usual, he read the *New York Times* as he ate his breakfast. The science section and the op-ed page usually stimulated him. He read these sections with passion and awe. He often thought, "If Jesus were around today, he would discuss and preach about topics such as these."

He maintained a living rather than historical approach to Jesus. "If the Church used the disclosures from the daily news in a contemporary way and showed the faithful in an interpenetrative way how the Good News story applies to contemporary culture, then people might listen more attentively. Instead in a fossilized way it continued to perpetuate the same boring story of hell and damnation."

The physical structure of ST. JUDE'S CHURCH was built with stone in a style typical of eighteenth century church architecture. The imposing edifice sent out a powerful signal of permanence. Originally, the altar, built with ornate Italian marble, served as the frontal display in the sanctuary, but later, the liturgy commission for the Second Vatican Council recommended that the table be turned around so that the priest faced the people and that the tabernacle be placed on a side altar so the faithful could worship privately. The Monsignor was not happy with this arrangement at all and insisted that the tabernacle be placed right square in the middle of the altar of sacrifice, what he considered its true worshipful place. This presented a problem, however: now that the priest was facing the congregation, his face unless he was tall was obstructed from the faithful.

It so happened that during Fr Pat's tenure in the parish, another parish priest, a very small man, could not be seen behind the tabernacle. Monsignor recognized that he either had to remove the tabernacle or require this little Italian priest to wear high-heeled shoes. But the people would faint in shock if they saw a priest walk to the altar wearing high heels along with his medieval attire. Fr Pat also sacrilegiously thought, "While you're at it, Monsignor, you should complete the outfit by converting the thurible into a purse and have the priest sling it over his shoulder." The very thought made Fr Pat laugh.

This hilarious dilemma was finally solved by raising the platform behind the tabernacle. However, in doing that, Monsignor created another problem. In helping the little Italian priest to look up at the congregation, all the other taller assistants now had to look down at them. In a church built on symbolism, this was much more damaging than a priest wearing high-heeled shoes!

Later that day, Fr Pat received a mysterious note in the mail with no signature and no return address. He wondered if it could possibly from Miss Prado. She was always up to something devious and made her feelings known that the Bishop should never have ordained him and that he was a disgrace to Catholicism. The note read: "You are not a priest but an actor, and if I might say, a poor one at that. I came here to pray, but you turned holy mass into a Broadway play."

Monsignor had scarcely acknowledged him for days. Fr Pat knew the pattern; this was the calm before the storm. But the storm didn't come this time. Very strange.

When he arrived home from his hospital visitation, a handful of telephone messages from the secretary greeted him. One of them was from the Bishop's office and read simply, "Call the Bishop's secretary." When a priest receives a message like that, he'd better attend to it immediately, Fr Pat knew.

He dialled the number. "Hello, Larry? This is Pat from St Jude's parish You called me?"

"Yes, Pat, I did. The Bishop would like to see you as soon as possible."

"Do you know what it's about?'

"No, I don't. What happens between a priest and his bishop is their own private affair."

"Come on, Larry. He must have said something to you," Fr Pat probed.

"When is it convenient for you to see His Excellency?" Fr Larry asked, ignoring the question.

"Anytime that suits him is fine with me. He's a very busy man, so I'll adjust accordingly."

"Fine. Now, let me see . . ." Larry clicked his tongue as he checked the schedule. "Would ten o'clock on Friday morning suit you?"

"Perfect."

"That's provided there is no emergency. You understand, Pat. You never know with a Bishop's schedule . . ."

"I understand. Thanks." He hung up the phone and immediately wondered what this could be about.

The first thought that pierced his mind was the most recent threat Miss Prado had made. That would explain the Pastor's iciness toward him too.

"Could it possibly be that Miss Prado has finally taken action on her threats? But on the other hand, maybe the Bishop wants to make me a pastor," Fr Pat mused. "I did apply for St Luke's Church, but I doubt if he'll give it to me."

St Luke's was a rich church, but Fr Pat wasn't interested in it for the sake of his own prestige. He simply wanted the freedom to express his creativity. He hated politics and money management. He had no expertise or inclination for that type of ministry. He knew money was necessary, but he believed a priest's priority must be the inspiration of his parishioners. When people were spiritually nourished, material support would follow. If he had the freedom, he would attempt through the miracle of photography to bring images from the ordinary world inside the church at Sunday mass. He wanted to teach people to connect spirituality to their everyday affairs and interweave the disparate and even despised lives of underprivileged people in foreign lands to their Western experiences.

"Africa is not so far away," he planned to say in one presentation. "It should haunt us that in our insane economy, a pound of dog food sells for more on the market of the human heart than a starving child in deepest Africa." He'd accompany this statement with a picture of the huge eyes of a hungry African child that would melt into the delightful eyes of a beautiful puppy staring out from a package of dog food. There were millions of such obvious ways to integrate the spiritual with the secular. He felt his calling from God was to do that precisely and passionately.

He very much wanted to talk to the Bishop about this mission, but he did not know the man very well. The present Bishop had been appointed to the diocese about four years before, replacing the Bishop who had interrogated Fr Pat many times about his esoteric views when the Vatican had moved the Bishop to a far more desirable sea by appointing him Cardinal of Baltimore. Fr Pat rarely spoke to the current Bishop and hardly even saw him except at confirmation time. Once he briefly spoke with the Bishop at the annual Catholic Charity Ball. He seemed an affable man from a distance as Fr Pat watched him mingle with the rich and the famous, but he had learned to never judge a bishop by his regal cover. One's adeptness with social graces could cleverly conceal greed. It was true that Fr Pat made the Bishop's acquaintance at their monthly conferences and annual retreat, but such meetings concerned ecclesiastical and liturgical matters rather than more personal issues. For those, usually the office of the clergy acted as intermediary between priests and the Bishop, but the fact that Fr Pat had now been officially called to the diocesan office indicated that the Bishop wanted to discuss something seriously personal.

Fr Pat had already worked in various parishes for nine years before the present Bishop was appointed to the diocese, so he had long since learned to keep a low profile in respect to those above him in the hierarchy. Bishops were a thorn in the flesh to Fr Pat. He had endured enough inquisitions to last a lifetime. It was a daily struggle to appropriately balance opening his mouth and closing it. In his daily ministry, he tried to keep the Bishop as remote from him as the Pope in Rome.

A PASTORAL BISHOP

Finally, Friday morning came, and Fr Pat put on his Roman collar. He felt hypocritical about wearing it, but he thought the Bishop would expect a dignified decorum. As he entered the office for the appointment, the Bishop kept his eyes glued on him but put out his hand and welcomed him to sit. The Bishop looked relaxed and, to Fr Pat's surprise, wasn't wearing his Roman collar, just a black clerical shirt with no collar. He looked like a normal man without his ecclesiastical trappings.

There was no sign of pomposity about him. His coat of arms hung next to a picture of the Pope, but apart from that, his office was minimally decorated, giving it an air of sparseness much more than luxury Fr Pat was surprised by this also. When he had last been in this office, the room was stuffed with all the trappings of elegance and luxury. He had often heard that the Bishop was a simple man, but he hadn't expected his superior to be as simple as this. Fr Pat's own apartment in the rectory was much more luxurious.

"Do you know why I called you in?" the Bishop asked.

"No," Fr Pat answered honestly, "but I have my suspicion."

"To get to the point, then, your pastor has made a lot of complaints about you, although I've heard many good reports concerning your ministry. In short, Monsignor wants you to leave St Jude's parish."

"Do I have the right to defend myself?" Fr Pat asked carefully.

"Of course you do," the Bishop said. "Every priest is entitled to due process. I try my best to be a just man, and in my eyes, a person is innocent until proven guilty."

"What charges has Monsignor brought against me?"

"Well, to be quite frank, heresy and blasphemy. Serious accusations, to be sure. If the accusations are proved true, the matter lies beyond my jurisdiction and will have to be presented to Rome."

The Bishop paused briefly. "But please relax. I have no intention to pursue such a course. I notice you are a bit of an outsider, and I like that. So was Jesus. I'm a very shy man, as you may have heard, and I've had my own struggles with my faith. At one point, I almost left the priesthood because of my doubts. To live is to question. I have rarely shared my reservations with another priest, except, of course, my spiritual director. Certainly because of my own pain, I can identify with what you've been going through. I've looked at all your records and listened to many of your sermons on the tapes which Miss Prado sends to me without fail every week. It seems to me that yes, you are a heretic, but for all the right reasons. What is heresy one year becomes the truth the next. I view my position of authority not as a means for self-promotion but as a way to allow you and a few other fine priests like you to exercise your vision. This Church of ours is out of touch with the real world. It needs renewal.

"I've heard about your fine work in the whole area of communications. I hear that you photograph exquisitely. We need to support men like you. I align myself with the passion which propel men like yourself. We all need prodding. I know you are good at what you do. You give a different perspective. It may seem hypocritical to some that I should continue in my role as Bishop when I myself doubt the very veracity of the

Church, but a man should be judged more by his motivation than his accomplishments. What may seem hypocritical to one may be paradoxical yet honest to another. If the Vatican knew my honest opinion I would be immediately dismissed. Perhaps in colloquial parlance I am an infiltrator, but my deviousness is energized by the conviction that I can do greater good by staying than by leaving. I play the Vatican at its own game not for myself but that young men like you with a new vision can survive in my diocese. If the outcome of my deviousness is good, then my very deviousness enables good to prevail. Even a week of goodness and compassion can outshine a hundred years of evil. I must protect priests like you, for the hounds will pounce on you as soon as I'm gone. We are yet again in the Roman catacombs. We whisper more than we thunder. You and I are in this together."

The Bishop stood up and opened a drawer of his desk. He pulled out a handful of tapes and scattered them all over the desk. Pointing at them, he said, "There you see. I have been listening to your sermons, even those from the Protestant churches that you lectured in. I listened to them not to decipher your heresy but to listen and learn from them. Life can be ironic, can't it? By sending me these tapes, Miss Prado in trying to destroy you by showing what she claims to be heresy, in truth and fact has helped you. Little does she realize it though. Contradictions help us to think more deeply. You are a man who lives outside the box. Your enemies have helped you. In truth they have refined you.

Jesus was an outsider and an outcast too.

Our Church no longer keeps its ear to the ground. We have become not only arrogant but also ignorant. Stupidity is bad enough but ignorance is inexcusable. I as your Bishop thank you. You have confirmed many of my own suspicions. As seekers of truth we are being refined together."

Fr Pat was shocked. He had never expected to hear such honesty from a bishop. He could not believe his ears. He knew that some of the spiritually thirsty people in his parish agreed with him, but never did he expect such an affirmation from a bishop.

"Thank you, Bishop. I'm honestly surprised. I really did not expect this response from any bishop in the Roman Catholic Church."

"Both Monsignor and Miss Prado, apart from sending in those tapes, also tell me you're cavorting with the Episcopalian minister's wife. They tell me she's a beautiful looking woman. What's at the bottom of that story?" the Bishop enquired.

"They exaggerate," Fr Pat said. "They see smoke and they cry fire. Yes, she is a very beautiful woman, and I enjoy her company. She's very feminine. She's an artist and a dancer, and she uses her dance to praise God. I've tried to integrate her art form with my photography and poetry. Together we create complementary expressions of the same prayer. We blend our creativity to give people a deeper experience of divinity. That's the tall and the short of the story."

The Bishop listened to Fr Pat's and then took a letter from the top drawer of his desk. He scanned it for a moments and then, laying it aside, said, 'They tell me that you allow Episcopalians to receive Eucharist in St Jude parish, that you preach more heresy in Protestant churches, and that you bring a lot of embarrassment to untutored Catholics who cannot intelligently defend the belief system of our Holy Mother the Church."

"That last point has never been my intention," Fr Pat said. "I had no idea such a thing was happening, especially in this ecumenical age. My whole approach to priestly ministry has been to bring people together to share our differences in a compassionate way. My aim has been to unify and never to destroy."

The Bishop took up the letter again and scanned it once more. Then, looking up at Fr Pat, he said, "It says here that you sound more measured in front of Catholics than you do before other Christian denominations and that you spend a lot more of your time in Protestant churches than you do in your own parish. Why do they say that, do you suppose?"

"In answer," Fr Pat said passionately, "I would tell my accusers that God has the same love for all of his creation. Protestant or Catholic, we are all one before the Divine. The energy of divinity is not discretionary; it seeps into all the corners and crevices of our world. Divisions in religion have been man-made, and they are stupid. God is interested in unity. The cosmos has always been one and will always remain so. It has ever been thus since the Big Bang. Division in our churches is anti-evolutionary, and it is time the religions of the world got their act together."

The Bishop looked very impressed by Fr Pat's passionate articulation. "But you haven't really answered my question," he said.

"I'm sorry, Bishop. I got carried away. I'm sick and tired of always having to defend myself. These accusations are wearing me thin. I know I might be wrong, but so what? I'm human. So long as a man has a pure intention, that's all that matters. The other stuff is trivia. Could you please repeat the question?"

"I was just wondering why you felt more comfortable in a Protestant circle than in a Catholic one."

Fr Pat thought for a moment. "I haven't really thought about it too much, but I suppose I feel more comfortable particularly with Episcopalians and Lutherans because they are more readily disposed to listen to me. Protestants are far more open to change than Catholics. They are more spiritually astute, it seems to me."

"Yes," the Bishop said. "The teacher comes when the student is ready."

"I try to bring balance into everything I preach," Fr Pat said. "I know it's very difficult for some older people to change their Religious perspectives, and I know that I won't persuade them to my rendition of the truth. We are all entitled to our own approach to God. My problem is that we should never live with a belief that has been coerced into us. Just as these older people don't believe my more radical ideas, there are millions of spiritually hungry and intelligent people who think the meta-myths of the Church are childish and manipulative. I try to assess the audience to which I am invited to talk, but no matter the audience, I always suggest that they look at reality from a different perspective. I probe more than prove."

"God knows this Church of ours needs a bit of probing," the Bishop said. "Now that I'm older, I'm more prone to discern than to disapprove. I would prefer to leave the diocese like this. Religion needs to be kicked out of its complacency. Your kind of disturbance is what's needed. It may sound like hell to the Vatican, but the best patriot is most often the critic. These Opus Dei people don't make life easy for us. They think I don't pull the reins hard enough. If they only knew my true thoughts, they would soon be on a journey to Rome with piles of money to get rid of me. But I've learned the game well enough to know how to survive in it. I'm a son of John XXIII. He was elected only to fill a gap, but did he ever surprise his electors. Had he lived longer, more truth might have reached the light.

Unfortunately, though the windows he opened have been closed again, and more tightly, I'm afraid. It's a tough time to be a priest. You are rare, and that's why I'll do my best to protect you. But I won't be here much longer. God only knows what suffering is still before you. Are you prepared for that?"

The Bishop went on, "'Too much suffering turns the heart into a stone', Yeats said that! I am not a glutton for punishment. So what should I do? Violate my integrity and live morbidly with the consequences? I cannot abort the sanctity of my own convictions; my values like yours, are chiselled into me, I would even say crucified into my mind. I am man enough to know that truth requires courage and trust. So I must carry on. We will survive. The truth always wins in the end.

I don't want to be crucified! Of course I don't! I would be a liar to tell you the opposite. I'm a coward, but who wouldn't be when confronted by a bunch of snarling dogs ready to tear him apart?

Rome is like a snarling dog. The Curia destructs much more than it constructs. I know they are after you. Miss Prado is a cute whore., But I will defend you. I promise you this. The most exquisite thing about the human mind is that good ideas can remain after a person's death to benefit all humans. The body of a man may be torn to shreds, but his ideas, if they further enhance the human condition, will become part of the world's accumulated wisdom. That is especially what I love about Jesus. He is my Ghandi, Martin Luther King, Mother Theresa, and Nelson Mandela all grouped into one. I will carry on or should I say we will carry on"

The Bishop's speech brought tears to Fr Pat's eyes, and he asked, "Bishop, what makes you carry on?"

"I am an old man now but am wise enough to know that learning never ends," the Bishop said. "As a man grows older, if he is really honest with himself, he will grow wiser and hopefully become a better person. I have learned that certainty answers nothing. Authority best serves others with the least interference. Now that I am older, my only future is the present. I treasure it. The older I grow, the more I take on the ways of a child. I use my imagination more and ask why continuously. You inspire me Father. It is men like you that give me purpose.

As you know, Father, I lost my lovely sister, her three children, and her husband in a terrible automobile accident five years ago. That catastrophe made me lose all ambition. Life is a fragile thing. What a paradox it is that the first time we begin to appreciate the gift of life happens mostly when we have been shocked into taking stock of its preciousness. Unfortunately, wisdom usually comes at life's end instead of at its beginning. If I were God, I would turn life precisely the other way around. I would give wisdom to the young and ambition to the old. But what is an old man like me to do? Compassion is my only option. Never ask me to decide your future. You are the master of your own destiny. You are your own ambassador."

The Bishop then stood up and rummaged through Miss Prado's tapes lying on his desk. He looked at the dates of a few of them before choosing one and putting it into a small recorder. "What do you think of this? A little vulgar, perhaps?" he asked.

It was the recording of Fr Pat's lecture on duality. His voice was clear: "The cosmos is one. Quantum physics teaches us this. Everything on earth is interconnected and interrelated. Nothing is secular. All is sacred in the one continuum. Contraries are complementary. Existence is a clash of opposites. There can be no light without darkness, no joy without pain, no courage without cowardice, no belief without doubt. All are part of the same reality.

There can be no God if the spark of divinity is not within us. Matter is saturated with divinity. A great Intelligence follows us everywhere. When I go to the toilet, divinity goes with me. A God who doesn't fart isn't very interesting—"

The Bishop turned off the recorder. "I'd like you to discuss these ideas on duality more with you." Then he looked at his watch and gasped. "Oh my God! I'm late for my next appointment. Larry should have told me, but of course, I warned him not to interrupt. Could you possibly send me an essay on the matter?"

"Of course, Bishop. I'd be happy to oblige."

A few days later, Fr Pat posted his essay along with a note that read, "Dear Bishop: I enclose herewith my essay on dualism. I have also included an essay on its necessary corollary, the spiritual dimension to quantum physics, for your perusal.

DUALISM

The two great pillars of Western culture, the Church and science, got it wrong from the beginning. The Church followed Aristotle instead of Plato. In so doing, we not only accepted dualism but even promulgated it through murder and terror. We divided spirit from body, mind from matter, immanence from transcendence. Aristotle separated all materiality and spirituality. This is dualism. The Classical Greek approach proclaimed that the earth is alive but God is outside of it. This is dualism. The Protestant Revolution held that Scripture was the domain of God and the material world the domain of science. This is dualism.

Dualism continued to reign. In the sixteenth century, a mechanistic view of the world emerged which proclaimed that matter is dead and inert, thereby killing God off completely. This total divorce, the philosophy of the so-called Enlightenment, was heralded in by the thinking of Descartes, whose famous phrase, "Cogito ergo sum," "I think therefore I am," separated the subject from the object, the mind from matter. The only truth was empirical truth: nothing should be believed unless proven objectively. Empiricism became the imperialism of the Enlightenment.

Materialistic science promised a techno-utopia here on earth. The Church promised a resurrected utopia in the next world. Dualism remains the biggest problem confronting Western Culture. Not only is dualism rampant in the clash between materialism and religion but within each pillar of Western culture.

Now, only rational, objective proof is accepted. Everything must be placed under a microscope or a telescope and scrutinized. All through the ages, until Descartes, room had been left for subjective experience, through belief in transcendence or an afterlife. But after Descartes, that approach was considered unenlightened. Religion became mere tokenism, a throwback to less enlightened times. Materialistic science became synonymous with sophistication. Transcendence became a taboo since it could not be proved. Religion was for peasants. Belief in an afterlife was nothing more than an opiate for the suffering or the regressive need of a child for its parent. Materialism dealt with the flatland of the provable and the profitable, gradually canonizing itself as the supreme master, and king not only of earth but of heaven itself.

Such a philosophy, because it so readily deals with the ego alone, caters much more to greed and selfishness, to accumulation and accomplishment, than it does to the necessary graces needed for refinement and civility. When a system divides in order to conquer, as the dominant force in Western materialist culture did, then inevitably new growling wolves arrive at the door.

A FRENCH MONASTERY

As Fr Pat wrote the essay, he was reminded of its points by two documentaries he watched consecutively. He had often thought he missed his true vocation when he joined the diocesan priesthood. Either the contemplative life of the Cistercian monks or the academic life of the Jesuits would have suited him better. His insecurity and lack of confidence proved more powerful than his desire though, and his fear of rejection deterred him from applying to either order. He could still recall almost every detail his visit with his mother to the Trappist monastery in Roscrea. The idea that his sister was thrown out of the milk parlour because she was a female still tickled him.

After that visit, his fascination with Cistercian monasticism was heightened further when a beautiful French woman in one of the parishes he served in fell head over heels in love with him. She had told him that her husband, a Hungarian intellectual, was not very impressed by the quality and content of his preaching., Her husband eventually became precipitously ill and was diagnosed with a virulent strain of cancer. He was given only a week to live. The French lady solicited Fr Pat to break the dreadful news to her husband.

It was imperative that he put all his legal affairs in order. She was very much in love with her husband, and her whole world was torn apart with the news of his impending death. The deeper her sadness and pain, the more Fr Pat was present to her.

As the grieving period moved from months into years, the bereaved wife grew to love and depend on Fr Pat. He had never been to France, so when she asked him to spend his vacation with her in her homeland, he jumped at the chance. He had always been enraptured by the beautiful churches and monasteries there. She hired a car and drove him to every sight he longed to see. He stood in awe at the magnificent cathedrals and felt totally inspired by the creative genius of men from ages past who were possessed by the fire of God. He marvelled at the Church of St Denis in Paris, where the round arches of

Roman architecture finally found a new expression in the astonishing arches of Gothic architecture.

As they drove through northern France, much of their adventure centred on the discovery of living monasteries, where the monks magnificently chanted psalms daily and bells still rang across the valleys, beckoning them to recall simpler and more serene times. However, most of the monasteries they visited, though still intact, were now little more than museums. The Spirit had gone out of them. Some of what Fr Pat called "dead monasteries", still magnificently situated on islands in the middle of lakes, had been turned into restaurants serving gourmet food. The smell of the incense from the thurable had been replaced by mouth-watering smells from the frying pan. The original purpose of these monasteries had been turned upside down, the thought of transcendence was now pitifully absent, and perhaps even frowned upon as unenlightened.

Fr Pat wondered what the monks would have to say about their chefs-d'oeuvre?

Often when Fr Pat returned to his room in the rectory at night, he felt weary and sometimes troubled by what he had encountered during the day. To alleviate the stress, he sometimes read or listened to classical music, but rarely watched television because, in general, he considered it a wasteland oversaturated with gratuitous violence. and catering to the lowest common denominator. PBS was the only channel he turned on, as he considered all other stations little more than propaganda machines. for the government. He felt deeply that a definite connection could be made between digitalized mayhem and murder and carnage on Main Street.

But recently, he had looked at the TV menu and noticed a documentary on *French Monastic Restaurants* was on. He wondered if any of the monastic restaurants he had visited (but had refused, on principle, to eat in) would be included in the programme. He turned on the TV. The documentary had already started. Synchronicity took charge, and the very first scene showed a beautiful boat full of wealthy European and American tourists sailing across the tranquil water of a lake towards the shore of one of the monasteries he and his French

95

companion had visited. He felt transported when he saw the pictorial of the monastery unfold. It was as if time stood still. He was sure he had heard the sound of the monastery bell tolling over the lake. The expanding ripples left in the boat's wake transmuted into the haunting plain chant of the monks.

But he was shaken from his reverie when the wealthy tourists disembarked on dry land. Their affected screams of delight, their empty vulgar chatter was not about the transcendent beauty of the monastery's architecture or the incredible natural beauty surrounding the enclosure. Instead they prattled on about something much more temporal: the food. All connection with the sacred or the eternal had been gluttonized out of them.

They babbled on, deeming themselves the crème de la crème, the real connoisseurs of fine food. They dismissed people of less delicate and refined taste as infra dig. These rich tourists never took a moment out to say a prayer. Surely the monks buried in the cemetery turned in their graves. Their hard work and craftsmanship dedicated to nobler purposes had become de-sacralized. Such was the madness of contemporary culture—vulgarity had become the new sophistication and the sacred as unenlightened and idiotic.

Fr Pat watched in horror as the gourmet chefs from the restaurant set their nets to catch hundreds of little singing birds upon their migration back to Africa. These birds were not much larger than sparrows. He felt nauseated as these little creatures were then killed, plucked, and eviscerated only to reappear as roasted appetizers on the restaurant's menu. These little creatures had made a heroic effort and overcome unimaginable obstacles as they sought out a warmer climate only to be struck down when, at last, they neared their destination. Some of them had spent the whole summer in Europe building their nests, selflessly rearing their young on insects caught with efficient and dynamic techniques They were attentive and faithful parents, and their undying zeal was to nurture and prepare their young for the long flight to a warmer clime. Driven by some inner calling, parents and offspring congregated together and then took off in flocks for their winter homeland. The pure savagery of pampered, gluttonous men and women put an end to these little creatures' lives. The tourists chewed on their small bodies without a thought for the poetry and sanctity of their little lives.

"Too many acts of savagery are applauded and supported by the entitled," Fr Pat thought. "The entitled are the blind. In a world with no moral compass, crime is crowned and vulgarity canonized. Our planet is evolving upside down. We rob the skies of new stories and silence our little songsters' Glorias. The song of the birds is necessary in a world nearly bereft of auditory beauty. We already have bulged bellies, but owned by the wrong species."

He switched the channel and again synchronicity was determined to increase his sensitivity. The programme on the new channel centred on the indigenous peoples of the Amazon whose habitat and sustainable way of life was becoming more and more threatened by the barbarism of corporate greed in its search for minerals. Fr Pat was mesmerized by the simplicity of these indigenous people's lives, separate from the outside world impoverished of the sacred. They only took from nature what was necessary and had built up a medicinal wisdom not learned from the white man but from their own accumulated association and intimacy with plant life. Their lives were interdependent and interconnected with everything which immediately surrounded them. They lived as a part of nature, not apart from it. Possessed by a deep reverence for all that sustained them, they gave honour and reverence to the trees, plants, and animals in the forest. They had absolutely no problem with the concept that all life is possessed by Spirit. Like all human beings, something within them made them reach out for something more. They knew that spirituality doomed the human race. Unlike people educated in the "civilized" world, intellectual distinctions and complications never hid the Spirit of God from them. They natively believed in transcendence. They did not practice meditation, they lived it.

At one point in the programme, the people needed a new boat in order to fish in the local river, as the old boat had sprung a leak and was no longer safe. The men of the forest selected a huge hardwood tree, but before chopping it down, they joined in prayer around its trunk. They conversed with it as though it was a living spirit and expressed profound gratefulness and appreciation for its longevity and providence. Alive with a collective unconsciousness, they had never compromised their will to believe in a higher power. It was as natural to them as the wood in their boats. Chopping down the tree was not a wanton act of butchery but one born from the sacred dimension and of pure necessity.

Comparing the two documentaries, Fr Pat felt that contemporary culture had become so twisted and insidious that savagery had become accepted as the new enlightenment and true enlightenment as the real savagery. Herein lay the clash between spirituality and egotistical mechanistic materialism.

† † †

His essay on dualism continued:

The greatest problem facing our planet is that power mongers and sophisticates have yet to learn that God lives in the forests and the ghettos more than in castles. When acceptance, gratefulness, peace, and reverence go out, in come greed, want, anxiety, turmoil, and fear. Scientific materialism loves us in such a state. Its profits are made on the back of greed which feeds the ego and the body. As a result, we have become a dis-eased people. We are not at rest with our Spirit. We are truncated. We are disjointed. We are not integrated.

Boredom and lack of purpose and morality take root in a culture so disjointed. The result is that we take drugs and commit crime to escape the ennui. While the needs of our bodies may be met in the wealthy West, never has our culture needed the integration of immanence with transcendence more. We are spiritually famished and impoverished. And far worse, we don't even recognize it. We cry out for completion by purchasing the latest gadget, but materialism at best offers us but lollipops. Our shopping malls have become our temples, and still we scream with anxiety. We have not learned yet the insufficiency of everything available through our warehouses and stores. Our lifestyle itself is telling us we are in a deep crisis. Despite the overabundance of ontological emptiness which Descartes and his successors have offered, our deepest yearning for meaning has not been satisfied,. We must look somewhere else.

Logically, we turn to the Church and religion, the other great pillar of our society. We need it for balance. The business of the Church, after all, is transcendence. It concerns itself with end times, the afterlife, and concerns immaterial. It is the flip side of the coin. What the Church must offer has no need for objective proof or the empiricism of materialism. Its realm lies outside the scope of the microscope or the telescope. It is not substantial. It cannot be measured. The Church's mission should provide what we need in order to complete our being. Thus the clash of opposites. Dualism has divided us.

But the Church itself, while acknowledging humanity's need for transcendence, is guilty of dualism So how can we solve our ontological problem? Where does the answer to humankind's quest for significance and truth lie? We need a new paradigm. We must get rid of dualism altogether, not only in scientific materialism but also in religion.

In what way is our religion dualistic? It may surprise you to hear that it is saturated with dualism. From the story of Adam and Eve to our lives today, our transcendence has been manipulated and punctured with what the Church calls the sins of the flesh. It was through St Augustine, not Adam and Eve, that the error of dualism entered religion. Augustine taught that original sin came into the world through concupiscence. The sin of Adam and Eve has contaminated humanity ever since.

Augustine claimed that human beings were utterly depraved in nature. The Council of Carthage in AD 418 confirmed this. It is surely an anomaly that celibates who know the least about human sexuality should be such experts in legislating about it. In an arena where humanity is most vulnerable, the misuse of power and control becomes most likely. Just as materialistic science cuts off transcendence, which lies in the arena of the spirit, so now religion cuts out the importance of the body in favour of the soul. Love ever since has been divided into Eros and Agape. Immanence has been separated from transcendence.

The here and the hereafter continue to be separated from each other. The dualism of Aristotle and Augustine continues to reign supreme in the Church. It has continued to exercise its hatred of the body through the ages by insisting on the need to be washed from original sin through baptism, through the encouragement of flagellation of the body in the middle ages, and, until recently, through the practice of churching women after giving birth. The Church has always insisted that this world is but a vale of tears.

Each of the two pillars which are meant to support society, due to their dualism, no longer serve that purpose, one for its dismissal of transcendence in favour of the body, the other for the dismissal of the body in favour of transcendence. We need a new paradigm.

So what must we do in a world exhausted by anxiety and bewilderment? Is there an answer? The Church still insists that matter, rather than being holy, is a hindrance to transcendence. It maintains that through matter sin first entered this world in the Garden of Eden and that only through the mediation of God's Only begotten Son can we receive reconciliation and cease the rupture—that this world needs supernatural intervention if it is to be saved from itself. Clearly, the scourge of duality will never be solved through the Church's insistence on its own version of reality

Clearly also the scourge of duality cannot be solved through atheistic materialism, which insists that there is no transcendent reality. Live life to the fullest while there is time for it, materialism preaches, for there is no God, and if there were, we would have no need of him. So grasp all you can; there is no point in reaching for more. Spend, consume, and enjoy. There is nothing else. This world is randomness. It came about by mere chance.

So where is the human race to find an answer to this scourge of dualism? Neither religion nor atheistic materialism, for the sake of its own survival, can abandon its position, as by doing so, it would destroy its own business.

Our incredible zeal for the marketing of material goods, based on the premise that the human heart is forever restless, has smothered the cry of the human spirit for meaning and purpose. Through its offerings of momentary distractions, the world of advertising has perverted the unquenchable longing stamped by nature on our soul. The world of advertising addresses only material consumption. Its fundamental flaw is that it manipulates transcendence for immanent reasons. It resorts to a power outside itself for its own selfish ends; it capitalizes on what is essentially spiritual for profit and material gain. In spite of the manipulation, the truth of the matter remains: "divinity defines us", as Shakespeare said.

We now see that neither religion nor materialism gives us an acceptable answer to our earth-bound experience. Will the tribal warfare between the two most powerful determinants in our world continue to torture us with anxiety and fear? Must we look forever upwards and outwards for meaning and purpose, as religion suggests or must we be content to say that God is merely a bankrupt Santa Claus, leaving us as cosmic orphans wandering in the dark? The human race had little chance of resolving this dilemma until intelligent men and women within the scientific community admitted in humility that perhaps scientific materialism does not provide the final answer., The seer, the subject, peering into the microscope or the telescope must be considered as much as the object under investigation. Contrary to the dualism of Descartes and sixteenth century materialistic science as a whole, this new scientific perspective put an end to dualism by stressing the interconnection and interrelationship between subject and object. A discovery can no longer be considered to be objectively true unless the subject is taken into account. Both subject and object are linked with each other henceforth. Subject and object cannot be separated. Finally the dimension of the human mind has been introduced as necessary to any objective study.

Quantum physics has put an end to dualism.

QUANTUM PHYSICS

Quantum means "lump" or "package", a package or a lump of information. We cannot receive this information until particles are joined together and interact with each other. It is through this interrelationship of particles that matter dances with life. The same particles which dance inside of you and me dance in all matter. What was given to any material object in the beginning was given to all material objects. We are all the recipients of the same stardust which the Big Bang initially spat out.

The name of this new science is quantum physics. Its main thesis is that *the whole is greater than the sum of its parts.* This insight is one of the most inspirational and inerrant observations ever to emerge from the mind of man. It has finally shattered the duality separating matter from spirit, immanence from transcendence, heaven from earth, the here from the hereafter. It tells us, in essence, that we are matter (quanta) moving into consciousness. Another way of saying this that our bodies (matter, quanta) have the potential for transcendence—invisibleness and ultimately nothingness. This is the true meaning of physical death. This is the language of mysticism.

Quantum physics is both microscopic and telescopic. It involves awareness of the micro—and macro-universe. It advances everywhere like an uncontrollable army. Life itself cannot conquer it because it is life itself. Quantum physics is concerned not only with wholeness but also with holiness. The local is tied to the non-local on a continuum, and as long as matter remains, the non-local is ever out there ahead of us. We mortals are emerging into the immortal. This one truth from the world of science substantiates all the inner workings of our world. This truth is sacred. When it is violated, malevolence shows its ugly head. The moment the construction of this primary law is tampered with is the moment of destruction.

Atheistic materialists may indeed sneer at religion, which they see as a scapegoat for this primordial construction, but in the end they are laughing at themselves because they also have presented a false saviour: its name is not Jesus but material consumption. Religion and scientific materialists each present a solution with a narrow perspective from opposite ends of the same spectrum. The problem is that there can be no solution to something that is already perfect. Quantum physics would be especially intolerant of the idea that God sent Jesus as mender of a system which does not need mending. The most telling truth about Jesus of Nazareth is that he remained ever faithful to the holistic law of the quantum. Jesus exemplified holism so much so that we now revere him as a wholey holy man.

Quantum physics invites not just wholeness but also holiness. One is not possible without the other. Corporations who exploit matter for the sake of profit beware—quantum physics will not tolerate such misguided intrusion into the very life of the atom. The particle must morph into the nothingness of consciousness; it cannot be used to substantiate the profit motif of misdirected men, for when it is, these men, be they clerics or bankers, become the devils among us.

The quantum is *the all in the one*. It unites. It joins the local to the non-local, thereby transfusing matter with a transcendence. Every possible bit of matter is therefore holistic and must be considered precious and sacred because it is interconnected and interrelated to our own bodies. The cosmos is one. Logically, then, if we kick or consciously destroy another person, we do so to ourselves because at the quantum level, we are all one.

Jesus spent his whole ministry trying to teach us this. He embodied the findings of quantum physics without even knowing it. He proclaimed, "All humans are brothers and sisters." Much of his ministry was devoted to the abolition of tribalism, which gestates through insecurity, and the urge of the ego to dominate.

Jesus preached the opposite, in harmony with the continuum. His magnificent aphorism, "Do unto others as you would have them do unto you," is the very spirituality which underlies quantum physics.

Hinduism, which has never entertained dualism, teaches that "thou art that": we respect ourselves when we respect others. The same law applies to all other matter on the evolutionary ladder. Forests, plants, animals, birds, all living creatures must be considered sacred and necessary for our survival. Nature itself is a scripture, and it is in our own interest that we listen to it. We each are but parts of the local embraced by some great non-local Intelligence.

As Meister Eckhart teaches us, "Apprehend God in all things, for God is in all things. Every single creature is full of God and is a book about God. Every creature is a word of God. If I spent enough time with the tiniest creature—even a caterpillar—I would never have to prepare a sermon. So full of God is every creature."

Walt Whitman echoes the point: "A mouse is miracle enough to stagger sextillions of infidels".

As Dostoyevsky tells us, "Love God's creation, love every atom of it separately and love it also as a whole. Love every green leaf, every way of God's light. Love the animals and the plants and love every inanimate object. If you come to love all things, you will perceive God's mystery inherent in all things. Once you have perceived it, you will understand better and better every day and finally you will love the whole world with a total, universal love."

Recently we have seen a prime example of the sacred bond between all living things. We learned that bees were disappearing at an alarming rate. At first glance, the bee appears to be an insignificant insect capable only of making honey. In itself, this is not necessary for humankind's survival, but miraculously, this little creature through its busyness and impressive dedication pollinates the plants that feed other creatures on the evolutionary chain, including ourselves. Without them, all life on our planet would quickly die. If in the future we are stung by a bee, it is far better to say a prayer than to curse this little creature.

Consider also the earthworm. Like the humble bee, it is of such staggering importance to the food chain which nourishes us that human life could not survive without it. The earthworm aerates the earth and breaks down bacteria, tasks that are essential for the growth of plants. The earthworm was the plougher before the plough was ever invented.

In the dense forests of the Northern United States and Canada, one often notices expanses of pox marked withering trees. At first sight these trees seem to be suffering from some disease, but then upon closer inspection one notices on the tallest branches, not yet withered, thousands upon thousands of caterpillars devouring the remaining leaves. One might be excused for reacting with sadness to the inevitable death confronting these stripped trees.

On closer inspection and analysis however, a scene of miraculous balance, interconnection and interrelationship unfolds. The little caterpillars, in devouring the leaves, create a corridor of sunlight to hit the forest floor, and thereby through photosynthesis energise green plants to grow on the floor below. These plants become the fodder and nutrients upon which deer, hare and other small animals depend for survival. In turn the lynx, the biggest of the wild cats in North America depends on these animals for its own survival. The interconnection, interrelationship and interdependence of the caterpillar and the lynx seem almost incredible at first sight. The same great energy seems to be flowing through everything. It behoves us to look more carefully.

When we look around us, we see material objects of all kinds which we usually perceive as solid and inert. But quantum physics teaches us that material objects are not, in fact, the way we perceive them at all. There is far more to everything than meets the eye. Quantum physics gives us a new perspective; it requires us to take a deeper look. We interpret reality from our own vantage point. We see everything as a linear, and the earth as flat, but if we were to journey on a rocket to outer space, we would see our planet as it truly is: a small blueberry among the multitudinous stars. The earth itself did not changed, but our perspective did. We no longer view things from the linear but from the lateral point of view. Life really isn't what it seems at all. Right now we are on a rocket ship called planet Earth, and it is hurtling through space around the sun at 66,000 miles per hour. But are we conscious of it? Do the seats we sit on register even a creak on the journey? No, it is so smooth that we don't notice the movement. Reality is not what it seems.

Stop and contemplate the fact that the sun is 93 million miles distant from Earth, so it takes the light of the sun ten minutes to reach us. What we see is already ten minutes old. We are seeing into the past. We are not used to such language; it sounds convoluted. But it is we who have twisted the truth, not consciously or deliberately, of course, but because reality does not speak to us directly. Even stranger still, all objects rendered by that same sunlight come to the retinas of our eyes upside down. With the marvellous machinery of the human brain, we turn them around. Everything is not always what it appears to be on the surface.

Quantum physics invites us to look at reality differently. If we were to take another journey on a rocket into the interior of the material world, we would get another perspective which would reveal a reality far different than the familiar. In taking us beyond the obvious, quantum physics shows us not dead and inert matter but particles not in and of themselves but dancing in interconnection in a relationship of energy. This, in reality, is how the material world works. We live amazingly, but we choose to stay stationary. We become lazy and want to stay in our own comfort zone. We refuse to take that rocket into a deeper reality.

Quantum physics takes us to the spot where the particle ends and consciousness begins. In so doing, it allows physics to jump into metaphysics—precisely where spirituality (not religion) begins. Quantum physics from a layperson's point of view is a very complicated mathematical system, but at its core, it breaks matter down into its smallest components. To begin with, there is the atom. the primary building block of matter, which comprises a nucleus, with neutrons and protons and electrons accelerating around it. In between is 99.8 per cent empty space.

Not satisfied with this, humans, in their eternal quest for a theory of everything, sought to break the atom down even further. Compelled by curiosity, they wondered what gave mater its substantiality. Scientists devised ingeniously complex atom smashers to learn what makes up matter. In their efforts, they have found the shadow beyond the substance. They've discovered six flavours of quarks and various other subatomic particles. The latest attempt to smash the atom even further is happening, of course, at the Large Hadron Collider, where scientists search for the Higgs boson, or the "God particle", adopting religious language.

With such breakthroughs in solving the problem of duality by joining matter and mind on a continuum, by moving quanta into consciousness, by clearly seeing the cosmos as one, our traditional support systems must now be toppled. A new paradigm is needed, one that no longer views religion and materialistic science as arch-enemies. Both systems must now face the serious challenge presented to them: materialistic atheistic science must now admit there is at least the possibility of transcendence and God in this world and that we are created for more than consumerism, whereas religion must now admit that this world is a sacred place which does not need to be altered by the intervention of a Saviour. Sin has not blackened it, the body is not evil, and God is with us. If we are to find transcendence, then the first baby step is here. We find and make heaven and earth within ourselves, from the light within us. Like all gifts, that light from within carries with it responsibility. How we use it determines our eternal transcendence and ecstasy. Guided by that inner light and the wisdom of human civility, we determine the invisibility of our no-thing-ness. Mystically we came, and mystically we go back to our original ground.

† † †

Fr Pat felt sure that his essays would make sense to the Bishop. He had found the Bishop to be a very gentle and humble man. Contrary to Fr Pat's expectations, the Bishop was incredibly open to a new paradigm. He had conquered the demonic power of ambition. He had accepted the invitation to forego the ego, having wisely learned that true internal peace, through the exercise of selflessness, enters a man's psyche to the extent that he forfeits control and power over the minds of others. It astonished Fr Pat that any Bishop in the Catholic Church could be so holy. Usually men were chosen because of their obedience in upholding the laws of an atrophied system or for their business acumen. As far as he could see men in the hierarchy were seldom selected for their spirituality. The Bishop, to Fr Pat's delight seemed more like a genuine human being than an autocrat. Fr Pat wondered how he sneaked through the net so cleverly set to fish out the creative and the holy, not to save them, but to dispose of them.

Perhaps in the beginning the Bishop was indeed an arrogant bird of prey but suffering had clipped his wings and instructed him to become a dove of peace and serenity. It would seem that the Bishop had finally learned what autocrats needed to know: peace is won not by war but through the spirituality of dialogue comporomise and diplomacy.

Fr Pat's duties on Wednesday, besides the routine of filling out of mass cards and other such office work, included a novena to Our Lady of Perpetual Succour. The service's attendance was usually made up of a preponderance of little old ladies. They were sweet, innocent, and delightfully warm senior citizens. He loved them and, insofar as he could without violating his own integrity, knew that he should never disturb their faith. These little souls were the apple of God's eye. Fr Pat thought they would never shoot a bullet from a gun or hurt anyone. Their only defence was their rosary beads, and they used holy water instead of agent orange.

Fr Pat felt he didn't have the right to change their views, and besides, unlike their fellow citizens enraptured by the gods of consumerism and the ego, they already lived transcendently. They had not reached the beyond matter through the dictates and rituals of an autocratic Church but through their own introspection and holiness. Without even realizing it, they had tapped into the God within themselves. They used the external only to better solidify the light they found within. Most of these elderly citizens, like their Bishop, had probably gained their wisdom and compassion through personal suffering, and although they might articulate their experiences as simply and superstitiously, in a totally different way from the sophisticated articulation of the Bishop, still they arrived at the same point: "I am in the hands of a power far greater than myself."

OF MAGIC AND THEOLOGY

After the novena, Susie Cameron, Mrs Best, and Lucy Esposito lit candles in the church sanctuary. Mrs O'Hara, another novena-goer, asked Fr Pat if she could speak to him in his office to set a date for her daughter's wedding. As they talked, Susie Cameron, Mrs Stanley, and Lucy Esposito knocked on Fr Pat's door. They were looking for mass cards.

"You'll have to wait for a few minutes until I'm finished with Mrs O'Hara," Fr Pat said. Then he closed his office door again. As he resumed his conversation with Mrs O'Hara, he heard the three other women chatting outside.

"If the wick on the candle burns up straight, that means the dead person in whose memory you lit it had gone straight to heaven," Susie Cameron said.

"Is that so?" Lucy Esposito said. "You learn something new every day! But what happens if the flame flickers or blows sideways?"

Mrs Stanley said knowingly, "That means that the soul of the departed has gone to purgatory."

"Lord have mercy," Lucy said. "Worse still, could it mean the soul has gone to hell?"

"No," Mrs Stanley said. "That only happens when the bloody candle won't light at all."

Fr Pat burst out laughing. Mrs O'Hara asked him what was so funny,

"It's just that those women out there have listened too carefully to my sermons on duality and quantum physics."

Fr Pat also looked forward every week to his discussions with the New Basalians, They were a great outlet for him, and even though at times he felt like a charlatan, he expressed himself freely, and the group accepted and loved him all the more for his honesty.

Miss Prado continued to crucify him for his heresy, no matter what he said. She detested not only the contents of his preaching but even the subjects about which he preached.

"Your duty as a priest is to preach the Gospel, not all these esoteric or hypothetical things," she scolded him. "Stay with the Church's dogma. What have kidneys and hearts to do with Church? They belong in the hospital, not outside of it, and certainly not in a consecrated church. You're no expert, Father. Are you trying to tell us you're a doctor? A lot of us are sick of hearing about body parts. Adam and Eve covered their body parts, and you should stop talking about them. The body is not holy; that comes from the Council of Carthage and St Augustine, a doctor of the Church and not a doctor of medicine. So please, honour the audience you are attempting to inform."

Monsignor and his ubiquitous appendage, Miss Prado, were trying to get rid of Fr Pat, but he knew that the Bishop wouldn't give him his marching orders. That decision was left up to Fr Pat himself, and when the moment came, he would do the honourable thing, but that moment, despite the opposition, had not arrived yet. Miss Prado spoke to him regularly, but Monsignor ignored him. He knew Fr Pat was still ministering compassionately at least to some of the parishioners, which in itself was his mandate. Fr Pat would continue at the parish for the time being at least.

"It is necessary to be foundational," Fr Pat said at this week's meeting of the New Basalians, "before we can build up an edifice sufficient to engender enough excitement for further discussion. We should discuss where the name of our group came from. Then, we'll proceed to a lecture on a subject we all have agreed upon, and we'll discuss the lecture's contents and expand upon it.

CHRIST AND THE JESUS OF HISTORY

"For this week's lecture," Fr Pat continued, "I'll discuss the difference between Jesus and Christ. Because of the way the Jesus' story has been transmitted to us, we join both names together, but this is the greatest mistake of our religious history. Jesus is the man of history and Christ is the man of compositional creativity. We know very few verifiable historical facts about Jesus of Nazareth, but hundreds of thousands of books have been written on the Christ of compositional creativity. There is a chasm between the Jesus of history and the post-Resurrection Christ. The question remains, how can we know anything about the historical Jesus since there are so few historical references to him? Is there really anything of historical significance we can know about him?

"The answer is yes. We can know a lot about the historical Jesus from cultural anthropology and compositional creativity. For instance, if we hear a wonderful story about Christ creating a super-jet out of a piece of tin, we know immediately that this story cannot be true because jets did not exist in the time Jesus lived. In the same way, we can know through cultural anthropology that the boy Jesus at the age of twelve could not have preached so eloquently to the elders in the Temple. He was a poor, illiterate peasant boy from a seriously deprived background. He was the son of a carpenter who could never have afforded to send him to school. To say that Jesus could quote Scripture in the manner the Gospel tells us he did is almost like saying he chatted on a cell phone. Culturally impossible, we say. So we dismiss it.

"We also notice that there is no portrayal of Jesus during his adolescence in the Bible except this one entry. This in itself indicates compositional creativity, as if the author wanted to make a connection between the infancy narratives and the beginning of Jesus' later public ministry when he was thirty. The preaching-at-twelve episode is a deliberate compositional attempt to join the entrance and exit stories of Jesus together.

"We should also notice that Jesus reportedly cried out in the Garden of Gethsemane, 'Father, why have you forsaken me? Take this cup away from me. Not my will but yours be done.' But this prompts the question, who reported these words of Jesus, since all of the apostles had fallen asleep? When trying to establish the story of the historical Jesus as distinct from the post-Resurrection Christ of the Church, it is important, as we have seen, to keep the tools of cross-cultural Anthropology and compositional creativity central in our study.

"Compositional creativity also plays an important role in the actual scene of Jesus' crucifixion. In literary form, great drama is born from a clash of opposites. There is always tension in great drama, and the story of Jesus' crucifixion is probably the greatest drama of all time. There is huge tension throughout its reportage. We see that a good thief and a bad thief are crucified on either side of Jesus. Do we take the scene as reported by the Evangelists as literally true? Do we accept that the crucifixion of Jesus, as reported by Matthew, Mark, Luke, and John, is historically accurate? We can, of course. However, it is more likely once again that the Evangelists were using compositional creativity in their report of the crucifixion and death of Jesus. Literary artists that the Evangelists were, filtered the historical facts through their own personalities in order to give emphasis to the centrality of the Jesus story, and they used this tension between opposites as a literary device to enhance their narrative.

Scholars who have intensely studied the New Testament story Of Jesus have said that about 18 per cent of his remarks are historically accurate. So we see how cultural anthropology and compositional creativity combine to determine historicity. The central story about this unique, compassionate man remains the same. Some of the details in the story, though not historically true, still contribute to the composition to enhance the importance of his uniqueness, perhaps even shockingly. The insights from the theory of evolution tell us that Jesus did not perform the sensational miracles accredited to him. This unique man did not come into the world to change water into wine. He came to change the selfishness of the world into a kingdom where the selfless heart prevails. He came to establish the Basalia, the Kingdom of God in this world. And this precisely is where the name of our group comes from.

We have to remember that the Gospels concerning the life of Jesus are at their core love poems. Words alone were not capable of describing the experience people had of him, so the authors resorted to metaphor and other literary devices to explain him and his revolutionary ideas. The writers of the Gospels, because of their intense belief in Jesus, often peppered their language with hyperbole, so the accounts of the miracles, in this sense, could very well be considered literary. We in our so-called sophisticated and enlightened century might be inclined to immediately dismiss the miracle stories as superstitious rubbish, and, indeed, atheists do just that. But we must realize that the miracle stories along with the infancy narratives are but the bathwater surrounding the baby. History must be careful to keep the core when it determines the periphery is no longer credible.

Fact still remains fact when it's separated from fiction, and that distinction is precisely what the discipline of history aims to make. We should remember that we often use hyperbole in our expressions, especially in our description of love experiences. For instance, you might hear a young man say as he attempts to explain his girlfriend's beauty, "You should see her eyes! They're the size of saucers!" No one in their right mind could ever believe that a girl with eyes literally the size of saucers walks among us. However, we understand the boy's meaning. This is how literary form works. We must bring it to bear to our reads of the love stories written as Gospels about Jesus of Nazareth and on the other narratives about his life.

Literary form is, of course, part of compositional creativity and further refines it. It also contributes to the historical Jesus.

Thus far we have seen that there are many ways to approach our discovery of the historical Jesus. As we know, the four Gospels of the Evangelists, Matthew, Mark, Luke, and John, were written some thirty to seventy years after the death of Jesus. We know from our own experience that in this time, the central story may very well have become more embellished or even diminished. The fact remains, though, that time affects the telling and retelling of all stories, especially if they're oral stories. We know from cultural anthropology that the stories and history of many communities were handed down from one generation to the next through oral storytelling. We also know from sociology that aphorisms and parables, because they are so easily remembered, must have been the form in which these historical stories were related to others.

All people live by such stories. We remember them best within our own families. When a loved one dies, we usually recount the memory stories of our loved one. It is part of the grieving process. So, too, with Jesus of Nazareth. All the parables or stories which he recounted in order to send a message should be considered historically true, and so should his aphorisms, or one-liners. These statements are memorable because they are succinct. Think of 'Turn the other cheek' and 'If a man wants your shirt, give him your coat as well.' In the oral culture of Jesus' peasant community, this is how his history was preserved.

In addition, people may have truly believed that Jesus was a miracle worker. Such superstitions were rampant in the culture of the time. Zombies walked about, demons possessed the wretched and convulsed their bodies. *Sheol*, or hell, was everywhere. Poor people in Jesus time were exploited not only by the oppressive Roman authorities but also by the Pharisees and other religious authorities. The people of Jesus' time screamed out in pain and clawed at this unique, compassionate man, pleading with him to give them some relief from their misery. He was one of the lowliest among them, a member of the artisan caste, an illiterate group ranked just above the undesirables.

He truly was one of them, yet there was something very special about him. He was gentle and compassionate. This son of Mary and Joseph, it seems, possessed a great gift for listening. He grew in wisdom from delving deeper within himself to find his own centre. The deeper he went, the more he found God within his own being and the wiser he became. His was not a wisdom that came from school and books, that prepared him for a white-collar job, that came from listening to the religious leaders of his day. In fact, it was quite the opposite: his wisdom came from turning the prevailing theocratic and political system of his day inside out. He found the truth within himself.

"'What does it profit you, if you gain the whole world and lose what is deepest about you, your own centre, in the process?' he asked. If Jesus were around today, he would probably say to us now, 'Why do you stuff people with stuff and make them snuff ontological death? The Sabbath was made for man, not man for the Sabbath. Why do command the tabernacles in your churches to house me? That is a lie. I never meant to become what you have made of me. You incarcerate me. Better to let men and women be free to find God in the tabernacle of their own hearts.'

But are the two pillars of our culture listening? No. They are terrified of the moaning and the groaning of contemporary people who are confused and over exercised by economic gloom. Lepers and outcasts stalk our streets still. Is anyone listening to them? We need another speech concerning the Jesus of history, preached in an applied way, to penetrate our lives. Never has anyone needed his revolutionary words more than contemporary society.

No one had ever spoken as Jesus of Nazareth did. His message and use of language was unique. He was an original, so much so, that his words penetrate our hearts and psyche to this day. No one had ever heard such a unique and original message spoken before in the Roman Empire. Not only was his message counter culture to the Roman Authorities but even more radically counter culture to the Jewish Religious establishment. The very originality of his message set him apart as an upstart and an outsider. There was a newness about him. This originality, newness and uniqueness in itself stands as a testimony to his historicity. He became a true international icon because of the originality of his message. Wise men, still follow his star, He emerged as a mystical giant. His breakthrough in the arena of spirituality is metaphorically akin to the breakthrough of Einstein in the arena of physics.

We have seen how through cultural anthropology and compositional creativity we can arrive at scriptural historical veracity. Cultural anthropology tells us to immediately dismiss the idea of Christ using a cell phone, yet it can also teach us to be inclusive rather than exclusive. For instance, the Samaritans in the time of Jesus were the most despised people of all, much like al-Qaieda in today's society. And yet, where do we find Jesus? Sitting by a well talking to a Samaritan woman, and compassionately, with due respect to her dignity. That in itself is an astonishing story. This would have been such a shocking scene in a culture which hated Samaritans, that members of that culture could only register it as remarkable. But through cultural anthropology, we know this story to be historically true, so it must be included in the Jesus story.

What is even more remarkable about this story is that not only did Jesus converse with a Samaritan but with a Samaritan woman. Within both the Samaritan and Jewish communities, women were considered second-class citizens. They were used and abused and appreciated only as the bearers of men's children and their slaves. Jesus surely was a revolutionary. In this one scene alone, he gave women dignity and defied the conventional culture of his time. He brought what was inconceivable into human consciousness, thereby revolutionizing his contemporary culture. His message cannot be allowed to fossilize and be kept in the firm grip of central control. Jesus' message is not closed but open and emergent. It is as dynamic today as it was in his own time. If we were to apply his message to contemporary society, he would probably say to our Church, 'Woe unto you for keeping patriarchy in your kingdom. Have you not learned yet that masculinity and femininity are integrated and interconnected? You cannot have one without the other. Cease your murderous dualism and learn the wisdom of unity. A church that is half is not whole.'

Jesus of Nazareth would similarly talk compassionately to and about homosexuals. Certainly, he wouldn't want men or women to turn each other into sex objects to gratify their egotistical desires with pleasure, but he would warn the intolerant of the world that they must cease torturing innocent people, for love, no matter the expression of it, is immortal and divine. Homosexuality is part of the evolutionary experiment. Love is the greatest aspiration on the human journey. To be born is to seek it. When realized, it is humanity's greatest achievement. It cannot be determined nor deterred by any force outside of itself. Its abode is the human heart and mind.

When love exists, God is happy with the integration, for a man or a woman has come home to his or her own centre. It takes far more than a piece of flesh to separate a person from the light within. When this separation is made dictatorially by the church or the state, the principle that the whole is greater than the sum of its parts is violated and injustice done. Variance occurs everywhere in nature, and the human species is no exception. Human sexuality exists along a spectrum, and all humans fall along that spectrum. There is no choice involved in genetic or psychic disposition. One cannot turn brown eyes into blue. Religious or political systems which so adamantly denounce an inborn characteristic should take to heart their most important mandate to dispense justice to everyone.

With the reverse approach, too, we can pretty accurately say that Jesus' proclamations metaphorically preached a revolutionary way of thinking. This attempt to separate truth from fiction is called *demythologizing*. All cultures have their great heroes, and as time moves on, more and more stories are told about them, each story filtered through the perspective of the one who is telling the story. As these stories accumulate, we end up with a much bigger story of the central hero than history can substantiate. This also happened with the story of Jesus. The storytellers wrote their compositions about him with great enthusiasm and even excitement because the central figure of their stories was a unique man. Never had such compassionate words been spoken before. He attacked the prevailing culture of his day and he criticized both the religious and political elite in such an original way that people were compelled to listen to him. He was interested in people's plight; he argued eloquently to bring them justice. He gave dignity to prostitutes, lepers, and the most disadvantaged. The spirit of the man could never fade from the stories circulating in his community about him even though, as time went on, some of the details were exaggerated. The central message of Jesus' compassionate spirit became so deeply embedded in people's memory that it became solidified. These bare bones of the story are surely historically true. We do have a history of this unique man through cultural anthropology. We know him centrally, even if some of the clothes thrown over him may not be historically accurate.

ANNIE AND MRS BEST

Mrs Best was a Jewish lady living within the territorial boundaries of the parish on a huge estate very near Miss Prado Who had very little contact with her except when they occasionally attended the same noonday mass. It was not unusual for Miss Prado to attend two masses every day. The one which Monsignor said at seven in the morning was, of course, obligatory, and she also attended the noonday mass depending on which priest said it. She had decided not to attend Fr Pat's noonday masses because she detested his spontaneous prayers and their application to the contemporary world.

These contemporary prayers you say are un-liturgical," she had told Fr Pat. "You must stay faithful to the Roman Missal, no more and no less. You distract people by allowing your thoughts from the outside world to intrude on the liturgy of the word. And besides, you give off the wrong liturgical message by placing the chalice on the altar of sacrifice before its liturgical time. Didn't you learn in your liturgical training that it is mandatory to separate the liturgical word from the canon of the mass? Surely you know the chalice can only be presented when the liturgy of the word has ended."

Fr Pat remained mute through her rant, but then he smiled. "Thank you, Miss Prado. I have immeasurably gained from your instruction." Inwardly, though, he thought about Jesus telling the Pharisees that they were searching for knots as the outside world was collapsing around them. Miss Prado had also complained to him for giving Mrs Best, a Jew, Holy Communion when she came up to the altar rails to receive it. The Monsignor had refused her, so Fr Pat should do the very same, Miss Prado had said, as Rome had insisted that no non-Catholics should ever be allowed to partake of the Eucharist. Fr Pat knew the law very well, but his heart spoke differently.

The case of Mrs Best was an exceptional one because, as Annie O'Connor had said, "The poor old thing is not quite with it. She has Alzheimer's and doesn't even know what she's doing." Annie O'Connor had been appointed as Mrs Best's primary caretaker, and by all accounts, Annie took her job very seriously. She treated Mrs Best like a baby. She washed her and she dried her. She put on her clothes and she took them off. She cooked for her and she fed her. A mother who finally gave birth to a baby after twelve years of trying could not have been more attentive than Annie O'Connor was to Mrs Best. The Best family loved their mother, and they loved her caretaker nearly as much. They trusted Annie enough to allow her take Mrs Best to mass at noon at St Jude Catholic Church. No one knew for sure whether Annie's daily attendance at mass had been a condition for her taking the job as caretaker, but regardless, Annie showed up every day in the church with Mrs Best in tow.

When Communion time came, she took Mrs Best with her up to the rail, and after receiving the Eucharist, Annie would whisper in Mrs Best's ear, "Open your mouth," and depending on the priest, he often placed the Host on Mrs Best's tongue, which made Annie a happy lady. But when it was refused, she could become fiery. Once she had railed against the

Pastor for his refusal. "There's no harm in giving Communion to this poor old woman. For God's sake, can't you see that if Jesus himself was around, he would have given it to her?"

This Friday, Fr Pat said the noonday mass, and as usual, Annie and Mrs Best came in. Annie tried to get Mrs Best to genuflect before taking her place in the pew, but Mrs Best had some difficulty bending on the one knee, as was customary, so Annie didn't insist. She always put kindness before all else in her dealings with Mrs Best. Both of them received Communion, and as usual, Annie Stayed after mass with Mrs Best by her side to say her novenas and rosary.

Fr Pat came out to put the sacred vessels away and tidy up the sanctuary, and as he looked about the church, he saw Annie deep in prayer and Mrs Best walking down the main aisle with her knickers down around her feet. His first instinct was to laugh, but then he realized that Mrs Best might trip, so he shouted, "Annie! Annie, for God's sake, look at Mrs Best! She'll trip."

He immediately ran down the aisle to rescue the old woman and Annie, disturbed from her mystical state, ran after him, shouting, "Oh, Jesus Christ and the Blessed Virgin Mary, save her!"

When Fr Pat stopped Mrs Best, Annie took her back into the pew and secured her knickers. As the two women were leaving, Annie made a double genuflection—she got down on both knees. Fr Pat thought this strange since such a ritual was only done at the exposition of the Blessed Sacrament in a monstrance.

"Why in heaven's name are you making a double genuflection?" Fr Pat asked.

Annie looked up from her crouched position and said, "Father, you are a very observant man." She pointed to Mrs Best. "I'm doing one for her and one for me."

A few days later, the Bishop called Fr Pat and thanked him for his insightful essays. He said he had found them challenging and interesting, but he warned Fr Pat to be prudent and allow others such as Monsignor and Miss Prado to follow their own paths to God.

"Keep up the good work," the Bishop said. "Critics and whistle blowers are the best of all patriots. But don't raise your head too high above the parapet unless you're ready to be assassinated."

At the next meeting of the New Basalians, Fr Pat continued with the theme of the difference between the historical Jesus and the Christ of compositional creativity in his interpretation and exegesis of the Gospels.

"We have seen why the miracle stories are the overly enthusiastic outbursts of a love language intent on expressing the inexpressible," Fr Pat began. "I am personally convinced that whenever we witness the suspension of the natural law in favour of the magical, we should always be suspicious. It has always struck me that when religion is at its most nefarious, sensationalism replaces a more enlightened appreciation of the ordinary. It would appear that the more we remove ourselves from the little routine, ordinary happenings of our lives, the more the God of the miraculous becomes alive to us, but true spirituality demands that we take the exact opposite approach. Miraculous interference with the laws of nature is anti-divine, and should miracles happen, they convince only the weak and not the strong. In truth, God lives in our eating and drinking, in our waking and sleeping, in our kissing and our lovemaking. True spirituality falls in the territory of the ordinary, and any religion that tells you otherwise is lying. Any religion that emphasizes the sensational and the extraordinary, thereby making them primary, is twisting God's truth. Ever since the Big Bang, life has been future-orientated and emergent according to the dictates of its own non-local inner Intelligence. To stall the Intelligence behind the natural process is to make God into a suspender rather than an enhancer.

With this in mind, how are we to reconcile the Jesus of history with the the Christ Redeemer story of the Church?

We have touched on the probability of compositional creativity used in the accounts of the miracles, and now we must look at the most miraculous stories of all—the narratives of Jesus' infancy. Jesus of Nazareth, according to the Gospels of Luke and Matthew, was born of a virgin called Mary in a cave in Bethlehem. Jesus did not become incarnate in the ordinary way that nature dictates; he was not conceived from the seed of Joseph. However, the carpenter, taking pity on the plight of Mary, married her under the guidance of the Holy Spirit of God.

Jesus came into world in an unusual and exceptional way since he, as the only begotten Son of God, equal to the Father in every way, could never be tainted by concupiscence or other sins of the flesh. He was born without sin. But he was born of the flesh of Mary and, therefore, it would seem logical that he must also be contaminated by the original sin of Adam and Eve. The Gospel makes no reference to this initial dilemma concerning Mary, but the Church of the post-Resurrection Christ, in order to support its own dogma on Christ's sinlessness, found it necessary to declare another dogma on the matter: the Immaculate Conception. According to this dogma, the God of divinity, from eternity, it seems, had chosen Mary to be his mother and exempted her from the original sin of concupiscence, and Mary remained a virgin pre, in, and post-partum.

This has been the teaching of the Church ever since. Even though the whole story is an assault on human intelligence. Catholics are still required to humbly suspend the gift of their intellect and accept it, giving over scriptural interpretation and inspiration to the control of the Church. The Church has put stopgap measures in to prevent further questioning. This has given atheistic materialists great fodder for their guns. How could anyone with the slightest deposit of enlightenment believe in such nonsense?

The same arrogance continues in Vatican pronouncements to this day, exercising it in the dogmas of the Assumption and the Ascension. Quantum physics clearly teaches that the most basic subatomic particle morphs as it leaps into consciousness, the territory of no-place-ness and no-thing-ness. But how in heaven's name can a material body still brimming with atoms find space in no-place-ness or no-thing-ness? Intellectually, it is an absurdity. Intangibility and insubstantiality are the ultimate essence of the material. This moment is but a time-and-place event in the eternal continuum. Knowing what we now know from quantum physics, Religion no longer has the right to keep the faithful in ignorant bondage. It must declare its meta-narratives as bankrupt. They make no sense in a world which through the findings of Science is growing ever more refined and enlightened.

So how do we reconcile the Jesus of history with the infancy narratives? The Church tells us we must still accept Mary as a virgin and Jesus as God's only begotten Son. We are told we must accept these dogmas as articles of our faith and that faith sees more deeply than intelligence speaks. But which article must we take on faith when one verse of the Bible seems to contradict another? Scripture tells us that Mary had other children also. How did they come about? How did she keep her virginity when James, the brother of Jesus, was born? Either she was impregnated by a living mortal man or James also was a child of the Holy Spirit, giving us two begotten sons to lead us. If that sounds unintelligible, then the only answer left is that Mary remained a virgin only post-partum with Jesus. But that is equally as unintelligible. The story the Church exhorts us to believe in is unbelievable. A God of intelligence would never compel us to believe it.

The belief which the Christian church promulgates is its own concoction. Religion prospers when the faithful are kept in ignorance. The longer religion can keep the historical Jesus incarcerated in its own interpretation of the Gospels, the longer it will maintain unscrupulous power and control over the faithful. The Church is a dictatorship, but unlike other dictatorships, it controls its subjects' minds more than their bodies. Materialism and Mechanistic science, on the other hand, controls our bodies to such an extent that our minds have become diseased.

So where are we to turn when an institution dedicated to spiritual direction atrophies the human mind? We can appreciate the story of Christ in mythic terms. But a myth is not literal nor historical,. We can accept Christ as an archetype through the tragic story of his death and Resurrection. It is a classic story. We see the tragedy of human death but also have hope for some sort of resurrection. The natural world supports this, since quantum physics allows for transformation. So the story oif Christ as an archetype is acceptable but not as a personal history.

All our lives we have been programmed to think that the Resurrection of Christ is a unique supernatural event in which, according to the Church the laws of nature were yet again suspended. But resurrection is the language of the continuum—the body leaves the material and transforms into consciousness, the emergent future of the particle. The mind and the spirit, intangibly and invisibly, cross the threshold of mortality into another dimension. This is the natural course of matter. Resurrection of the body, though, is most unlikely. Quantum physics teaches us that the particles which add up to a unique entity will probably never come together again.. As far as we know particles come and go ever expressing themselves in new form. What is of importance and significance is not so much that particles coalesce but that the Great Intelligence energises all, no matter the expression. We think of the afterlife in an anthropological way and want experiences such as closeness to our beloved departed to become the reality For sure though we will not experience our departed loved ones in a physical way when we transcend and transform. Particles belong to earth and no longer cloak us when we leave earth. All we can say is that through transmutation there can be no emptiness or sorrow in the all in the all that is nothing, in the all that is poetry, in the all of our circuitous journey.

We shall no more crave a bottle of cheap wine from a supermarket when our cellars are already full of the best French wine.

It is impossible to add something to that which is already all.

Through quantum physics we are unapologetically informed about the possibility of life after death.

But where is the applause from either religion or secular materialism for this possibility?

Surely it is a much more encouraging, hopeful and enlightened thesis than the one offered by atheism.

Surely it is time for a new paradigm. We need a spirituality of higher consciousness. The story of Jesus can provide this. Not only does it speak to us about the transformation of the human ego from selfishness to selflessness but it also speaks about the transformation of life through death into a deeper experience.

We can easily appreciate the Gospel narratives in an overarching and archetypal manner, but not through the Church's misconstrued meaning that promotes only its self-interest. We are fascinated by the infancy stories because they sound so human, and all these miraculous happenings surrounding the birth of Jesus also ignite our imagination. There is a romance and a beautiful naturalness about an adoring mother bending over her baby and wrapping him in swaddling clothes, a big, strong carpenter supporting and protecting her, animals breathing out hot air to keep the crèche warm, shepherds on the hills keeping watch over their flock. This is the perfect setting for a Hollywood movie with a happy, cosy ending.

"Unique as this story seems to us, however, it is not original. Cultural anthropology tells us that it echoes both Greek and Egyptian myths. The infancy narratives of Matthew and Luke in particular were based on stories from these two great antecedent cultures. The profound mysticism of ancient Egypt deeply influenced both Judaism and Christianity. Hundreds of thousands of tourists flock to Egypt every year to see the pyramids, temples, and tombs in the Valley of the Kings, enchanted by the architectural achievements and the superb artistic expressions, yet so many of them misunderstand the intent of the messengers who created them. If ever a place on planet earth were saturated with religious symbolism it is Egypt, but most Westerners who visit these unbelievable sights fail to associate them with the human spiritual quest.

The pyramids were built as places to perform funeral rituals. Ancient Egyptians considered our present world secondary, calling it the *near world*. In their minds, it was only temporary and far less significant than the *far world*, so they buried the pharaohs with magnificent adornments, including furniture and food, to accompany them on their journey to the far world.

The story of Adam and Eve has its beginnings in Egyptian mythology, and the Jews and then the Christians adopted it. The Egyptian myth starts in a garden where everything is perfect, but soon human greed lets sin in. It is then up to humans to repair the fracture and restore balance. There was no duality between the near world and the far world: harmony existed between them, and sin disrupted this harmony. Life existed inside of time and the dead existed outside of it. Paradoxically, the world of the dead was considered the source of life, and the dead were truly believed to be alive in another realm.

A tombstone from 107 BC reads, 'A trifle only of life is this world, but eternity is in the realm of the dead.'

The Christian church converted the story into a tale of dualism, dividing the near world from the far world and revising it so that because humans corrupted the world, they could not restore the harmony between the worlds. Intervention from the far world was needed for that, so God sent Jesus, His son, as a ransom to mend the rupture. It took supernatural, divine power in the person of Jesus to pay restitution for the split. Ever since the revision, Christianity has maintained that matter needs the redemption dispensed only by divine intervention.

From cultural anthropology, we recognize the inspiration for the Christian Salvation story. Through compositional creativity, the Christians then twisted the Egyptian myth, dividing the near world of matter from the far world of the spirit, thereby creating a dualistic split.

Christianity is also informed by Greek tradition, which, contrary to the Egyptians, put their gods outside of creation. The Christian Church capitalized on this divide.

In ancient Egypt, the sun had eternal significance and was central to their mythology. Because of its ability to create and nurture, Egyptians anthropomorphized it in their myths. To them, it was the light of the world, the king of kings, the unseen creator of everything in the near world. Life in the underworld was but a journey into the sun, the outer world. Starting around 3000 BC, the Egyptians worshipped Horus as the sun god and believed that he had an enemy called Set. Horus fought Set every morning, banishing her from the day, only to have her return in the evening and banishing Horus from the night. Here we see the clash of opposites, light versus dark and good versus evil, but they exist as part of one reality, no in duality.

The early church, as it applied its compositional creativity to the historical Jesus, kept the Egyptian meta-myth but did not adopt the message of unity. We see the story of Horus the sun god transformed into Jesus' birth in December, on the date of the solar equinox. From there, the church used compositional creativity, borrowing from myths extant in various parts of the world, for the rest of the details of Jesus' life: that he was born of a virgin, that a star in the east led three kings to the birth site to adore Jesus; that Jesus was a teacher at twelve, had twelve disciples, performed miracles, was crucified, and was resurrected on the third day. The details of Jesus' life parallel exactly the details of the life of Horus., the Egyptian Sun God. The church also borrowed from the ninth-century BC Greek stories of Dionysius and the Indian stories of Krishna.

The Evangelists in their compositional creativity capitalized on this ancient mythology and applied it to the Jesus story, but this application was not historical. Instead, it was filtered through and expanded by storytellers impressed by the central historical man called Jesus of Nazareth. It is vital to remember that there were many versions of the Jesus story in the early stages of Christianity. There were Christiani*ties, not just Christianity.* One of these came from a group called the Gnostics, who stressed that truth can only come through knowing, from the light within, not through an outside intermediary. However, the problem with Gnosticism was that knowing required learning, which was not available to the masses.

As the initial Christianities merged into a single Christianity, the story of the historical Jesus came under control of an entity that contaminated it with a mucky mixture of fiction and fact, myth and truth. To those who sought sensationalism, the miraculous doings of Christ and his role as Saviour and Redeemer took centre stage. In the amalgamation of Christianity, the church also saw its opportunity to politicize spirituality, thereby turning it into religion. It made the central message of Jesus into a commodity with itself the sole dispenser.

You need Jesus as your Saviour and Redeemer,' the church tells us, 'but we hold the rights to salvation. You cannot expect redemption without receiving our stamp of approval. "I give to you the keys to the kingdom. Whose sins you shall forgive, they are forgiven them, and whose sins you shall retain, they are retained."' What a perfect avenue to power and control!

Those in power declared the Gnostic Gospels heretical and, in AD 313 at the Synod of Antioch, burned them because the Gnostics rejected authority, preferring to walk an individual path guided by the light within. A little later, in 325, the Council of Nicaea unalterably dogmatized the Synoptic Gospels, and thus the historical Jesus became Christ the Saviour. The story of the compassionate historical Jesus was now secondary to the meta-narratives which surrounded him, a deceitful regime of religiosity turning this astonishing, courageous man into an outrageous deceiver by making the meta-narrative stories into historical fact.

The Council of Nicaea mainly concerned itself with the question, who is Jesus? Is he human or is he God? Arius maintained that he was not the only begotten son of God as the Gospel of John claims but was, rather, a son of God just like the rest of us, as supported by the text of John 14: 28: 'The Father is greater than I'. If God was greater than Jesus, then Jesus was not equal to God. Instead, like all of us, he came into being after the Father and, therefore he had a beginning, making him a finite being like the rest of us. The Council of Nicaea did not agree. They condemned the Arian view as heresy, and sent Arius into exile, confiscated his works, and executed those in possession of these works.

The opposition forces led by Alexander of Alexandria centred their argument in the Gospel of John also, in 17: 21: 'That they all may be one; as thou, Father, art in me, and I in thee, that they also may be one in us: that the world may believe that Thou has sent me.' These homoousians (with *ousia* meaning 'essence') argued for hypostasis, for the consubstantiality of Jesus with the Father. They were of the same substance and essence, and therefore Jesus was the true God, co-eternal with the Father, begotten of the same substance as the eternal Father. Thus the historical Jesus became an avatar.

At Nicaea, the Christian meta-narrative of virgin birth, crucifixion, Resurrection, and redemption, based upon the ancient myths of Egypt and Greece, were morphed into articles of faith and, with the consubstantiality of Jesus and the Father, incorporated into the Creed we say in every mass to this day. These myths became historical facts.

However, because there was such quibbling among the council as to whether Christ was divine or human, Emperor Constantine, for the sake of unity in a fragile empire, though not a voter himself, pressured the Church to accept consubstantiality, making the first step to join church and state. In time, the Church seized all the power of the secular state and became the final authority not only over people's souls but their bodies as well.

The story of the historical Jesus became so obfuscated that the words which he used to condemn the scribes and Pharisees could justifiably be directed at the Church which he was supposed to have instituted. This world does not need to be redeemed by the intervention of an external God. Jesus was far too much in touch with his own centre to stoop to such stupidity. Throughout his ministry, he unceasingly proclaimed that the Kingdom of God lay inside. For example, Luke 17: 20-21 says, 'The kingdom of God does not come with observation. Neither shall they say, Lo here! or Lo there! for behold, the kingdom of God is within you.'

Jesus called us to an integral appreciation. Come home to what you really are, he said. Come home to the light within you. The meta-narratives with which the Church has imprisoned Jesus must be abandoned in the interest of historical truth. Spirituality belongs to everyone, and each person finds his or her own way to God. The only mediator is the ceaseless yearning of the human heart for completion.

The Pharisees and the scribes took the keys of knowledge and hid them. They have not entered the kingdom and they do not allow in those who wish to enter, as Jesus said in Matthew 23: 13. Surely these are dire warnings to the Christian Church, which has fallen flat on its face. It says little of importance to a struggling world searching for meaning. To the mind of contemporary culture organized religion is of little relevance. In a world where material growth has far outstripped internal growth, we run the risk of annihilation. We must integrate the material with the spiritual if there is to be peace on earth. The separation of one from the other is the cause of all our consternation. We will apply integral solutions to our global problems or we will perish.

Quantum physics teaches us this. Because it focuses on the whole, it is about hierarchy and is thereby vertically orientated. In contrast, the horizontal approach of the materialists is illusory. We must integrate the temporal with the eternal if we are to bring balance and harmony into this world. As Benjamin Franklin warned, 'If we do not hang together, we will hang separately.' If ever there was a man conscious of the vertical and aware of its consequential connection to the horizontal, it is Jesus of Nazareth. He was unconventional and counter-cultural.

As Albert Einstein said

"A human being is part of the whole . . . the universe, a part limited in time and space. He experiences himself, his thoughts, and feelings, as something separate from the rest—a kind of optical delusion of his consciousness. This delusion is a kind of prison for us, restricting us to our personal desires and to affection for a few persons nearest us. Our task must be to free ourselves from this prison by widening our circles of compassion to embrace all living creatures and the whole of nature in its beauty"

If a new paradigm is to emerge, then Jesus will have to be rescued from being viewed as a rescuer. Instead, we should see him as a leader on the compassionate journey into interiority. He lived courageously and unselfishly. He freed himself from the prison of his own ego knowing that he himself was but a part of the whole, and he showed us how to become truly integrated.

"In 1945, ancient scripts called the Nag Hammadi Texts were discovered in the Egyptian desert. These text included the works of Plato, various hermetic texts, and the Gospels of Thomas and Mary. These Gospels give testimony to the fact that there were various expressions of the Gospel in early Christianity, showing that there were multiple Christianities, as each author of a Gospel had his or her own following. In reading the Gospel of Thomas, which recalls comments Jesus made, we can clearly see why a church interested in power and control would immediately burn them. This Gospel especially stresses Jesus' message of the light within.

"We read from the Gospel of Thomas: 'Jesus said: "If you bring forth what is within you, what you bring forth will save you. If you do not bring forth what is within you, what you do not bring forth will destroy you."'

Jesus's disciples ask him, '"when will the new world come?"', and Jesus answers, '"What you look forward to has already come, but you do not recognize it." In another part of the Gospel, he says, "'The kingdom is inside you and it is outside you. When you make what is inside you and outside you one, then you will become sons of man.'"

In the Gospel of Mary, Jesus says, "'Be on your guard so that no one deceives you by saying, 'Look over here, look over there,' For the child of true humanity exists within you. Follow it. Those who search for it will find it. Go then and preach the good news.'"

From these texts it is clear that the Church has chosen a scripture best suited for its own end.

The Gnostic Gospels tell the story of Jesus the enabler, but the Synoptic Gospels tell the story of Jesus the Saviour, downplaying the Jesus of the downtrodden and overplaying the Christ of the miraculous.

"The original message of Jesus is simple. It lifts the human spirit out of its physical misery and gives dignity back to the individual. It invites his followers to seek what is essential, for this is the way to become integrated, happy, and fulfilled. But the Council of Nicaea changed the story. History was forgotten and Christ became mythic.

Arius opposed Nicaea and was exiled to an inhospitable island. Then, in 381, when Theodosius was the Roman emperor, heresy in the Church became heresy in the state as well. Church and state became so entwined that the property of heretics could be seized by the Church. How hypocritical that a religion which is based on a man who said 'Put away your sword, for those who use it shall perish by it' should torture and murder men and women in Jesus's name. The Church itself was a terrorist, all in the name of a compassionate man.

The Church turned the crown of thorns which Jesus wore into a mitre made from the finest thread. The staff of the good shepherd became the Pope's golden crosier studded with precious stones. Jesus' rough-hewn wooden cross became a gilded one. The tattered burlap sack which the Nazarene wore became an ermine shawl. And as though these morphs were not enough, this self interested Church handed out bracelets of salvation to the faithful, which turned into manacles of oppression.

It is important that we recall here the purpose of our study. Centrally, we are trying to discover the historical Jesus. This is not easy, since little is known about this unique man historically speaking. But through disciplines such as cultural anthropology, compositional creativity, and mythology, we can come closer to the historical truth. Further, we can learn of the history of Jesus from the Nag Hammadi texts found in the Egyptian desert. But is there anything more which can aid our investigation? Yes! The Dead Sea Scrolls found in Qumran in 1947give us vital clues.

"These texts make it clear that the primitive Christian Church was, at heart, Jewish. Jesus was Jewish: he lived as a Jew, found his identity in Jewish culture steeped in a land which oppressed not only by the secular culture of the Roman Empire, which bodily exploited the people, but also by the religious culture of the scribes and the Pharisees, which spiritually exploited the people. The Jesus of history found the culture in which he lived insufferable. He became an outsider, then a protestor and a non-violent revolutionary. He probably belonged to a group analogous to Amnesty International, although in his day, such a group would have been mystically orientated, concerning itself with the great unknown and the non-local Intelligence viewing the universe as balanced and integrated. Jesus most certainly was a Jewish mystic caught up with transcendence. We gather this from our overall impression about his character.

There is debate about which mystical group he belonged to. Since he was so tolerant of women, some scholars suggest that Jesus was a member of a group of nature worshipers called the Therapeutics, as, unlike the prevailing Semitic culture, this sect included women. They also gave homage to the sun. Other scholars say that Jesus was a member of the Essenes sect. Scholars do agree, however, that the primitive Christian Church had its genesis in mystical Judaism. The Dead Sea

Scrolls indicate that compassionate thinking and mysticism existed among the sects that wrote them, particularly the Essenes. In these texts we see parallels between the Essene Teacher of Righteousness, who was put to death by his enemies and was expected to be resurrected, and Jesus of Nazareth. The mysticism of the suffering Messiah is also clearly delineated in these texts. So, these these texts suggest the foundational inspiration for the story of the death and Resurrection of Christ the Redeemer. Thanks to the Dead Sea Scrolls, we can now say that the Jesus tradition is Jewish, but the Council of Nicaea made Jesus mythic.

Fr Pat stopped here. "We still need at least one more lecture in our effort to discover the historical Jesus," he said, "but that's enough for tonight. Our next lecture will be on the difference between the Gospel of John and the Gospel of Thomas."

Miss Prado, of course, was delighted with the regime of the unbending conservative contemporary Pope The Church had begun to undo the catastrophic mistakes of Vatican ll This was the only way to control the stampede of horses gone wild with a sense of their own importance. The Vatican had reverted to the principle that truth was always what the Church says it is and cannot be changed. The Second Vatican Council was now a distant memory, and the time had arrived to emphasize the core teachings of Catholicism once again.

Miss Prado clutched the new Roman Missal as though it were worth more than a thousand pounds of gold bullion. She praised its new words. "Much more traditional," she thought. "Much more in keeping with a Church renowned for aesthetics and art. Not at all tacky. This is a worthy improvement on those faddish attempts liturgists have made in recent years to address the public.

"The faithful were much more reverent when the Mass was said in Latin.
We should bring it back" she ranted

While there was an awful lot of work still to be done, especially concerning the awful dress of the faithful when they attended mass, yet this new Roman Missal was a wonderful beginning. The Church was finally moving in the right direction again. She thought of the huge dedication and tireless work which the sensitive breed of intelligent men in the Vatican had expended in its publication. They had had to reconcile contradictions, of course, and refine difficult interpretations of complex issues with precise wording best suited to the concept.

The Monsignor, who was usually ruffled by any change in the liturgy, as he had been during the tabernacle debacle, now quite willingly accepted the new approach. After all, it was more in keeping with tradition. Finally the Church was no longer moving forward but backward. He liked that. He said his daily mass as usual on the Feast of the Immaculate Conception. Orthodox priest that he was, he read the Offertory Prayer:

"Grant, O Lord, on this the feast of the Immaculate Conception of the Blessed Virgin Mary that we profess her on account of her prevenient grace to be untouched by the stain of sin so that through her intercession we may be delivered from sin."

Fr Pat thought satirically-

"How poetic. What a masterpiece in a world plagued with terror and the doomsday scenario of nuclear war, when people are troubled with recession and anxiety, wandering around spiritually impoverished. This prayer will surely convert the unaware, raise their spirits, and give them the promise of holistic integration! How clever of these men in the Roman Liturgical Department to be so original and relevant! Their inspiration must surely have been born of perspiration and their aspirations born through a feeling of asphyxiation.

Bravo, bravo to you alert and attuned liturgical men
for your literate liturgical sense. We applaud for your
noble achievement."

The only problem was, when Monsignor saw the word *prevenient* he stumbled and stuttered. Oh, what a shock!.

135

I've never come across 'prevenient' before. It's very close to 'preventive'—A word, I am most familiar with. Forgive me Oh Blessed Virgin Mary, I didn't mean to accuse you of using birth control"

At Fr Pat's next meeting with the New Basalians, he continued as promised with his lecture on how cultural anthropology and compositional creativity informed the historical Jesus.

"Tonight we really hit at the heart of the matter," he said. "There are differences in the narratives of the Synoptic Gospels. The Gospel of John stands out from those of Matthew, Mark, and Luke. We can see this clearly not only in John's loftier language used but also in a marked shift in tone. John divinizes Jesus. As we saw, the Council of Nicaea used John's Gospel as evidence to reach the conclusion of consubstantiation with the Father. John's portrait of Jesus most admirably suited the power hungry Church bent on centralization.

As a result of the many Christianities in the primitive Church, we can see an even greater contrast to John's Gospel in the Gospel of Thomas than in any of the others in the New Testament. According to John's Gospel, Jesus is an avatar. He is portrayed as God, penetrating human time, carrying with him the complement of the Godhead, having been sent by the Father to redeem the world. His words 'I and the Father are one. As you, Father, are in me, so I am in you' speak to hypostatic union.

The Gospel of Thomas, however, though consubstantial in its essence, takes a totally different approach. There is a growing consensus that the Gospel of Thomas predates the Synoptic Gospels of Matthew, Mark, Luke, and John. The opening of the Gospel of Thomas states, 'These are the living words which the living Jesus spoke and that Didymos Thomas wrote down.' We see immediately that the Gospel of Thomas is not hierarchical, it is horizontal. It is democratic. From there, it directly tells people that they are masters of their own destiny and that they should look to their own inner light for guidance. It is very practical instead of passing down dogma from others to become dogma for yourself. Thomas's is the truest of all orthodoxies, as it purports that the wisdom of God is as amply poured out on us as sunshine. We see this in saying 42 of the Gospel of Thomas, when Jesus says, 'Be passers-by.' In two short words, Thomas tells us, metaphorically, not to enslave ourselves to the inferior concerns of material entrapment.

Again, in saying 3, Jesus says, 'When you come to know yourselves, then you will become known, and you will realize that it is you who are the sons of the living Father.'

The Jesus Thomas presents is a true educator. He brings out from us what is best within ourselves. It is already there inside of us. He does not stuff us dogmatically; he does not force us. Instead, he invites us. He tells us that God's work must become our own. The Jesus of Thomas is intuitive. He speaks in koans (paradoxical phrases), such as 'We receive by giving. He leaves room for the imagination and is open to possibility. He uses metaphors and tells parables. His thinking ascends to a greater consciousness.

The Jesus of Thomas most admirably complements the findings of quantum physics. Jesus would never have heard of such a thing, of course, but he lived it. He was far ahead of his time. The Jesus of Thomas is very approachable, the kind of man you'd like to invite to your table. He's accessible and lovely to listen to, expanding the possibility of our own horizons, blessing our dreams, and installing hope. The Jesus of Thomas is affirming and encouraging. He would never damn us or judge us.

The Jesus of John, on the other hand, is definite and definitive. When he says something, nothing more can be said, and no further endorsement or explanation is needed. You cannot improve on orthodoxy. Revelation is finished. He lets us know, 'God entered the world already, and I am God's word to you. I have already told you everything; there is nothing more. I am the truth, I am the way, I am the light of the world.' How can you improve on 'I am the Resurrection and the life. I and the Father are one'?

The Jesus of Thomas, in contrast, is not haughty or arrogant. He says to us, 'Of course I don't presume to have total wisdom because that comes from shared experience. Your light within is your own, coloured by your own insight. You are a part as I am a part, but we are not apart. We bring together our own parts to create the whole

In the saying 24 of the Gospel of Thomas, Jesus says, 'There is light within a whole person of light, and it lights up the whole universe.' He goes on in saying 50, 'If they say to you, "Where did you come from?", say to them, "We came from the light, the place where the light originated through itself. If those who lead you say to you, 'The kingdom is in heaven,' then the birds of heaven will precede you. If they say to you, 'It is in the sea,' then the fish will precede you"'" (verse 3).

"'The kingdom of God does not come visibly. Nor will the people say 'here it is' or 'there it is' because the kingdom of God is within you and it is without you'" (verse 113).

A famous Sufi poet, Rumi, confirms the wisdom of Thomas though he came from an entirely different culture. He has this to say: 'There is a force within that gives you life—seek that. In your body there lies a priceless jewel—seek that. Oh, wandering Sufi, if you are in search of the greatest treasure, don't look outside, Look within, and seek that.'

The Gospel of John is a lecture on the orthodoxy of divinity. It is closed, whereas the Gospel of Thomas is open, saying that God is not finished with us yet, that there's always the possibility for more revelation. John's Jesus is more intellectual and less emotional. John's Jesus is of the head, whereas Thomas's Jesus is of the heart. John was hell-bent on moving Jesus to a higher realm, to enlarge his story. He admired Jesus so greatly that he wanted him to take on the characteristics of God. He used compositional creativity—metaphor and hyperbole—to get his message across.

The Gospel of Thomas, on the other hand, does not usually use such literary devices. It tells the story of a compassionate man who lived simply and had no need for regal adornment. He had no agenda; he was not ambitious. The Jesus of Thomas is so ordinary and believable that he has no intrigue about him. His goal was simply to lift the mind of his followers to a more Integrated view of life.

Of these two Gospels, historically speaking, John' s Gospel is less credible. It does not resonate with our view of reality. The Jesus of Thomas sounds more real and positively addresses much of the scrutiny historical science would impose upon him. The Gospel of Thomas has no adornment, just sayings. Thomas made little use of compositional creativity, and his rendition of the Jesus story is therefore minimalistic. It gets to the core of Jesus' life without embellishment.

John, of course, did not like the Thomas rendition. In it, Jesus was far too human for John's taste, contradicting his central theme of the divinity of Jesus. In John's story, Jesus is different from us, but in Thomas's, Jesus is one of us. For this reason, John tells the story of the doubting Thomas, eliminating his adversary from the scene in which Jesus appears to the apostles after the Resurrection, where the gift of the Holy Spirit Was given to the Church. As a consequence, Thomas was no longer a part of the apostolic succession. John, it seems, was as much a politician as he was an evangelist! It's horrendous enough that the messenger was murdered, but more horrendous still is that his message was murdered with him."

MARY—A SOUL RATHER THAN JUST A BODY

Fr Pat knew Mary very well, as she was on his sick list, so he visited her home at least once a month to administer the Holy Communion to her. She looked forward to his visits because she loved to chat with him after the religious rituals were complete. Mary herself was little more than a conventional Catholic; she often referred to herself as "religiously retired. She didn't possess a rosary and displayed no religious symbols in her house, not even a crucifix. When her husband, whom she loved intensely, had died, her comfortable world was shattered and she was shredded with grief.

She once said to Fr Pat, "Where is he now? I can't believe he's dead, but he is gone. I cannot find him. He seems to be nowhere. Maybe from no-where he'll reach now-here! Life is a mysterious thing." Half of her life had gone away, and at this time, she began to question her own life, Had it any meaning? What was her purpose? Would she ever enjoy her husband's presence again or the ecstasy they experienced in carving out their generous love?

Through all this, her grandchildren remained the apple of her eye, and the moment her youngest grandson was born, she fancied him and sanctioned him as though he were a theophany, a thunderbolt from God. He was unique, never seen before in the annals of human history. He could do nothing wrong in Mary's eyes.

When some women first saw him in his nursery crèche, they noticed his wonderfully long fingers. One woman said to Mary, "His fingers are beautiful! I bet he'll grow up to be a writer."

When Mary later told this story to Fr Pat, she added, "It's a good thing he didn't blow a fart or else she would have predicted he'd grow up to be an astronaut!"

They both laughed hysterically. This reminded Fr Pat that compassion and a sense of humour grew to the same extent that the ego diminished. Love gave us all the ability to laugh at ourselves Mary was a frightfully intelligent and articulate woman, and she gave Fr Pat many insights into his own character as well.

She spoke at length to him about the clash between selfishness and selflessness. "The ego and the selfishness which materialism causes is winning the day in our society," she said. "What this world truly needs is something like the love which existed between my husband and me. Love involves give and take, fighting and crying, exchange and compromise. Never can love end in war. Nothing is solved by killing. Sometimes, perhaps, a solution can be hurried along by the threat of a pointed gun, but not if the person pointing it intends to kill.

All this talk about collateral damage is bullshit, she went on. "It's a cover-up for murder. How can our generals live with themselves? What an irony that one of our own great war heroes should be so easily moved to tears by the death of his pet poodle while at the same time not caring a whit about the little Vietnamese children he murdered. And what about the mental and physical consequences people are still suffering because of the Agent Orange that was poured on them? And what about these dreadful drones and the depleted uranium America used in Iraq? Those innocent people are as precious in God's eyes as we are, yet we never pray for them in our masses on Sunday, when we strike our breasts with our mea culpas. Is the love of God confined to our own shores? Surely our generals must be haunted by the terrible atrocities they caused in our name.

War is mostly caused by Imperialism and ambition; not to spread democracy. Even now, do our warlords not hear the screaming of the innocent Vietnamese children in the wind? What about all the mental and physical deformities now appearing in Iraq long after we have gone, leaving their country plundered? Does the sound never enter our leader's inner territory? They have committed mortal sin in my name. May God forgive them."

Mary was in a rage, but Fr Pat knew she would never act violently, for that would undermine her point, that injustice had to be fought with love. He knew she would channel her anger into something constructive. She had vowed never to own a gun even though so many of her neighbours had at least one in their homes. She didn't have the organization skills to establish a planetary revolution of love, yet she had the courage within her own being, according to her own inner light, to be unconventional.

She had confirmed to Fr Pat that great love could be accomplished in small ways. It was viral. The love she once spent on her husband could now be transferred to her grandchildren, and they, in turn, could multiply it in many manifestations. She loved her grandchildren unconditionally, and what she received from them she gave back to them a hundredfold not with things but with herself. She didn't realize it, but her life had become a prayer. She didn't need rosaries. The pictures of her grandchildren adorning her home were her icons.

She had pointed each grandchild out to Fr Pat with enthusiasm and excitement. She was in love with every one of her children's progeny. She tired him with her chatter about them. She fretted that they were growing up in a culture of mayhem and violence. She wondered how, for the first time in modern America, where children are brought up on abundance, they could possibly cope with insufficiency?

"American children don't have the necessary discipline for survival anymore. They know little about natural sustainability, their school curricula prepares them for work but not for life. Religion has failed them too. They are growing robbed of values necessary for the development of civility and culture."

"The great flaw in American society," Mary said, "is that we have spoiled our children. We've brought them up to view everything as an entitlement rather than a blessing. I try to do things differently for my grandchildren. Instead of presents, I give them my presence. I try to show them that the best things in life, the natural things like the sun and the rain. the leaves on the trees, the little miracles all around us, are free. Still, artificial concerns saturate our minds. Our world has become make-believe, with stage effects having become our wonders. We take our values from the illusion of accumulating commodities. We have removed ourselves from the natural world and so cannot learn its lessons. Sustaining values have gone out the window. When the smog of manufactured illusions enters our homes, it ruins our imagination and our gift of wondering.

We don't know how to play anymore. Worse still our gadgetry takes over our imaginations the more violent it becomes, and this violence increases to justify the existence of video games and substitute for their inability to satisfy. Why do our children have to be trained to be killers when it is written by their own inner light to be lovers? That inner light tells us not to kill but to love immediate family members and to extend this love to others That is how community begins.

"Mary, you are a wonder" Fr Pat said

"I could not agree with you more.

"I can't change the world's motivation to murder and kill" Mary said "but I can instil the value of love in those I am most responsible for, making it possible for them to multiply this love through other channels. We all have to start somewhere. I start in my own kitchen, where I sit and chat with my grandchildren.

This country has truly been a great experiment. It was innocent once and full of good politics, but it has lost its way. It's like Europe was before the Second World War We have become the new bully boy with our empirical attitude and without even realizing it our civil rights are becoming more and more tampered with. There's no money to be made out of forgiveness though.

Can you imagine if just one nation on earth was founded on this one principle and truly tried to live it, how inspired the world would be"

In spite of Mary's worries for the future of her grandchildren, she remained positive and focussed on their accomplishments and promise. She believed in them. She truly believed that compassionate love was so potent that it would fill the earth with new berries, allowing the world to live from the one tree.

"Ah, Mary," Fr Pat said, "can't you see that what's in your heart is your own beautiful humanity? You yourself are an inspiration I have not brought Holy Communion to you nearly as much as you have given it to me."

When Fr Pat made his next visit to Mary's house, she seemed sad. "Is there something the matter?" he asked. "You look sad and tired."

"I'm a complicated woman," Mary said. "I'm trying my best. I wasn't always the woman that you know me to be. If you look close enough, you'll see some wounds that have yet to heal. But I've learned that I must forgive.

143

I.'m worried about my daughter Carmel. She doesn't remember what I've done for her. Her two small children are my little pets, and it's a shame what's happening to them. I'm terribly worried about them, too. They're still adorably innocent but as shrewd as you'd like. I know they're listening and drinking all the toxicity in their house into their little minds.

It's awful. Carmel uses more foul language than I've heard in my life. I don't know where she learned it; certainly not from me and certainly not from her father. He was a kind man. Carmel won't even come with me to say a prayer at his graveside. Sometimes I wonder if it's because she's learned that he wasn't her biological father. But he adopted Carmel when he married me. He loved me. He saved me. No father could ever love a child as much as he loved Carmel.

He and I worked hard all our lives to send each of our children to college, and now they're all living their own lives scattered across the country, except Sally, who lives just down the street. We wanted to give them a good education, which was something we never had ourselves. I worked as a waitress, and let me tell you, you have to serve a lot of dishes to pay for an education. My husband and I learned our lessons the hard way, and in retrospect, I think it was the right way.

. My daughter is not a kind woman. The other day she threw a glass of wine in my face and called me a fucking bitch. We never reared her to be like this. How could a child ever say that to her mother? Where did all this anger come from?? We worked so hard for their education that we often left them alone, but I always prepared dinner for them. We did the best we could. Sometimes I have thought our children took on an inferiority complex since most of their school mates came from filthy rich families

"Anyhow, Father," Mary continued, "I am terribly worried about my two little grandsons. Their father is even worse than Carmel. He has this macho attitude and comes from a very wealthy family. He grew up with a silver spoon in his mouth. He may have had a good schooling . . . . Catholic education right through college, but he too is spiritually illiterate. Carmel married him, because he was handsome and rich.

They bought every kind of war game and violent toy that you can possibly imagine for those children. The whole scene really scares me. Their lifestyle is the total antithesis of what I believe in. You know how opposed to war and violence I am. If their father ever takes them to a park at all, he lets them turn it into a shooting gallery.

That reminds me: a shocking thing happened a few months ago, and I saw it with my own two eyes. The two boys have pellet guns and Carmel thinks nothing of allowing them to use them. All she says is, 'Now, honey, be careful.' Of course, her husband, macho man that he is, even encourages violent play. To his eyes a pellet gun is just a toy." 'That's how you teach them to become real men' is what he said. Well, anyhow, the two boys and their father went out to shoot pellets in the back yard the other day, and in walks a stray cat. The children shot at her, so in terror, the poor little animal ran up the nearest tree. But they kept shooting pellets at her, as they laughed and hollered. They were having such fun, but then I came out and put an end to it.

"I screamed at them, 'What are you doing? I am ashamed of you, trying to kill a poor innocent animal that has done no harm to you. Don't you realize what you're doing? That cat can feel pain just like you can. How would you like to be on the receiving end of a pellet gun?'

I don't understand this new generation. There's no respect for anything anymore. But it's no wonder! Families don't sit around a common table to share a meal anymore. Carmel's husband Tony just sits around watching football and drinking beer.

She doesn't even prepare supper for him since she's too busy watching soap operas or yapping on the phone to her college friends. You should hear her language. It's just awful!

She put a DVD on the other night for me and the two boys. She had already seen it and thought it was hilarious. It was called *Bridesmaids*, if I remember correctly. Oh, Father,

I've never seen such a filthy movie in my whole life. I was embarrassed to watch it. How a mother could ever expose her two little children to such vulgar trash is beyond my imagination. What is this country coming to when something vulgar and disgusting is considered hilarious and something beautiful is considered uninteresting and boring! What is happening to society?

Of course, I stood up and objected to the movie's content. I told Carmel that it was disgraceful to subject her children to such garbage. Then I invited the boys to come outside and play on the front lawn.

Carmel just yelled at me, 'This is my house and these two boys are my children! They are to obey me, and I don't want you interfering. I wish you would stay at home. I don't need you anymore. My sons are well behaved until you come around. Then they become rambunctious.'

"But let me tell you, Father, when she wants a babysitter, I'm the first person she calls. I am no more than a nanny to her. She can be an angel to her snobby friends, but I see a different side to her. She's like a devil to me.

, She uses a new way of talking. I don't understand her or my grandchildren half the time, especially when they're talking about this computer stuff. She's always talking about the latest fashion. God how can people have such small minds! If she isn't on the phone she's out shopping, leaving the boys in my care. She's gone half the time, always out at some fancy restaurant with her college chums. In a way, I'm glad. The house is more peaceful when she's not in it. Although she accuses me of making the boys misbehave, I know I calm the boys down. I try to teach them about God.

They love it when I tell them stories especially about growing up on a farm and all that. Children need to hear such things. They love hearing about the fish we would catch in the river. I tell them how the milk they drink comes from a cow that munches grass and then uses its belly like a factory to transform it into something completely new They don't listen to me as much as they used to. They've changed, and too quickly, I think. We don't let children be children anymore.

I usually do the laundry for Carmel, but when I haven't found the time, she goes into one of her sulks and of course takes her anger out on everyone around her. She thinks an educated woman like herself shouldn't be a housewife. God forbid that she get dirt under her nails.

Sometimes I think she considers her boys more of an intrusion than a blessing. Although she's never said it, I think she would prefer to be without them. I don't think she has the heart for motherhood.

One day I didn't have time to do the laundry. She had been gone all day, God knows where, she never tells me, and she got angry and took her anger out on her husband. She yelled at him, 'Get up off your fat ass and help me with this goddam laundry!'

"he replied, 'I'm tired. Can't you see I just came in from work? As usual, there's no dinner waiting on the table. What were you fucking doing all day anyway? Yammering on the phone, I suppose, or out there somewhere with those other fucking bitches!'

"I tried to calm things down, but he shouted at me, "Quit interfering! What do you know anyway? You're nothing but a white-trash, low-class cunt! Why don't you get out of my house and leave us alone?"'

Fr Pat had listened attentively to everything she said, and then he asked, "Is there anything I can do to help?"

"Oh, Father," Mary said. "I would love it if you would speak to them. It's my grandchildren that I'm worried about."

"I'll try, Mary. I'll try," Fr Pat said.

He felt inadequate. He could be very articulate, but some situations were so overwhelming that they left even him. speechless. He knew that some problems, if left to fester, would only get more serious, and all he could do was apply a Band-Aid to a gushing artery. If he were to tell Mary's daughter and son-in-law that their problem was basically a spiritual one, they would look at him as though he were growing horns. It was bad enough to be spiritually impoverished, but if they couldn't even recognize the this how could Fr Pat make make any sense to them.? It would be like speaking Chinese to an Indian in the jungles of the Amazon or trying to explain the danger of cancer to someone who couldn't appreciate the scourge of a rebellious cell.

Where would he even start with Carmel and her husband? He didn't know if it was even possible to reach them. He would have loved to read a few poems to them, perhaps one poem on missing the light that included the line "Men go home because they do not know,". But then he became frustrated as he realized he couldn't start there because their materialistic culture had little tolerance for poetry. It played no part in their culture. If he could only help them understand this one poem, he knew the result would work more wonders than a thousand hours of psychoanalysis,

Brendan Kennelly:

I knew the world is most at ease
With acceptable insanities,
Important nothings that command
The heart and mind of busy men
Who, had they seen it, might have praised
The light on Portobello Bridge.

Fr Pat thought further about poetry. It is only the spiritually attuned who understood poetry. Without it, only the literal, the visible, the tangible, and the material exists; the vision, the pleasure, and the treasure remains hidden. He Could not talk about spiritual matters to Carmel and her husband, simply because to their mind ":That stuff belongs to Church'

The master arrives when the student is ready and they certainly were not ready.

Materialism prevents the eye from seeing beyond the surface. Where commodity is king, poetry and a sense of interiority recede, imagination and wonder are smothered, and humans end up as little more than well-behaved zombies. How can the music of the earth be heard in a culture so removed from nature? Children rarely intimately encounter the miracles which feed them? In such a culture, children's imaginative minds so disposed to curiosity and make-believe are stripped of their intuition and inspiration much more than they are enhanced their toy gadgets. How can a culture truly be great when it overly emphasises profit and money.

Such a country may considered itself religious, but it definitely is not spiritual. A country without poetry and spirituality is anti-evolutionary. To deny the possibility of true spirituality is like saying to the singularity before the Big Bang, "Put your dust in the bin. We don't need you any longer."

Fr Pat thought that Mary's daughter, like others in her culture, had chosen to give her full attention to the material, ignoring consciousness, putting her on the path to neuroticism. Mary's daughter was a victim, but far worse, she didn't recognize it.

Atheistic materialism, although promising utopia, is as nefarious and terror-driven as the Christian and Muslim fundamentalism which it so vociferously opposes,. Carmel, her husband and children had fallen into a fundamentalism, not so easily recognized, because it was culturally accepted as politically correct.

Fr Pat understood precisely the cultural dogmatism ingrained in the minds of Carmel and her husband. Could the vicious cycle cease in the case of the two young boys? Or was it already too late.?. According to Mary their young minds were already indelibly scorched. They already had entered exclusively into the land of the ego.

Mary said, "Just yesterday, little Jimmy ran up to me and pretending to have a gun, he shouted, 'Bang bang!' I said to him, 'Jimmy, I told you to stop those games. You know I don't like them. God didn't give us life so we could shoot one another.'

Then Jimmy pulled up his undershirt to display a machine gun he had painted on his little belly. I said to him, 'Jimmy, what did you put such a horrible thing on your skin for?' He answered, "grandma that's the way the army does it.

Don't you know the marines dress in camouflage before they sneak up on you. Then they shoot you"

Mary paused and began crying. "I tried to tell my daughter that the boys shouldn't be playing killing games, that it would be far better if she and their daddy took them out to the park and showed them the swans and the ducks. But my daughter answered back, 'They're only boys. Do you want them to grow up like sissies? Anyhow, it's only a little game.'"

Although Fr Pat had never met Mary's daughter or her family, he felt he knew them. They were like so many others who were good people at heart but who had been battered to death by materialism and consumerism. Like so many Westerners, their being had become less important than their having, leaving them dehumanized and dis-edified. God was absent from their world. They rarely entertained a metaphysical question. Anthropomorphism coloured their total perspective. They segregated themselves from any question concerning a higher purpose. To them, God was, at best, a convenience in times of need; otherwise, Divinity scarcely played any part in their lives. Mary's daughter and her family were but a manifestation of the ontological disease which pervaded their culture.

Fr Pat lamented this, for a world without spirituality is a world without meaning. Compassion is learned through the realization that all that living things are interrelated. We are but a part of the natural world. We cannot live apart from it.

The sweeping brushstroke which paints the portrait of contemporary Western culture is materialism, and it blots out almost totally the best portrait of our potentiality. We have lost the ability to appreciate what the poets and the mystics see, and until we learn this, we remain apart from not a part of nature.

He thought about the famous words of Chief Seattle: "This we know the earth does not belong to man, man belongs to the earth. This we know: all things are connected like the blood that unites us all."

Chief Seattle said also, "All things are connected . . . . The whites, too, shall pass—perhaps sooner than other tribes. Continue to contaminate your bed, and you will one night suffocate in your own waste.

> You whites . . . didn't understand our prayers. You didn't try to understand. When we sang our praises to the sun or moon or wind, you said we were worshipping idols. We saw the Great Spirit work in almost everything: sun, moon, trees, wind, and mountains . . . . Did you know that trees talk? Well they do . . . . [They'll talk to you if you listen. Trouble is, white people don't listen. But I have learned a lot from trees: sometimes about the weather, sometimes about animals, sometimes about the Great Spirit."

These ideas came across in an American Indian prayer as well:

> The Creator gave us the sun, our elder brother. It's his duty to give us warmth and to nourish the life-giving foods that we planted on earth. And as we see the sun come up this morning, it shine on us, keeping us warm. He's doing his duty, and for this, we are very grateful. So let us put our minds together as one and thank the sun for still performing his duty, and let out minds be that way.

Fr Pat thought about these points further. "Ours is a world of disruption and disconnection," he mused. "Both the Church and materialistic science have dismembered us. Autocracy is an atrocity and because of it, we do not appreciate the music and the spirituality running through everything. Our materialistic world cannot deal with the higher dimension of invisibility and nothingness. What we see is only the tip of the iceberg in the universe.

"Materialism's fakery has replaced the sights, the sounds, the smells, and the tastes of nature and has thereby removed us from what is real. Our phones and our automobiles now mobilize but not our minds.

We have become very lazy in respect to spirituality.

Through gadgetry we disassociate ourselves more and more from the natural world and what is real

"As Einstein said, 'He who cannot wonder and be wrapped in awe is as good s dead,' and as Socrates said, 'The unexamined life is not worth living.'

Scientific materialism and religion have made it almost impossible for us to examine and wonder at the mystery. Both systems are monological—each has its own point of view. Both systems are closed. Neither represents the whole truth. Quantum physics, on the other hand, teaches that in our search for truth, the human race must become dialogical on its journey into the trans-logical. A country without inner sustenance cannot learn vulnerability. When we lose the sense of wonder, we are left grasping and lustful. Such a nation no longer has the idealism and innocence of its youth; it has grown up into a monster. A culture has to be conscious and grateful to become great.

Fr Pat turned to his bookshelf and opened a book of poetry by e. e. cummings. He read:

> i thank You God for most this amazing
> day: for the leaping greenly spirits of trees
> and a blue true dream of sky; and for everything
> which is natural which is infinite which is yes

He thought further, "Any empire which banishes the idea of God from its constitution is not integrated. It cannot experience peace without recognizing some great non-local Energy. Prayer has the power to remove arrogance and restore harmony, and every great civilization before us has used it for this purpose." This brought to mind St John of the Cross's words: "You might quiet the whole world for a second if you pray. And if you love, if you really love, our guns will wilt."

Fr Pat would have loved to tell Mary's daughter and her family that one found the anchor for the universe within the self, but how could he say A, B, C to a person who had never heard of the alphabet or worse still, saw no need for it? Where there is only glitter and neon light, how can one explain the shadow cast by the candle?

He thought further and then came up with his answers. First, he'd explain that young children's minds were tabula rasa, etched with everything they were exposed to, bad as well as good. The toxicity they absorbed as children would remain with them for the rest of their lives. Second, he'd present the idea that the bodily scars from child abuse were easily detected, but more insidious and less obvious were the mental scars that remained with children for the rest of their lives. Third, he'd point out that if parents could realize the true potential of the unique gifts placed in their care, then our world would have many more Mozarts and Michelangelos. It was a frightening thought that someone blessed with such potential might never use it or even notice it.

Having collected his thoughts and asked Mary to mind her grandchildren the following evening, Fr Pat called Mary's daughter and made an appointment to see her and her husband then. When he arrived for the meeting, he found that their home was the usual house owned by young upwardly mobile couples. The door of the three-car garage was open, revealing that it was filled to the brim with stuff, an SUV and a Mercedes tucked inside with small power boat nestled next to them. Hockey sticks and about a thousand Yankees hats hung everywhere. He noticed a bag of golf clubs but, interestingly, no gardening tools.

Carmel greeted Fr Pat, and when he asked about the tools, she responded, "Oh, Tony hates gardens. So we don't have any tools. Our gardener brings his own with him when he comes"

"You also have a housekeeper to do the cleaning as well, I presume," Fr Pat said.

"Oh no, my mother does that. It's very difficult with two boys in the house. They're terrors at this stage. It's a full-time job trying to watch them."

"I can imagine," Fr Pat said. "It seems more of a vocation than a job."

"I've never heard it put like that before," Carmel said. "Do you mean it's like becoming a priest?" Not waiting for an answer, she led him inside. "Let's go to the living room, Father. My husband, Tony, is waiting for us. It's more comfortable there than in the garage anyway. I wish I could have let you in by the front door, but you came in by the garage before I knew could, and now you are seeing all this mess in the den. It really is embarrassing."

Fr Pat looked around. The boys had taken over the den with toys, making it even worse than the garage. It was stuffed with gadgets toys and guns, guns, guns everywhere. Machine guns, pistols, rifles, sawed-off shotguns, pellet guns, you name it. War video games were scattered all over the floor. *Playboy* magazine lay on the big armchair where Fr Pat presumed Tony sat.

"I know it's a disaster, Father," Carmel said. "I try to tidy it up the best I can, but then Tony and the two boys mess it all up again."

Two huge flat-screen televisions sat against one wall, placed only a few yards apart and each connected to a video recorder.

As they walked through to the living room, Fr Pat could see that Tony and the boys were nervous.

"Take a seat, please, Father," Carmel said. "My mother tells me that you like tea. Would you like a cup now? Or maybe since you're Irish you'd like some whiskey?"

Father Pat smiled and said, "Please don't stereotype me. There are a few of us, maybe twenty out of four million, who don't drink at all."

Tony and Carmel laughed.

"I didn't mean it that way," Carmel said.

Fr Pat then held out his hand and introduced himself to Tony, then he sat down and looked about.

The living room was simple to say the least, decorated with delicate taste. Even though it was almost minimalist in its design, Quaker or early American, Fr Pat saw, it as elegant. It was as though Carmel and Tony came right out of a glossy magazine. They didn't match his preconception. From what Mary had told him, he thought they would look like hippies and would show contempt for the finer things in life, expressing their house and dress as unconventional.

Instead, Tony was a very handsome tall man with a big frame, but typical of someone his age, he had the beginnings of a beer belly. Carmel was dressed casually but with a refined flair that was neither ostentatious nor understated. She looked beautiful.

Fr Pat wondered if he had been cast as an actor in some surreal movie. "Can this be the same couple on the brink of collapse that Mary told me about?" he thought. To his eye, everything seemed perfect; not a detail had been overlooked. But Mary had told him enough. Life is not always what the eye beholds.

Beautiful external appearances often camouflage interior ugliness and emptiness.

To arrive at the core of their unhappy relationship, he must invite them to look inside themselves. If they could put a stop to their own rot, then, naturally, they would stop the infection from spreading to their children. Their problem, and its solution, were a classical example of how quantum physics applies to spirituality as much as to materiality. The cosmos is one, Love is caught more than it is taught.

Fr Pat knew he would have to show Carmel and Tony that unresolved love in a parent soon becomes the child's problem. How could one give love when an addictive invader in the guise of a lover had stolen one's mind and heart away?

"Mary told me that you're planning on separating," Fr Pat said.

"That's true. We've discussed it many times, Father," Carmel said, "and we tried it for two months once but then we got back together."

"You know the old tug of war," Tony said. "I missed Carmel. Before that, the sex was good. So good, in fact, . . . that's when we conceived our second son. We thought that maybe having another child would glue the goddam relationship together and make the marriage work. But it didn't happen that way. Within about three months, we were back to the way things were. Fighting, fighting, fighting."

"He even wanted me to abort the baby," Carmel put in. "But being a Catholic, I refused."

"But Tony's a Catholic too," Fr Pat said.

"He's only a kind of one," Carmel said.

"But if both of you are only a la carte Catholics, then why am I here? How can I help you?" Fr Pat asked.

"I don't suppose you can really do anything, Father. It's up to us, isn't it? But it's good to talk. Sometimes another opinion helps us to do what's best," Carmel said.

"We'd like to try one more time," Tony said,

"For the kids' sake," Carmel added.

"Are you sure that's your motivation?" Fr Pat asked

"Well, you know, the boys need a father," Carmel said. "Not that he does too much with them. But they do watch football together."

"Do you do anything else with them, Tony?" Fr Pat enquired.

"You know, the usual man stuff," Tony replied.

"Like what?" Fr Pat asked.

"Well, you know. I teach them how to be good Americans," Tony said.

"And how do you do that?" Fr Pat probed further.

"I teach them that this is a great country, except for what's happening now with all these foreigners coming in. We have our own kind of low-class whites. We don't need to let others in. This is the white man's country. We founded it and have worked to make it what it the most powerful nation on earth. We're the envy of the world. That's why so many foreigners come over here and take our jobs from us."

"So you think might is right?" Fr Pat asked.

"You're goddam right I do. We're the best country on earth. The second amendment of our Constitution gives us the right to bear arms" Tony said. "I know it's anecdotal but I strongly believe that is the reason we have become so violent," Fr Pat said. Then he turned to Carmel and asked, "Do you agree with Tony?"

"On the whole, honestly, yes, I do I think this country is the best in the world. Our government is always trying to bring democracy to everyone overseas, and what do we get back but a bunch of dead Marines," she said.

"So you think the United States is over there to spread democracy? Fr Pat asked

"Damn right about that. You hit the nail on the head, Father," Tony said.

"You don't think the government has an ulterior motive?" Fr Pat asked.

"Ulterior motive? What do you mean?" Tony asked

"What about oil?" Fr Pat said.

"Ah, I've heard a lot of dickheads say that before," Tony responded. "But that's shit. We have enough oil in this country to last us the next thousand years. All we have to do is go get it. Haven't you heard about fracking and sand oil?"

"At any cost?" Fr Pat retorted "You believe we should just soak it up from the bowels of the earth and pollute the bed we sleep on?"

"Look, Father, this country was built on capitalism. It's ruled by the law of supply and demand. It's the best system ever. It's done a lot of good, and that's why we have plenty of everything. Name a better system.

Do you see this house? Do you see anything wrong with it? My children have everything they want. They ask for something and they get it. What other country in the world can brag about that?"

"But don't you think there's something amiss when all the good things of the earth flow overwhelmingly in one direction?" Fr Pat asked.

"I don't know what you mean, Father," Tony said.

Fr Pat turned to Carmel again. "Why did you marry Tony, Carmel?"

She smiled. "Well, to tell you the truth, he's a hunk. I know he has a beer belly now, but the moment I first met him. I lusted after him. I could hardly wait to go to bed with him."

"Why don't you still feel that way?" Tony asked. "The other night when I really wanted you, you told me to take my fucking hands off you. I had to masturbate."

"You shouldn't be talking like that in front of a priest, Tony," Carmel said.

"Sorry, Father," Tony said, "but let me tell you, she's a cute whore. She had her eyes on my money as soon as she met me. She knew what she was doing. I spoiled her in the beginning, but the more I gave her, the more she wanted. She hasn't changed. She always gets what she wants only to stuff half of it in the closet. She doesn't even take it out to dust. But still she's never satisfied. She always wants sex or a new dress. Go upstairs and look in her closets. I am sure you'll find a hundred new pairs of shoes in there."

"Well at least it's better than spending money on drugs or drink," Carmel said. "At least I can look and my clothes after I've bought them. I can touch them and I can smell them and I can see them. But where are your drink and drugs, Tony? They're gone. They're invisible! You have nothing to show for all the money you've spent on your beer except your fat belly. And you're teaching the boys to grow up to be boozers just like you. I've seen them tasting what you leave in the bottom of your cans, and you don't do anything to stop them."

"We're all addicted in some way or other," Fr Pat said.

"I'm not addicted," Carmel said.

"Well what about all those pairs of shoes?" Fr Pat said.

"Don't listen to Tony. He exaggerates everything."

"Well, how many pair of new shoes do you have?" Fr Pat enquired.

"I don't really know. I've never counted them. Certainly not a hundred!"

"Give a guess," Fr Pat said.

Carmel thought for a moment. "Maybe seventy," she answered.

"You see, Father? It's just like I told you," Tony said.

"Oh, shut up, Tony. You're no saint. I'm not addicted like you are."

"You're really not addicted?" You're either a liar or stupid. Maybe you can't count!" Tony snapped.

Carmel sneered, "Just you wait a minute." She left the room and came back with two plastic bags. "Yeah, you're not fucking addicted!" she shouted as she dumped the empty beer cans and gin bottles from both bags onto the living room floor. "Please, explain this to Father."

There now, Father, you can see with your own eyes what she's like. She gets into a rage over the slightest thing. I'm not saying I'm a saint, but how do you live with a maniac?"

"Let's at least be civil with each other," Fr Pat interjected.

"Just look at the beautiful Persian carpet that she made me pay ten thousand dollars for. Look at the state it's in," Tony said.

"Well, it's not like you ever clean it. All you do is sit on your fat ass. Besides, if you emptied your trash like I asked you numerous times, none of this shit would have happened and the carpet would be clean now."

"If she's not nagging me about the carpet then she's barking about something else," Tony said.

"You love your beer more than me."

"She drives me crazy!" Tony shouted. "She gets everything she wants but then harps on me about having a few cans of beer as I'm watching a football game."

Fr Pat sighed. "That reminds me, why do you have those two huge TV sets in the den?"

"Well. you know the way it is with children," Carmel said. "Especially boys. They're always fighting. They both want to watch a different programme and play a different video game. To stop them from fighting, I bought them each their own TV."

"So, you live in your own comfortable paradise," Fr Pat said, "yet neither of you seems to be happy. What do you think is the underlying cause of you unhappiness?"

"I guess it's because we've fallen out of love with each other," Carmel said.

"You don't think that maybe you have a spiritual problem? It seems to me that you're attached to things rather than to something deeper which would give meaning to your lives."

"Like what?" Carmel asked.

"Well, like your children," Fr Pat said.

"Of course," Carmel said. "That's why we're going to give it another try. For the children's sake. I told you that already."

"But your relationship is toxic. If you keep on acting like this. your children will miss out on the most important thing in life. and that's your love," Fr Pat said.

"I give them plenty of love," Carmel said. "I'm always kissing them. I cook for them and I feed them and I bring them to school and I buy them ice cream and pizza, whatever they want. What more can I do? When they cry, it's me that they come to because Tony told them they have to be tough, that Marines don't cry!"

"But that is not necessarily love," Fr Pat said. "And in Tony's case, it certainly isn't. Love is selfless. Love only works if you work at it. When it arrives, you'll recognize it. It will free you from the iron cage in which you're trapped."

"But we're in no cage," Tony said. "We're free as a honey bee."

"But, Tony, we're not happy. My mother is right. We need help."

"Oh, for Christ's sake, don't quote your mother to me!" Tony said. "She's a lump of shit, and I've told her so to her face. And you, Carmel, are no better than she is. You're nothing more than a dumb blonde with a college education."

"As long as you behave like this to one another you are in an iron cage," Fr Pat interrupted. "You'll never get out of it until you cease all your fighting and your cursing and your drinking and let go of your attachment to material stuff. It has to stop. You've been drugged by the dopamine these temporary pleasures give you. Ask God to help you. When you look to this higher power, the rows between you will disappear. Do you realize what an awesome gift you've been given in your sons? But their two young minds soak in everything they hear and see, so you'd better be careful. I hope you don't fight in front of them. The greatest calamity anyone can suffer in this world is to be misdirected while still an innocent child. As far as I can see, you're directing your sons to grow up to be as unhappy and un integrated as you are. It is a fierce thing to be parents.

The future of the world depends on you. According to the attention you give your sons, they grow up to be a Hitler or a saint. Such is their potential. Do you understand me?"

"Sort of," Tony said. "But, Father, seriously, apart from all that you said about the cage, I know why you're here, and we should get down to basics 'cause I have to go to work to keep my bitch happy. All she wants is my money. 'I'm tired of your body,' that's her latest whinge."

"What I see is that you both use each other as objects. Tony, you use Carmel for her body, and Carmel, you use Tony for his money. You both see each other as something you can barter for. You've turned love into a commodity."

"That's the way it's done, isn't it? Everyone does it the same way," Tony said.

"No, they don't." Fr Pat said. "I'm afraid it's going to get like that if we continue to live without spirituality, though."

"I don't understand why you have to bring religion into everything," Tony said. "The Church is always sticking its nose into my bedroom."

"I agree with that," Carmel said. "What do those old farts in Rome know about sex anyhow?"

"They know about paedophilia." Tony chuckled.

"I'm not talking about sex, I'm talking about love," Fr Pat said.

"What's the difference?" Tony said.

"Well," Fr Pat began, "sex can be divine when it comes from love. Otherwise it's just an animal act. Even the dogs in the street do it."

Father Pat took out a piece of paper from his jacket pocket. "This is something my father wrote to my mother a long time ago. This is what I think love is." Fr Pat read:

> I will live for you
> If your mouth is parched, I will give you water to drink.
> If you are cold, I will cover you with my own coat.
> If you cry, I will cry with you.
> When you laugh, I will laugh too.
> Your pain will be my pain
> And your joy, my delight.
> I will stay beside you forever,
> No matter the cost.
> I will anticipate all your needs.
> Your footsteps falling on the stairs as you come up to bed at night
> Shall be unique, unlike any other footstep in this world.
> Your voice and your call
> Shall be sweeter to me than a symphony.
> We journey into the future together
> And even if there are twists and bends upon the road,
> Our one heartbeat shall halve our sorrow
> And double our joy and happiness
> In an eternal tomorrow.

"Isn't it beautiful!" Carmel said. "I always did like poetry."

A moment of silence went by, and then Tony said, "I know why Mary sent you She's more worried about our religion than about our marriage. I know I'm not a good Catholic, but she makes me sick with that religious stuff" "You mean spirituality" Fr Pat said.

"They're the same thing" Tony said.
"She tries to indoctrinate the boys too much.
I don't like her interfering.

Religion turns boys into cissies.

I don't believe in confession or wipe the plate clean. That's magic!

I don't believe in that stuff anymore. I can see that you're a good man and you're just doing your thing. I expect that of you, but don't include me in it. I think going to mass and all that sort of things is for women and wimps. It bores the hell out of me. Sometimes I have to go because Carmel makes me do it, especially at Christmas and Easter, but even then, I stay at the back of the church and smoke a few cigarettes. I don't think I've said a prayer since my confirmation."

"And what about you, Carmel? What do you think about spirituality?" Fr Pat asked.

"Well, Father, I have to say, I do believe in something, but I don't know what it is. Just like Tony, I don't often pray. I think it's all a lot of wishful thinking. I really don't think God is listening. This evolution stuff seems to make a lot of sense. We were monkeys and then we became humans, and that's it in a nutshell. Nothing more to say. Just drink, eat, and be happy, Religion bores me too, and like Tony, I haven't said a prayer since CCD, except when my father died. I do the bare minimum when it comes to church. A lot of women who do go are just a bunch of hypocrites. I send in my envelopes to keep the boys registered since they'll need their baptismal certificates when they receive their first Communion and when they get married. I love First Holy Communion, though; I must admit it. I wish the boys were girls just so they could wear Holy Communion dresses for a day. You must think I'm crazy, Father, but you know women. We can be too feminine!"

"Do you think there's a solution to your problem?" Fr Pat asked.

"I guess therapy," Carmel said. "I'm going to a shrink already, but Tony won't come."

"The human brain is a wonderful machine," Fr Pat said. "It can produce serotonin twice the strength of that manufactured in a laboratory, and at no cost, I might add. Miraculous happenings are occurring inside the human body all the time and we're unaware of them. The same is true of the mind. It's always available but we may not be aware of it. But we can have a different kind of serotonin that brings peace not only to the body but also to the mind. It is the archenemy of spirituality. It is a million trillion times more effective than all the cures prescribed in the world. When psychoanalysis doesn't include it, it fails miserably. It is an essential ingredient. It cures broken relationships. Without it, unity is impossible. It brings body and soul together and treats them as one." Fr Pat paused. There was silence in the room.

"Sounds wonderful," Carmel finally said. "Where can we buy it?"

Six years later, Mary fell ill. Fr Pat visited her in the hospital, and Carmel called the next morning to say that her mother had passed away. Their children were now teenagers, and Carmel and Tony had divorced, Carmel was now living with another partner. The evening before Mary's burial, Fr Pat visited the funeral parlour where her remains were laid, and he finally met Mary's three other children, two sons and a daughter. They indeed had a strong family resemblance. Just by looking at them, Fr Pat could tell that they were very successful. He learned that one of Carmel's brothers was a very successful surgeon in a big hospital in Las Vegas, that her other brother was the chief executive of some big corporation, and that her sister, Susie, was a lawyer. Fr Pat didn't know, and didn't dare enquire, if Carmel's brothers and sisters knew that Carmel was only their half-sister, but what he discovered that they considered Carmel the black sheep of the family. Her siblings had tried to distance themselves as far as they could from her, but Mary's funeral had brought them unwillingly together. They indicated that they considered Carmel to be dim-witted, as they mentioned she had scarcely graduated from college, even though Mary and her husband had given them all the same chance in life. The rift had intensified when Carmel married Tony. They thought he was a redneck totally outside their social class. To Carmel's siblings, he was rude and dumb and embarrassing. Even though Carmel had now divorced him, they were still worried he might show up at the funeral.

Fr Pat could certainly feel the tension in the funeral parlour between Carmel and her family. All of Mary's grandchildren seemed to get along admirably, so perhaps they didn't know or even care about the strained relationship between their parents. Carmel's boys looked like teenage movie stars, and they had the personalities to match. If they had been scarred psychologically by their parents' relationship, there was no evidence of it, and the rest of Mary's grandchildren seemed happy, although a few secretly cried, and all were neatly dressed. Now Fr Pat knew why Mary loved them.

They all told him tales about the impact their grandmother had had on their lives. She had cuddled and nurtured them in a special way. They could never forget her. She had touched each of them indelibly. It seemed to Fr Pat that Mary's spirit was moving through them. He was sure that she had not gone away at all; she had merely been transformed. Her love was alive and kicking inside of her family like a baby in its mother's womb. But if he said that to anyone there, they would have surely thought him mad. Still, her love expanded in an ever more embracing circle, like the ripples in a pond. Love had such power to carry on.

Silently, Fr Pat prayed, "Mary, stay with your grandchildren. They still need you. They are the future. May you go with them." The joy and beautiful innocence on their faces had to be an epitaph for Mary's love. He prayed that their idealism would never be destroyed by school or Church.

Fr Pat spoke with Susie, who told him that she and Carmel didn't speak to each other because Carmel had put her through hell. "We wanted mother to move out west with us, Susie said, but she refused, saying that Carmel's two boys needed her. Carmel put poor mother through hell while she was still on earth and that's the reason for our not speaking to one another.

"Why is Carmel so different from you and her brothers?" Fr Pat asked.

"Well, as I'm sure you know already, she's only our half-sister," Susie said. "Mother had her before my father married her. I'm sure the difference is due to genetics. That may sound awful, but just look at the difference between her and us."

"I'm not sure about that," Fr Pat said. "From what I've read, genetics doesn't determine the behaviour of a child. That's learned; it's the result of nurture rather than nature."

"But Mother and Father were very good to her. Father adopted her when she was only four. He gave us all limits and stressed education and obedience, but he did it in such a loving way that his strictness didn't really bother us. He treated Carmel just like he treated his biological children."

"Her poor behaviour may be the result of a traumatic experience she went through when she was young and vulnerable," Fr Pat surmised.

"What are you implying?" Susie asked

"You can draw your own conclusion," Fr Pat said.

"Are you suggesting that she was molested as a child?" Susie asked.

"I don't know, of course, but it is a distinct possibility. It's happened many times before. Perhaps that's why your mother ended her first marriage. I'm only suggesting it as a possibility since I do know that when innocence is crucified, we go on wailing for the rest of our lives from the pain of the nails hammered into us. It can turn a mind suicidal or else push it to non-conformity. Maybe that's why she let Tony treat her like a dumb blonde. I heard him call her that once. We'll pay all kinds of compensations just to keep us from remembering."

"Carmel was always impossible," Susie said. "She scalded Mother's heart, and I think that's why I almost hate her. Smoke, drink, drugs, abortion, you name it. I don't know where she came from. She always had a mind of her own. She only married Tony because he had money and good looks. Mother begged her not to do it, but she wouldn't listen."

"Where did all his money come from?" Fr Pat asked.

"Inheritance, he says, but I'm certain he's in the Mafia," Susie said.

After his conversation with Susie, Fr Pat drifted to a corner to observe the mourners. Mary's sons were very distinguished-looking men. They exuded professionalism and remained aloof throughout the visitation. They didn't seem as approachable as Susie. Fr Pat would have liked to speak with them more personally, but they were too busy welcoming their friends and family members.

A flash of insecurity came over Fr Pat. How could he address this group in an intelligent way about Mary? Out of respect for them and, indeed, anyone, he couldn't resort to clichés, easy answers, or stopgap theology to speak about their pain and separation. Perhaps, like so many members of their generation, Mary's children were post-Christian and, like Nietzsche, considered religion to be a pox on society and all priests liars. Or maybe they believed that, as George Bernard Shaw once remarked, "The closer the church, the further from God."

In a culture centred on external beauty and focussed on being forever young, death was the ultimate terror. It was intolerable to a lipstick-and-rouge culture. It had to be covered up at all costs. We camouflage the soil with a green plastic rug which we pretend is green grass. And for God's sake, we never allow our children to hear the awful thud of the earth as its hit the coffin lid. In contemporary culture, what was natural is now considered reprehensible and removed as far as possible from its true representation. Obscuring the lessons of nature and treating them as suspect is a molestation of truth.

Death is the very antithesis of everything vibrant, passionate, and acceptable to our beauty-centred culture. Mourning and grieving are not allowed; fakery is preferred. Deceit becomes endemic when the reality of natural processes are obfuscated. We have become disjointed and unintegrated.

Fr Pat hardly recognized Mary in the coffin. She was all painted up as though she were going to a ball. He had never seen her in such a rig-out before. As he knelt before her coffin to pray, he silently wondered what had happened to the beautiful, dignified, simple woman he had known for the past ten years. Her body had been contoured to fit the expectations of a culture which distained death. The mortuary technicians had manufactured a pretty fakery. There was no lesson to be learned here; Mary's body had been dolled up into a hoax. Instead of reminding those assembled of dust unto dust, this teachable moment had been twisted to express the reverse. This was truly a misuse of poetry. The deadness of it all had been turned into a mockery of its reality.

Throughout our lives, we gave ourselves over to escapism, and even now it looked to Fr Pat as though we were again prevented from facing our own mortality. The truth remained: we were but a part of and not apart from nature. To disassociate ourselves from the natural world is like saying to the earth, "I do not want the seed and the grains of your fields. I spit out the graciousness of your fruits and vegetables. I can go on living without your meals." To cover up death in this way is like covering a winter tree with plastic leaves and turning on a fan underneath to simulate and stimulate a fake breeze.

"We are out of tune with our planet," Fr Pat thought. "A culture with a more holistic view, one with its mind more attuned to the processes of nature, would celebrate death as much as birth. It would see them both as transformations. By spiritualizing, we turn our mourning into dancing. Mary would want it that way." She never owned a rosary beads and never said the rosary, yet this religious symbol was wrapped around her hands as she lay in the coffin. Her dead body told a different story. Through her spirituality, she became a living rosary.

SCIENCE AND DEATH

Stop all the clocks, cut off the telephone,
Prevent the dog from barking with a juicy bone,
Silence the pianos and with a muffled drum
Bring out the coffin,.
(W.H. Auden)

Life is a petticoat about death.
(James Stephens)

Physical death looks like an insult. The eyes which looked so lovingly upon us are closed now; the arms which once cuddled us and the feet which once walked with us on our journey have given up their purpose. They have shut down the windows and blown out the candles. What darkness! The lips which once kissed so tenderly are closed now. She speaks no more. The hands which once made bread and fed have said no to the bakery oven. The fingers which tempted the needle and thread through the cloth have closed down their factory. The voice which played as much music as a bird's song has thrown away its violin and piano. The smell once more sweet than the star gazer lily has wafted away into the sands of the Sahara. The desert is pregnant with nothing. No greenery anywhere. We cry, unrepaired in our grief. We are robbed of our energy like a deflated tyre. What good is a bicycle tour when our mode of transportation has been taken away from us? The Sunday in our week is missing. There is no rest or peace prevalent. Our love has been assassinated. We are left with nothing but the exercise of ennui. We shake our fists.

What use are eyes if we cannot see? Sounds terribly bleak, doesn't it? But just because we can't see the sun beyond the clouds doesn't mean the sun isn't there. If we journey in an aeroplane beyond the clouds, we get a new perspective. We see that the sun is there after all. Death asks us to take a journey into a new perspective so that we will see differently with a new vision more powerful than the sight of our eyes. We are held too much to the familiar. Even in looking at what seems familiar to our eyes, it is obvious that life holds out many surprises for us.

For example, our bodies are built with atoms, but each atom contains 99.98 per cent empty space. So, the matter of all the bodies in the world, if condensed into that space, could be held in our two hands. Incredible, we say. Another surprise comes from our vision. An object needs to reflect light for us to see it. Because it takes ten minutes for sunlight to reach our planet, we do not see objects as they really are but as they were. Even in the realm of matter, we do not always look beyond the obvious. We have to make a leap to really understand.

When we take notice, we see that life is an oscillation. Our very heartbeat tells us that we go in and out all the time. We only come back because we have first gone out, and we go out in order to come back in. Life is just like that—it thrives on its opposite. It is never dualistic. Opposites operate with the same energy; they are one. Half of the moments in our daily lives are dead ones. To live is to embrace both life and death in the one system. We cannot have one without the other. So why should we be so terrified of death when we have spent half of our lives practising it? It is the on and off of the lights on a Christmas tree that give us the illusion of movement. We cannot have life without death. We go away as much as we stay.

Spirituality asks that we also make a leap beyond the obvious before we can understand. We are too limited by our small perspective on reality. But we feel more comfortable with what is familiar, we feel more at home with our perception, even though scientific facts tell us a different story. The possibility of a larger horizon can be disturbing. None of us likes to leave the familiar and move out yonder. Change is often challenging and troublesome.

When we face death, we are asked the biggest questions of our lives: Where has our loved one gone? Is this thing called an afterlife merely the happy ending to a children's fairy tale? Is God just as fictional as Santa Claus? Are we cosmic orphans wandering in the dark? Or might we be instead creatures invested with divinity, heirs to a kingdom etched eternal? Is life meaningful or is it absurd?

Every person born into this world must somehow posit these questions to reach his or her own answers about being. We are inclined to stick to the familiar answers. It is easier that way. We like the familiar because it is explainable and tangible and evident as it is. But is reality truly as we perceive it? According to science it is not. If we want to perceive it as it is, we must take a journey of discovery into a different perspective. In order to get into the correct perspective, we must leave the familiar. It is only by looking at things differently that we can find the truth.

Materialistic science is dedicated to what is called *observable phenomenology*, that is, seeing the material objects in our everyday world. This is the boundary of mechanistic scientist's discipline. Their practice is reigned by measuring, by scrutinizing objects under a microscope or through a telescope. Such scrutiny can go either inward through the microscope (into the micro realm) or outward through the telescope(into the macro realm). Materialistic science restricts itself to studying the things of this world only. It is orientated towards the object, the observed, and never towards the subject, the observer. Its main aim is to discover the truth of the object by reason alone. In order to believe in anything, it must be empirically verifiable.

The science of matter has been taken on the attitude of a god since the sixteenth century. It rules the West, for our culture has submitted itself to it and accepts it as the only truth. It ignores the idea of God. There is little room for mysticism or transcendence in such a culture. Objective materialistic science tells us we should not believe in anything we cannot prove. Its eschatological conclusion is the absurdity of life. There is no life after this life. God is dead. The same fate awaits us all. Life is a random thing; it just evolved through the coincidental meeting of different vapours and chemicals spewed out by the Big Bang.

We have moved so much in the direction of Scientific materialistic Atheism that it now controls our life, We have become so brain washed that we pay little heed to the fact that this approach spells ontological death. We are embarrassed by the fact that possibly we may have a divine dimension. Even when we do admit the divine to ourselves we seldom have the courage of our convictions to speak publicly about it. We see little connection between our private spirituality and the world at large Yet it is spirituality which moves humankind into a higher realm. Martin Luther King, Mother Theresa, Ghandi, Nelson Mandela took their spirituality seriously and were not afraid to proclaim it. Whether we like it or not, we are doomed to be spiritual. We are strong wired for God. This tug lies within each one of us, even atheists. This unquenchable longing is part of our collective unconsciousness.

It is of vital significance and central to the whole theme of this book that we connect, our inbred unquenchable longing, collective unconsciousness and what is called The Perennial Philosophy together. All three essentially point to strengthen the possibility of a Great Non Local Intelligence that we call God.

Because we are limited by our temporality, a rational proof for the existence of God is impossible. All we can do is use metaphor or myth to hint at what lies beyond the curtain. There is no proof, but there is intuition. Faith is one great intuition. It is all that we have, but always remember it has been sparks of intuition which have led to some of the greatest discoveries on our planet.

Myth and metaphor give veiled explanations of the truth. They are more Divine than they define. Rationally all we can speak about is life as we know it here on earth through our physical bodies. Our minds can and do project however, but they do so out of the experiences we have in this world. In other words we anthropomorphize. We impose on another realm our understanding and conditioning from this realm. When we believe, we paint heaven with the colour of our humanity. We make a blind leap from one reality into another. We do this because we believe that this life bespeaks an eternal one. It is not just temporal. This life is not only transitional but it is also transformational. This is the process of faith. It is the cornerstone of belief. However, there is not and cannot be any proof that this approach is rational. To believe or have faith cannot be objectified as atheistic materialism requires. Herein lies the dilemma between the materialistic consumer orientated world and the world of belief and spirituality.

The flatland of materialistic mechanistic science reduces everything to a flatland. There are no valleys or mountains in this approach. There is no horizon to be reached and nothing lies mysteriously on the other side. There is no room for playfulness and imagination. The only conclusion is ontological death. With the hubristic approach of atheism, possibility is wiped from the human races' ability to imagine a new heaven and a new earth. This approach puts an end to dreams and turns reason into a despotism.

It most certainly remains true that any sensible person should not accommodate faith or belief in and after life to the detriment of hard scientific facts. We now realize in this respect how the Church made such a catastrophic mistake in the case of Galileo. But quite equally scientific materialism cannot and must not destroy humankind's capacity to dream and approach life spiritually.

Paradoxically, perhaps one of the greatest proofs that God exists is the absence of God in our contemporary world. Never more have we accumulated trinkets and gorged ourselves on the flush of the earth's precious gifts, and yet never have we been so unhappy and empty. There is a vacuosness to contemporary existence. We seem so bored and stressed with our existence always in search of the latest toy to entertain and replenish us.

Something elemental is missing. An unquenchable longing for something more erupting inside of each one of us. Our collective unconsciousness tells us we are incomplete. Intuitively, without ever articulating it, we seem to recognize, beyond rational proof that some Great Non Local Intelligence is stalking the Universe.

When we connect, God's absence and all the evil extant in the world, we are inclined to make a connection, which may be but anecdotal, but non the less reasonable. Perhaps it is telling us that as Dostoyevsky said: "If God be not, then this world is but a vaudeville of devils.

Furthermore because of the perennial philosophy, which again goes beyond rational proof, the fact that throughout the ages and in so many different cultures, the whole idea of a spirit world is present and rampant.

Scientific materialism may be spelling its own demise if it does not balance power and control with respect and prayer.

IT IS DUE TO THE MAGNIMINITY AND BENEVOLENCE OF DIVINITY THAT WE HAVE THE FREEDOM TO DENY THE EXISTENCE OF GOD.

While most of us do not want to embrace the conclusion of ontological death, we encourage its predominance by the way we live our lives. We seem to want a happy ending to our story but we refuse the detachment that is necessary to achieve it. One has to be courageous to believe in transcendence. We must take the risk and trust a perspective different from that of our materialistic culture, which promotes a grasp-and-accumulate mentality and proclaims itself to be the only truth.

At best, we only give lip service to God and the possibility of transformation. Ours is a God who jumps in and out of our lives according to our demands and schedules. Our God is just another amenity. Our God is an a la carte God. Capitalism has taught us to think this way.

So, faced with the most fundamental choice of our lives, must we choose the objective proof that materialistic science demands or may we choose transcendence, a higher form of life beyond the material? It would seem that we cannot entertain the idea of further life until we first understand death. By forfeiting the gloomy conclusion of materialism, we must adopt a spiritual solution to find truth. To do that, we must take on the full dimension, subject and object, to study the possibility of transcendence. Whereas materialistic science concerns itself with the object alone, transcendence demands that the subject be involved in addition to the object in every search for the truth. The observer as well as the observed must be jointly involved. By introducing the subject into the equation adds a dimension. It is at this point precisely that spirituality enters the picture. In scrutinizing the eye as object, we may find a cataract and remove it so that the eye may have better vision. But vision is intangible, it is invisible. It is not a thing; it cannot be found in a place. It has gone into transcendence. It would seem, then, that the future is already here: we are already capable of transcendence In the way we use our senses.

The material, one end of the continuum, has shifted into the immaterial, the other end of the continuum. They are joined, interpenetrating, and interconnected. The organ of the eye has been joined together with the gift of sight by some non-local Intelligence or great Energizer. Our senses tell us that we can believe in some great force who energizes us. The body may die and corrupt into another set of atomic arrangement, but the transcendent dimension to our unique experience continues on. Our immaterial spirits have instead gone into a deeper knowing and another way of being. Quantum Science provides us with this possibility.

Mechanistic science can give us marvellous insights into our universe and new cures for our bodily diseases, but it cannot tell us anything about the subjective experience of our senses. Mechanistic science may tell us much about the ear, but it has not language to explain the experience of hearing. It may tell us much about the human foot and hand but is incapable of describing the experience of human touch. It can tell us much about the nose but it cannot describe the experience of human smell. It may teach us much about tasting but it has no tongue capable of describing the human experience of taste. Mechanistic science does not have the language for experience. It tells us how but cannot tell us why. It has no language for our essential composition, the very dimension needed for completion. Instead, it gives us a terminal answer, one carved out of that which is temporal. It is powerless and helpless when confronted with the possibility of infinity. It turns life into a flat land. When robbed of its spiritual complement, life becomes boring and provides an easy entrance for ennui. Mechanistic science tells us that experiences of love and laughter, pain and anxiety, hope and joy, tasting and seeing, touching and hearing, are nothing more than electrical currents in the brain

As Erwin Schrodinger said, "The scientific picture of the world is static and closed. It gives me a lot of factual information but it is ghastly silent about all that is really near to our hearts, that which really matters to us. It cannot say a word about red or blue, the sensation of bitter or sweet, feelings of delight or sorrow. It knows nothing of beauty, the ugly, the good or the bad."

Who wants to live in such a horrible mechanized place? It seems, however, that we overwhelmingly like it. We support it unconsciously by bowing to the dictates of the marketplace. Coke advertises "Coke is it", so we buy it. But Coke cannot tell us what "it" is. Does the advert mean "Coke is God"? Every time we choose superfluity over necessity, we put the ego before love. The culture of mechanistic materialism encourages us to do this, and it is very good at getting us to do it. Materialism is the real culprit in the divide between rich and poor because it requires inequitable distribution of the planet's resources. There is something diabolical about a system in which a desert country such as Dubai can have ski slopes while the poorest countries of Africa do not have food to put into the hands of their starving children. We also read in the paper of a very wealthy woman in California who had a whole staff to take care of her pet poodle and commissioned a palace more than a house to be built for the dog, to the tune of fifty million dollars, with four or five specialists attending to his every need for his entire life. She employed a vet, a groomer, a house attendant, a cook, and a nutrition expert full-time. giving them huge professional salaries for their service. A system of spirituality would never tolerate such vulgarities. Like quantum physics, spirituality recognizes that we live in a world of vibrating atoms and interlacing fields, that all life is interconnected, and that at our deepest level, we are brothers and sister and mothers and fathers to each other.

Materialistic science has no language for the experience of love or the cry of the human heart for meaning or purpose. It is mute with respect to joy, pain, hope, and transcendent belief, and when pushed to its logical conclusion, it takes away with it the joy, the hope, and the belief this world gives us. It leaves us in a world more concerned with profit than a world worth living in. Western culture has turned everything upside down. In a world obsessed with concern for the ego discussion about what it means to be human is, at best, marginalized.

Our spiritual dimension is a persona non grata, unsuitable for social discourse. We have thrown the baby out with the bathwater. Mechanistic materialism reduces us to genetic automatons. We curse the dirt splashed on our spotless clothes but do not notice the muck dribbling out with our curses.

Atheistic materialism has neither tongue nor title in the arena of the spiritual. By its very nature, it is exclusionary. It deals only with materiality. Science has indeed been masterful, and made our bodies more comfortable

Through molecular biology, science has brought us antibiotics and other medicines to address our bodily ills. Through mechanical engineering, it can now offer us new hips and new hearts. Never in the history of our world have humans had the hope of relief from and eradication of so many diseases. For the past century and a half, materialistic science has proclaimed it can explain everything, but it will take more study and experimentation first. Mechanistic science proclaims that it is the only wonder in the universe. Of its recent technological achievements, the computer and the mobile phone take precedence as the greatest expression of man's genius. Mechanistic science and all its accomplishments have so captured our imagination and attention that we no longer have time to meditate on deeper and more primary issues.

Mechanistic science considers itself the only part worth considering in the whole. Never once in its extreme prejudice can it tolerate the dimension of transcendence, when, in fact, quantum physics tells us unapologetically that consciousness is connected on the one continuum to its predecessor, matter and that the world of the mind cannot be separated from the world of the body. To know everything about the brain is first to recognize that it is attached to the mind. To reduce the brain to a special location under a microscope in order to study it is metaphorically the same as taking a car for a test run with no fuel in it. Materialistic science, reduces the inscrutable complexity of the brain by its own limitations. It declares that the brain must be studied as a mere machine which came about by the random linking of a string of chemicals spewed from the Big Bang. In its conclusion about natural selection, it leaves us with a brain without a thinking mind. It robs us of the possibility to conceptualize, wonder, and feel astonished at the marvels of the natural world.

As Richard Dawkins said, "It is absolutely safe to say that anyone who does not believe in evolution is ignorant, stupid, and insane." It would seem that the very mind which gave us this insight is the same mind which condemns its own thinking. Within the confines of natural selection, there is no mind and there are no moral or ethical laws, no eternity, no free will, no ultimate meaning. Just human self-determination."

"Nobody comes, nobody goes, it's awful," Samuel Beckett

The world of natural spirituality cannot be held down by the exclusionary restriction of atheism. Its territory is a continuum, with body and spirit joined together, brain and mind joined together. Matter is part of the holiness of the complete structure. Everything is sacred. Nothing is secular. Cro-Magnons, the first early modern humans, in using their minds conceptually expressed through their art the integration of brain and mind. At the quantum level there is separation, but that separation, like the separation at birth of a mother from her baby, is a bursting forth from a tomb. Death is also a bursting-forth experience; it too is an enlargement. It is a transformation and not a termination. At the quantum level, we remain a part of each other. Mechanistic materialism spells ontological death. Spiritual materialism spells only the possibility of further glory.

A HYMN TO MATTER

Blessed be you, mortal matter: you who one day will undergo the process of dissolution within us and will thereby take us forcibly into the very heart of that which exists . . . . You who batter us and then dress our wounds, you who resist us and yield to us, you who

wreck and build, you who shackle and liberate, the sap
of our souls, the hand of God, the flesh of Christ: it is
you, matter, that I bless.
(Pierre Teilhard de Chardin)

The transcendent aspect of the human person certainly must be invited in as an honoured guest to our debate about what it means to be human. We live more attuned to materialistic science than we do to our spirituality. Materialistic science has it too easy because it markets the human body and not the human spiritual component. We are programmed by mechanistic science that happiness is found in having, whereas the root of our ontology is being. God is our original ground.

Transcendence begins with the material. The beyond is already here in the ordinary. Experience teaches us that heaven is already within us. It starts where the foot falls but cannot be observed by our telescopes or our microscopes. Instead, we need the discipline of spirituality to discover it. The experiences we enjoy in our materiality indicate to us the connection between spiritual experiences and matter. The scientific world of quantum physics now suggests the interconnection between matter and spirit through consciousness.

We Westerners should take notice: we have disassociated ourselves from the natural processes, cutting off the body from the mind. We have truncated ourselves. Matter matters most in our society, leaving us to torture nature. We cut down our forests. We pollute our air. We soil our soil. We pour chemicals into our waterways. We kill off our wildlife by making their habitat uninhabitable. When matter is king, we exploit nature for ever increasing profit, all the time sucking the sap out of nature and ignoring sustainability.

Money is God in the West, which is governed by fifteen massive global corporations that make all the rules so that most money flows into their own coffers. Profit is their reason for living. The more they profit, the more they applaud themselves, for profit is a self-congratulatory system.

When profits weaken through decreases in consumption and accumulation, profiteers engineer demand by turning medicine, crime, and war into money-making machines. They create competition in the name of efficiency, but the economic system which these gurus have created in their own interest is a horrendous failure. They rape nature instead of listening to it. They breed obsolescence into everything the manufacture. And breed most function out so that we will be tempted to repurchase an object when it has received only slight modification, thereby continually increasing their profits.

A profit-driven economy is a monstrous system of inefficiency, and the dump hills and landfills of our world are its symbols.

Wall Street never takes a walk in the forest for the right reason. It does not know how to listen. If it did, it might hear a whisper telling it that nature's efficiency is superior.

The great minds in science and art have much to teach us about nature. Einstein said, "He who cannot be wrapped in awe is as good as dead."

St Irenaeus said, "The terrible pity is what dies within a man while he is still living."

"Live in the fields and God will give you lectures on natural philosophy every day" Emerson

"Am I not partly leaves and vegetables and mould myself?"

(Thoreau).

"To see a world in a grain of sand and a heaven in a wild flower, hold infinity in the palm of your hand, and eternity in an hour" (William Blake).

Nature joins everything together. It promotes interrelationship and interconnection. It tells us the cosmos is one. The profit motive is its very antithesis. It only divides. Listen to the trees in the forest and the leaves will chatter, "I am related to you. I am your sister. I am your brother." \

If you go to the shore, the waves will say to you, "The sea is your cradle." Death is natural, but the profiteers on Wall Street do not want us to face the truth of the human story,. They earn more profit by promoting their propaganda. Nature has been doing its job for the past fourteen billion years. We had better listen to it instead of scientific materialism.

We are in a tomb of our own making, and if we want resurrection, then we had better listen to Jesus, not the person the Church has taught us to believe in but the great teacher who preached the spirituality of nature: "Look at the birds of the air; they neither sow nor reap nor gather into barns, and yet your heavenly Father feeds them . . . . Consider the lilies of the field, how they grow . . . even Solomon in all his glory was not clothed like one of these . . . God [who knows your needs], will he not much more clothe you?"

Jesus was one of the greatest quantum physicists, sustainable economists, and psychoanalysts of all time. Spirituality was his economy. He did not come to preach that he is the Saviour of the world; rather, he preached that nature is our saviour. Quantum physics concerns itself with the solidity of matter, what underpins life as we know it. Is there any material building block smaller than the particle? From studies conducted in particle colliders, particle physics tells us that the particle moves into consciousness along the one unifying continuum. Science itself now suggests that when matter disappears, consciousness takes over. Life as we know it moves from substantiality into insubstantiality. The future of physics is metaphysics.

The material becomes consciousness, which, at heart, indicates transformation rather than termination. This happens at the precise moment when material death appears. Quantum physics would seem to indicate that there is only life and more life. There is no separation, no end. What is deepest about us carries on. There is no duality in life and death; they are part of the one system. We are future-orientated, it seems. We are emergent. Death is but a transformation in which we crawl into a deeper life having left our material shell behind.

It is difficult for us to see this because we must look beyond the obvious, beyond the prison of our anthropocentrism, our own limits on limitlessness. We cannot even imagine this, for we keep ourselves too constricted to enter the world of the mystic. Death is transformation from thing into nothing. We must leave a place for no place, travelling from the visible into the invisible. We are destined to become nothingness, which is another name for physical death. We are destined for invisibility, as we exchange our visibility for it.

It seems the mystical approach has been correct all along. In its deepest sense, it tells us that some non-local Intelligence has been living inside us as invisible nothingness. Quantum physics presents this possibility. The mystics say, "I carry God with me. Transcendence is my destination. My me is God. Thou art that."

We ignore this, but we do so at our own peril. In our ignorance, we listen to a louder voice more insistent on addressing the needs of the ego instead of that inner voice which tells us of the insufficiency of all available things. Whether we like it or not, nature will have the final say. We are but recent visitors to planet earth. It has done without us for 95 per cent of its life and it can do without us again.

Our culture of scientific materialism grows ever more vociferous and tenacious. In doing so, it becomes more corporeally incompetent and diabolical. It has already taken our souls away. The problem seems to be overwhelming as more and more economic pressure is applied to each of us. We can solve it if, as individuals, we choose to abandon this system. We still have the gift of free will, and we must use it to make the significant choice that confronts us. Do we make the connection between body and soul, immanence and transcendence? That is the great spiritual question. Do we see the one in the other?

Lest we think that if we choose the spiritual side of the equation we are living spiritually by going to church on a Sunday morning, we must know that true spiritually finds its expression much more in the ordinary than in any cathedral reserved for Sabbath worship. True spirituality is attained not by huge heroic acts but by the little ordinary ones we perform every day with a pure heart. God comes to us in bits and pieces, incrementally and never at once.

Scientific materialism divides everything. It is dualistic by its very nature. It takes spirit out of matter; it separates the brain from the mind. It is an expert in the art of dualism. Its success has led to endless chatter about the economy and politics. Through its trickery the needs of the ego and the profit motive may be met, but our souls go empty. Economic enrichment is not the only test of a person's success or worth; spiritual enrichment leads to a better world.

Attunement to the natural rhythm of the earth alone will bring us resolution and rest. Nature teaches us this. So many people nowadays come home exhausted and miserable from the pressures the working environment imposes. Our mechanistic culture and its economy may give us enough money to put food on our tables, but in the process, it rips apart the most essential of all bonds by separating mothers from their children, often leaving children to fend for themselves, and it separates fathers from their children as well. Because of the work ethic prescribed by a mechanistic culture, modern fathers spend on average fifty-three seconds a day with their children. We know that money is not the ultimate answer, for peace, serenity, and happiness cannot be bought with all the money in the world. They come from what already is inside of us.

Money cannot force us to be happy, and there is no point in shoving money into the coffin as we are taken under. When we are stressed, we often go back to nature to calm ourselves. We take a walk in the woods, watch ducks swim in a pond, listen to the birds chirping in the trees. Contact with nature brings integration back into our being. The call is primordial. When we lose our connectedness to the natural world, we lose all. A lot of rich people are unhappy precisely because they listen more to the garbled messages of materialism than to that inner voice which teaches us about insufficiency of all that is available.

Our God is a patient god, and nature is God's law. If we do not listen to nature's whispers in all living things, then we will drop of our diabolic nuclear bombs, ending God's experiment with us. God will go on with or without us.

Scientific materialism is so gluttonous that it intends to devour all the energy not only on earth but also in the cosmos. We have become like greedy caterpillars on a head of cabbage. Our spirituality asks, Are we little more than a virus? Jesus tells us we have such dignity in the sight of God that he counts the very hairs on our head and considers us of much more worth than a flock of sparrows. However, humankind's idolatry to a false god will end God's experiment. If the end comes, it will be due to our own stupidity and ineptitude. Divinity is within us.

Mechanistic materialism has nothing to say about transcendence. It is incapable of entering into the realm of the spirit. It can only tell half of our evolutionary story, and like religion, it only tells us lies as stopgap measures. Both systems thrive on their meta-myths, but transcendence is about experience and not about details or explanation. It cannot be defined, and its only orthodoxy is the truth of its own telling. It is internal and eternal to each of us. So put all your yapping aside, be it religious or materialistic. Spirituality has but one language: poetry. "The priests of the twenty first century shall be the poets," James Joyce said.

"My language and my sensibility is yearning to admit a kind of spiritual or transcendental dimension. But then there's the reality . . . The complacency and the utter simplification of those things into social instructions. That's what's disappointing," Seamus Heaney

Our over materialistic culture produces kitch instead of art.

Our narcissistic Church is more interested in Orthodoxy than poetry.

Both systems have failed the deepest yearnings of the human heart for beauty, truth and sustainability.

Little do the gurus of empiricism realize than in their drive for objective proof they murder creativity. Through their lines of productivity they give us preassembled objects reeking with the worms of inbred obsolescence, and which provide but little else than visual illiteracy. Instead of a vessel of beauty and unity our sense of morality has been severely crushed into a shattered pot beyond the hope of useful repair. We yearn for paradise only to remain as scattered shards. A society without cohesiveness is one without hope. A society which cannot reinvent itself creatively is as good as dead.

We need a new paradigm if we are to reinvent the human story, and to do this we need the articulation and the vision of the artist. Unfortunately though both the authorities of Church and State have relegated art to the fringe as lkittle less than cute nonessential. Pure literalism reigns in both ecclesial and secular realms. All possibilities of imagination have been ruled out. The poetry of life wears but a beggars mouth pleading for a hand out, violins have lost their strings, drums their goat skins and pianos their ivory keys. But how can there be poetry again without music and hope? Art is an expression of the sacred and divine. Its feet are on the ground but the puff from its throats of glory reign transcendentally. Art lifts the emotions and the spirit to fly into a language— less domain of utter inscrutability. Experience is all in this singular domain where speech is no longer necessary and languages obsolete. Understanding synergistically expands without explanation. Only Serenity, tranquillity and harmony monopolize the silence.

Both the Church and the Scientific world have themselves to become harmonious and cooperate to create a space where the linear and the lateral meet complimenting each other. By embracing art we can create a glorious testament to the human races' highest ideals for peace and serenity.

Neither Church nor state is taking its vocation seriously. Both are infidels, Neither provides an intelligent answer to the problem of ontological death. Poetry, and the arts in general on the other hand, excavate the real world rather than just preaching escapism. Poetry deals with the incommunicable thirst for the incomprehensible. Poets, like mystics, concern themselves with the dispossesedd the weary and the wanderer.

Poets place their feet on staid ground but transport us to the door of transformation and transfiguration. As D. H. Lawrence told us, "When we get out of the glass bottles of our ego, and when we escape like squirrels turning in the cages of our personality and get into the forests again, we shall shiver with cold and fright but things will happen to us so that we don't know ourselves. Cool, unlying life will rush in, and passion will make our bodies taut with power, we shall stamp our feet with new power and old things will fall down, we shall laugh, and institutions will curl up like burnt paper."

We have been co-opted for too long. We behave like robots We have given over our intelligence to the wrong brokers. Neither religion nor mechanistic science can answer our ontological question. Only Quantum physics and its attendant consciousness can do that for us. The answer to the question of our physical death is already within us. Poets and mystics make the answer more clear for us.

"Plant sequoias. Say that your main crop is the forest that you did not plant, that you will not live to harvest. Say that the leaves are harvested when they have rotted into the mould. Call that profit. Prophesy such returns. Put your faith in the two inches of humus that will build under the trees every thousand years. Listen to carrion—put your ear close, and hear the faint chattering of the songs that are to come" (Wendell Berry).

Poetry is always more than what it says. It is transcendent more than literal. When it speaks, it turns words into music. It enlivens and energizes. It mixes our stardust with the potency of ecstasy. It suggests more than it explains. It is rooted in the earth but its spires point to the heavens. Parable and the simile, metaphor and paradox are the horses which draw its wagon. It is a sacrament more than a utensil. It catapults the limited seen and obvious into the invisible, illimitable nothingness of wonder and imagination. It takes us round trip from nowhere to nowhere, but it condescends to make one stop at the station called now-here which in itself is no-where.

Mystics teach us that like birth, death is a breakthrough, but into invisibleness. Birth and death are part of the same cycle, but in death, we do not have the language for the transformation. We. cannot imagine nothingness or invisibleness. We remain anthropocentric and restricted. But our imagination can take us into another realm of reality. The mind behind the beholding of the dust is not dust, though the brain be such. Spirituality knows and quantum physics suggests the possibility for a new way of perceiving. When we make the journey into our invisibleness and our nothingness, then we will know that the dead go nowhere, and until we learn this, we remain un-integrated human beings. Mary Frye shows us this:

> Do not stand at my grave and weep, I am not there
> I am a thousand winds that blow,
> I am the diamond glints on snow,
> I am the sun on ripened grain,
> I am the gentle autumn rain.
> . . .

Francis Nnaggenda also shows us this:

> The dead are not under the earth
> They are in the tree that rustles
> They are in the forest that groan
> They are in the water that runs
> . . .
> The dead are not dead.

When we listen to the mystic poets, Celtic spirituality and Egyptian mythology, somewhere deep within ourselves, we recognize that the penumbral is the breeding ground for light and life. The world of the dead is indeed the world of the living.

† † †

Fr Pat knew that if he had been living in the middle ages, he would have been tortured and executed by now. The Catholic Church would never have tolerated the heresy spouting from his mouth. He also knew that if he were to continue in his role as priest, then he would have to either violate his own integrity by telling lies or else maintain his integrity without compromise. The latter would mean confrontation, and he wasn't very good at that. He was grateful for the Bishop's patience and understanding in giving him time to ponder his situation. If he were to leave, it would be his choice; the Bishop would not order it. Fr Pat knew he believed that one's own consciousness was primary, and if what is primary were violated by an institution, then one should be courageous enough to abandon the club which one formerly supported. But it was often more difficult to leave than to join.

Intellectually, Fr Pat was already living in a new paradigm, but emotionally, he had not severed from the old one yet. He took pride in the magnificent heritage of the Catholic Church. Until recently, it had always been a great supporter of the arts, and its music, sculpture, stained glass, painting, and architecture. These expressions were some of the greatest artistic achievement in human history. The wonder of it all transported one into the embrace of the divine. Standing before some of these heavenly achievements, one could not but be moved to tears. Fr Pat loved Renaissance art and wished for another in the Church, but such art couldn't evolve from a past theology; instead it had to express the experience of the contemporary. Art was stimulated by freedom, not restriction. It could not express itself in the atmosphere of contemporary religion. He felt the Bishop would agree with him about this.

In their second meeting, the Bishop had advised Fr Pat, "Create new stained glass windows with your beautiful photography. Go on showing us life as it must be considered so that we can become more alive and awake. Go on writing your poetry. Our theology is far too small to lead us into transcendence. We need the art of the insubstantial to set us on the right track." Fr Pat admired the Bishop as a visionary.

He remembered the Bishop saying, "Critics are the truest of all patriots," and Fr Pat agreed.

Monsignor and Miss Prado exhibited the very antithesis of this viewpoint. They wanted to keep God bottled up. Like them, with the exception of the Bishop, the Church was growing more and more conservative and reverting to the dualism of the old closed system. Monsignor and Miss Prado waited and waited for an announcement that the Bishop had dismissed Fr Pat from the parish or, better still, that Rome had defrocked him, but to their consternation, such an announcement never came. So Miss Prado continued to make life at the parish of St Jude challenging for Fr Pat.

He continued to say mass even though he no longer believed in consubstantiation. However, he did not think this hypocritical, as he did so to recall the Last Supper and to memorialize the most magnificent, moral man he had ever heard of. Jesus was a poet who had the courage to actualize what he believed in. Fr Pat looked on him as the brother who walked the same road as he did. On that road then as now, people were crying and laughing and dying. People in the time of Jesus cried in the same way we cry. "Where are you, God?" they said and we say. "Why don't you show your face to us? We have no meaning or purpose in our lives without you." Like his brother Jesus, in attempting to answer these questions, Fr Pat felt called to lead a life of ministry.

Through all this, he still looked forward to his lectures to the New Basalians. He enjoyed the privilege of sharing his insights with them and hearing their insights after the lecture. They had chosen evolution as their next topic for discussion, and Fr Pat took much delight in preparing the lecture:

EVOLUTION

The Enlightenment of the sixteenth century sent waves of uncertainty through the West, rocking its religious belief system. New insights from the scientific world dealt strong blows to the Greek view which looked upon God as an outside creator. From the insights of mechanistic materialism starting

189

in Descartes' time, the elite of the Enlightenment preached that there is no God.

Life comes about merely randomly and by chance. The only empiricism acceptable is what comes from reason. This scientific approach studies the object without any consideration for the subject who studied the object. Thus objective science became supreme. Objects were studied under what is called special location, leaving no room for the possibility of the non local This mechanistic, mathematical approach to life became the only basis for truth, thereby ushering in atheism.

Later, Darwin's theory of evolution added more zest to Atheism. Darwin's theory of Evolution demonstrated the emergence of higher forms from lower forms. Subsequent organisms became more complex than their predecessors. Life came from genetic mutation and was processed by natural selection. The idea of a creator either transcendent or immanent was excluded from the picture. With this view, mechanistic science seemed to deal the final blow to religion. Mechanistic Science has held this theory ever since. It is the prominent theory now taught in non denominational secular schools.

But even as acceptable and widespread as this theory is, it still has some problems. For example, no fossils have so far been discovered to directly link humans *Homo sapiens* to their earlier ancestors, such as apes. There is also the problem of the Cambrian explosion, which happened 550 million years ago when multi-cellular creatures suddenly appeared in magnificent and varied expressions. Many species appeared at once without appearing to have passed through different stages of the evolutionary process. There is also the problem of the structure of the eye, which has basically remained the same without seeming to have mutated.

Despite these problems though, evolution as we know it in the scientific mechanistic sense tells us for the first time that we are evolution, conscious of ourselves. Starting with the stardust that exploded from the Big Bang, evolution has brought us through many incarnations to get us here.

Through our process of becoming more, we have stepped from *cosmo-genesis* (world in process) to *bio-genesis* (sentient life in process) to *noo-genesis* (mind in process). This last stage is where we now find ourselves. We have been emergent all along, going from simplicity into complexity. Our evolutionary story thus far tells us we are future-orientated. Mechanistic science, however, tells us that this is the end of the human story. We have arrived at the stage of natural selection.

Richard Dawkins tells us "that all life, all intelligence, all creativity and all design anywhere in the universe is the direct or indirect product of Darwinian natural selection."

Stephen Weinberg analyses this view, saying, "The more the universe seems comprehensible the more it also seems pointless," and Jacques Monod adds to this, saying, "The ancient covenant is in tatters. Man at last knows he is at home in the unfeeling immensity of the universe out of which he has emerged only by chance." So, in general, the atheistic view of life conspires with mechanistic science. The ascendency of atheistic materialism over the last three centuries has left no space for interiority or inscrutability. Mechanistic science dismisses the fact that humans are attached to a mind. It is our mind which distinguishes us from our evolutionary antecedents.

Scientific atheism considers the mind as nothing more than the electrical circuits of the brain. With this theory the possibility of a non local intelligence is denied.

But people of a spiritual orientation ask, Why does matter alone matter? Why does evolution have to stop with the brain? Why is the brain the last possible expression on the evolutionary ladder? Why is the brain the last possible genesis of natural selection. Evolution is emergent, producing more complex new expressions of life all along its path. The appearance of *Homo sapiens* put us at the mind stage of the evolutionary push. But why must our evolutionary story end here? Can it not emerge further?

Is the evolutionary story true, merely because it overcame the stumbling block and stop gap measures of mythological religion, which it viewed as superstitious, incredulous and stupid?

> Can we have a narrative which respects the finding of objective science while at the same time it provides space for the possibility of interiority which by its nature is subjective and spiritual?

Why must our evolutionary story end with natural selection? Can it not be emergent into something deeper? Quantum physics says yes it can! The death of the physical body begins the story of the possibility of emergence into a higher realm. Beyond this threshold, we can make no other material prediction. Quantum physics, in agreement with many mystics, teaches unapologetically that matter continues to emerge into consciousness. While the brain may cease to function, the mind continues on.

Quantum physics, in reality deals a death blow to Atheism in that it tells us life continues and moves from the material particle into something insubstantial untouchable, non local and invisible. Quantum physics respects the movement or process of the physical into the metaphysical.

It respects imminence while providing a possibility for transcendence. It makes matter and non matter one.

The beauty and eloquence of nature and the conclusions of quantum physics bespeak a marvellous creative non local Intelligence. Evolution marches on into no-thing-ness and invisibility This is precisely what the Mystics say.

As spiritual creatures, we denounce quite readily the conclusion of atheistic materialism, but what about the conclusion of religion, a sort of the pie-in-the-sky solution? A proper understanding of the emergent evolutionary story puts an end to the meta-narratives of Christianity as well. Evolution tells us we have emerged from stardust into *Homo sapiens*. The evolutionary plan from the beginning has worked rather splendidly and is still accomplishing its mission to move from simplicity to complexity up the ladder to a greater expression of perfection. It seems to accomplish this through some great Intelligence within matter itself. No extraordinary external force turned apes into humans. Instead, *Homo sapiens* evolved incrementally, emerging from what was already within us.

Until Darwin's theory of Evolution appeared, the Church, in keeping with the story of Genesis, proclaimed that God spontaneously and directly created human kind. The theory of Evolution tells us that man and woman evolved incrementally. The Church until recently paid little attention to immanence and put all of its eggs into the basket of transcendence. It separated heaven from Earth. It considered the world as little more than a staging post, a jumping off point into eternity. It proclaimed itself as the one true answer to the question of our humanity and mortality.: it proposed transcendence at the cost of immanence. Many viewed this answer, which incrementally became dogma, as an insult to human intelligence an equated religion with superstitious un-enlightenment. Religion offered, as Graham Dunstan Martin said, "a spurious knowledge, superstitious belief in nonsense angels and devils. It offered ignorant credulity. It preached obedience and incuriosity. Through inquisition and torture it sought to suppress new questions and new understanding. It sided with the rich, with the ignorant and the complacent, and was against the lively and the inquisitive."

Scientific materialists viewed religion in general as anti-intellectual and people of faith as superstitious and simplistic. In casting off the yoke of religion, mechanistic science dismissed the potentiality of the human mind to imagine and wonder, concerning itself only with humdrum problem solving. Facts were facts and there was nothing more to life. The brain was nothing more than a machine. Nature was there to serve humans, even to the point that we could torture it. It was as though life was just a block of Italian marble with no potential for a *David* or a *Pieta* within it. "We eat well. We drink well. We live well But we no longer have good dreams," Michael Ignatine.

Through mechanistic science, it would seem, we can find and prove everything except ourselves.

Darwin's theory of evolution, told the world that God was not the direct creator of the myriad expressions of nature; instead, those expressions came about from mutations within nature itself. God was not necessary. Genetics had a mind of its own. Each species carried its antecedent genes with it but expressed itself differently by adapting to its unique environment, passing on genetic mutations through natural selection.

The theory of evolution paints a picture of cruelty with one organism fighting another tooth and claw. This seems to be true to an extent, but there are also many signs of cooperation in nature, as seen in the honey bee, which we mentioned in a previous lecture. We might also mention the helpful role leeches and what we consider disgusting, flies on dung heaps. It is difficult for us to recognize flies as disinfectants. They and their worms devour rotting carcases. Leeches clean out festering wounds by eating up pus. The panoply of observable phenomena like these tell us that nature is not incidental. It seems to be driven by some form of intelligence.

Mechanistic science would never admit this.

It could never consider humans as slaves to a supernatural master. It's claim is that we are proud sons and daughters of nature, controlling and shaping it for our own use and benefit. Since the Enlightenment, mechanistic science has remained king. Without even realizing it, we pay it homage. But the atheism which the Enlightenment imposed, instead of cleansing us, has increased the pus of our existence with stress, anxiety, boredom, fear, and lack of meaning or purpose. We have tortured nature so much that we are threatened and terrorized to our deepest core. Through our tampering with the atom our greatest achievement has become our greatest atrocity. The USA, to say nothing of Russia has stockpiled enough nuclear weapons to destroy the earth three thousand times over.

Science has had marvellous success in improving the harshness of a cruel environment, which allows hunger, disease, and suffering to reign. We must give science its due recognition for the marvels that it has delivered, but we should take care to limit our praise, for mechanistic science without spirituality will not provide the whole answer to the human dilemma. It can only tell us finally that life is a random thing. Nothing has meaning.

There is darkness without and darkness within. There is no splendour, no vastness anywhere, only triviality for a moment, then nothing,

As Bertrand Russell said,
"man is the result of a purposeless and natural process that did not have him in mind,"

Mechanistic science's conclusions about the evolutionary push have become our great new cosmological mythology. Science is its own pope who proclaims the infallibility of its own truth. Its truth now prevails almost everywhere with more adherents than the three monotheistic faiths put together. It has seduced China and India and other emerging profit-prone nations. Like air, it invisibly oxygenates our lives. It has destroyed our dreams, crippled our poetry and our mysticism. It has left us no reason for laughing or singing. It has separated the parts from the whole. Despite all the enlightenment it gives us, we cry out for something more. Our minds tell us we have been cut off, we are no longer integrated. We surely need another dimension to restore balance and rescue us from our intoxicated madness.

The spiritual dimension to human existence is so despised in the arenas which most touch our lives that we run from it as though it is an affront to our intelligence when, in fact, it is the primary informer of ethical judgement, refinement and civility. We are too embarrassed to publicly embrace it lest we be considered brain tormentors or mental terrorists. The separation of our spirits from our bodies is now so complete that materialism and all the stuff that comes with us is our only language.

It is time for a different exchange than the one we find on Wall Street. Our schools teach facts but never essentials, neuroscience treats the brain but never the mind-boggling mind. We treat the heart, the lungs, the liver, the kidneys as machines but refuse to recognize the whole person they sustain. We learn all the technical terminology to name a foetus but consider none of the profundities of its gestation.

The materialistic approach which teaches only facts is tedious and uninteresting. We need the spiritual dimension to make learning exciting. Materialistic facts become hell when separated from the possibility of heaven. A party is dead when there is no sense of celebration in it. Everything must be in balance. The whole world will jump with laughter and courage when the spiritual dimension of the mind is again balanced with matter. Life will take on a new glow and we shall be glad. We will be integrated when we welcome home this prodigal son. in each one of us. Voltaire, who rightly dismissed the religion of the Church as tyrannical, proposed an enlightened spirituality integrated with matter as the system with which to bring balance to the human enterprise:

> "The most powerful evidence for a divine hand, is as ever, the wonders of the natural world. From the meanest of insects, the disposition of flying wings and the feelers of a snail, we see design. We have a mind and we are intelligent. This has not been formed by crude, blind, insensible happenstance. There is certainly some difference between the ideas of Newton and the dung of a mule. Newton's intelligence comes from a higher intelligence."

Astoundingly, the arrogance materialistic science imposes on Western culture is finally being challenged by its very own discipline. New genetics is challenging evolution's idea of matter as the only dimension worthy of study. The Human Genome Project has discovered very little difference between the genomes of humans and mice. Mechanistic scientists were expecting to find that every variation in the genome could be explained by natural selection. But it did not. It was left in a quandary. Evolution now was pointing towards consciousness. The brain points to something beyond itself and so too does the genetic code. Both indicate inscrutability, a territory unexplainable by mathematical formulas and only by experience. Like the human mind, genetic mutations can no longer be understood as matter alone.

The human brain, which accounts for about 2 percent of our body mass, consumes 25 per cent of our energy. It is not the product exclusively of natural selection as mechanistic science says, for if it were, we would never have developed language or the ability to create or appreciate art. This would seem to confirm, then, that a spiritual vision was on the right track, all things considered.

Unfortunately, the Church pushed the culture of the West into a different kind of a fishing net. While it included the mind and the transcendent, it did so at the expense of matter. Religion was as dogmatic as mechanistic science, and its teachings as fundamentalist as those of atheistic materialism. The Church imposed the unnatural on the natural. It manipulated the truth of the Jesus message, adapting and twisting the story to suit its own agenda. The compassionate Jesus was turned into a man of dogma consistent with the Church's lust for control and power. If Jesus was in our midst today, he would reject the Church's teachings as much as he did the mouthings of the scribes and the Pharisees.

Jesus never once compromised his own identity. As a struggling man who suffered like the rest of us, he hammered out his theology on the anvil of his own personality. His wisdom came from interiority. Through contemplation, he found compassion. The non-local Intelligence didn't favour him in any exceptional way; he took the ordinary route on the evolutionary journey. Those who follow him so revere him precisely because he was truly one of us and no more divine than the least among us. He, too, had to follow the process which emergent evolution demands, and through him we know that the ordinary way is the way of God. Never can there be a suspension of the natural evolutionary path, for God cannot violate what God is!

We must discover that all the energy we will ever need is already inside us. Jesus realized this and explained it better than anyone else: "The kingdom of God is inside of you. Just tap into it." The Church twisted his story, however, and turned him into Christ, superimposing the supernatural over the natural as though God made a terrible mistake in the creation.

In the Church's story, Christ is a deus ex machina, which makes the myth of Jesus much more important than the real facts of his life, making him a magician much more than the man that he was. No wonder Einstein and others have deemed the Church's manipulation as terribly childish. It is time for a new paradigm. God's original evolutionary plan could never be violated by his Son's disruption. Such a Son, serves the Church's ends much more than God's. Christ became the scapegoat for the Church.

Once the Church manufactured Christ, it owned the rights to his story, allowing them to modify it as they wished. Making him into a Saviour and Redeemer suited its purposes splendidly. The Church teaches that evil came into the world through the original sin of Adam and Eve. This sin disrupted our evolutionary journey, disconnecting God from his original plan. In order for God to energize the world once more a reconciliation was needed., As the story goes, God sent his only begotten Son as a ransom to set us straight on the evolutionary path again.

But if an omniscient God knew from the very start that his plan would unravel, then why did he allow it to happen? Some might argue that it happened because God gave us free will and we willed our own demise. However. that, in turn, implies that God became dissatisfied with his own evolutionary plan. The spirituality of the poets and the mystics tell a different story than the one promulgated by the Church. Instead, they tell us that sin is very much a part of the natural world. Humans commit sin, so it is humans who can eradicate it. He who has sunk the lowest is capable of climbing the highest. Sin is part of the interplay of agony and ecstasy. The tooth and the claw can be very creative,. Our most sincere compassion can spring from our worst sin. If we do not cooperate, God is helpless. The whole is already within us. God is here in our squabbles and our prayers. We are not apart but a part.

The Church put God outside of his own creation, splitting heaven and earth. The Church's story is dualistic. However, quantum physic teaches us that the whole is greater than the sum of its parts; that God is inside creation, not outside of it; and that life exists on a continuum from matter to consciousness. The teachings of Christianity violate these principles. Quantum physics tells us that evolution has been working very well all along and does not need an outsider to correct any flaw because it has no flaws. It runs like a river into the sea. Outside interference would only misdirect evolution from its destiny, and the story of the Christ as Saviour and Redeemer is conscious interference. It tells more about the deceitful manipulation of man than it does about God the creator. The reality is that the whole continuously embraces the parts; the whole is not outside but within all the parts. The human race has been divine from the very beginning.

God is inside of us and it is up to us to make God come out of us. Only then shall we truly dance. The Gospel of Thomas says, "You will not know Jesus until you know how to sing and dance." The historical Jesus did precisely that: he allowed the God inside of him to come out and dance. He did such a fantastic job of it that two thousand years after his physical death, he still lives in our memory. "The kingdom is within you," Jesus said, recognizing his own Godness. He devoted his whole ministry to sensitizing humans to a higher consciousness, and he did it as a mere man, no more infused with divinity than the rest of us. If he was extraordinary in any way it was in the way he exercised his ordinariness.

Quantum physics, in essence, teaches us that the same energy which actualized Jesus' compassion exists in each of us. What we need to do is spiritualize it into reality. "If I as a mere human can do it, then you can also," Jesus says to us.

Whereas the Christ of religion violates God's evolutionary plan, the Jesus of history shows us the orthodoxy of the natural and the ordinary. Quantum physics and the evolutionary process have outlined the push into consciousness, and suggest the possibility of movement from matter into transcendence. Energy is tangential and it is also radial, It can be both immanent and transcendent. This is the essence of the spiritual journey. It is estimated that we use only fifteen percent of our energy. The rest lies wasted. Jesus of Nazareth was a man who lived out the whole potentiality of his energy. He lived what he preached This same man invites us to move from war into peace, from hatred into love.

The earth is groaning from exploitation and destruction, but if we could follow Jesus as our non-denominational leader, then this planet would become more serene and tenable. We do not even have to know the name of Jesus to follow him; his spirit spurs us on. He threatens no one. He invites us to come out of ourselves. His message is non-sectarian, defying our tribalism. "That they all may be one," he said. Only when both religion and secular society follow the way of interiority which he proclaimed shall God's experiment with us show results. This is the future of our evolutionary journey.

Many thinkers have similarly decried the falsity of religion:

"The danger of religious faith is that it allows otherwise normal human beings to reap the fruits of madness and consider them holy . . . . We are, even now, killing ourselves over ancient literature" (Sam Harris).

"The immense majority of intellectually eminent men disbelieve in Christian religion, but they conceal the fact in public, because they are afraid of losing their incomes" (Bertrand Russell).

"The spectacle of what is called religion . . . has filled me with horror, and I have frequently condemned it . . . Almost always it seems to stand for blind belief and reaction, dogma and bigotry, superstition and exploitation, and the preservation of vested interests" (Nehru).

"Religion is excellent stuff for keeping common people quiet" (Napoleon).

"Religion has actually convinced people that there is an invisible man living in the sky who watches over everything you do, every minute of every day. And the invisible man had a special list of ten things he does not want you to do. And if you do any of these ten things, he has a special place full of fire and smoke and burning and torture and anguish where he will send you to live and suffer and burn and choke and scream and cry forever and ever till the end of time. But he loves you" (George Carlin).

The Catholic Church may be a bitch, but fundamentalist Protestant sects are its mongrel pups. Christianity has taken such a turn for the worse in these sects that the historical Jesus must be turning in his grave. At least the Catholic Church has given posterity the glory of Renaissance art.

The proclamation of the Christian Gospel since then has deteriorated to such an extent that it now appeals mostly to the illiterate who know nothing and care not to learn anything about literary form or the marvellous ongoing findings of science.

An example of this can be found in Christian Fundamentalist hell houses. In Colorado, a horrendous assault on human enlightenment has emerged because of a literal interopretation of Scripture. These hell houses were devised to scare the living daylights out of young churchgoers to teach them what would happen to them if they sinned. Actors dress in scarlet and parade around like devils, playing the part of a different sin. One plays homosexuality, another abortion, and so on. Sulphurous secretions and agonizing screams set the scene. "Come and be traumatized so that you can reach heaven," it tells followers. If this is not child abuse, then what is it?

Even worse debauchery, comes from a Southern Baptist church which declares itself Christian. It calls Catholics "Cat-u-licks", inferring paedophile priests. But it has an even greater prejudice against homosexuality. One of the items on sale in its Christian bookshop is called a Sissy Kit, and parents are encouraged to take one home if they have any suspicion that their child might turn out to be homosexual. Basically, it is a torture kit containing whips, chains, and various other implements. As a preventive measure, parents are advised to feed tuna fish and anchovies to their suspected pre-sodomite children, the idea being that such a practice will make young boys accustomed to the odour of fish which this church claims to smell like a woman's vagina. This is the depth to which fundamentalist religion can bring us!

Ask any of these Southern fundamentalist Preachers, which version of the Bible they read and most likely they will answer "The King James version." Little do they realize that King James was homosexual.

As was outlined earlier, the Bible cannot be read literally. The Old Testament concerns itself with mankind's relationship with God,. It embraces the Jewish perspective of life which was extant at that time. We need to go back some thousands of years and vest ourselves with a Jewish mind, in order to understand it. We need to consider the cultural anthropology of that epoch. The birth of a child in the Jewish community of that time was considered a communal blessing because it increased and multiplied the Jewish population. In those days it was culturally understood that the man's seed was a mini-baby and the woman's womb was but its incubator. To waste the seed through ejaculation was looked upon as a heinous crime and doubly so when two men performed this act together. It is in this cultural milieu that homosexuality became taboo. Notice that Lesbianism was not condemned because women were considered as mere incubators.

In order to fully appreciate the implications of this cultural taboo on homosexuality, it is also important to take into consideration other laws prescribed in the Book of Leviticus. For instance Leviticus also condemns the eating of pork and shellfish. To wear a garment with two types of fibre or inscribing a tattoo on the human body was also prescribed as hateful. The question must now be asked why do Evangelicals and Fundamentalists only consider homosexuality as heinous, while ignoring some of the other laws of Leviticus. Most likely they enjoy their pork and shellfish as most of us do.

If homosexuality was considered a burning issue, then almost certainly Jesus would have broached the subject Even if he did, his compassion and tolerance would be more embracing than his condemnation.

Fundamentalist Protestantism as well as the rest of Christianity must learn that the Bible was written by people and not by God. It is the story of man looking at God much more than God looking at man. It is not fully relevant to the complexities of our contemporary society. Many people have given up on their belief in a benevolent God because of all the pain and suffering in the world. The barbarism of the Second World War turned many otherwise good people into atheists. They echo Nietzsche and say "God is dead." But if we look more closely, we will see that a lot more suffering in this world is caused by the barbarism of man than by God.

The Evolutionary push has given people free will, which has proved a very necessary attribute in what it means to be human.

We have the freedom to construct or destruct; it's our choice. Certainly the destruction of war and our inhumanity to each other is due to our human will much more than to God. Our free will also means that we have the power within ourselves to act as though God lives within us, as St Catherine did, and recognize that "my me is God." We cannot blame God for our own stupidity.

We learn from quantum physics that evolution favours death not as an end but as an emergence into consciousness. A watermelon seed grows to twenty thousand times its own weight when it is sown. Who are we to deny the potency of the seed? In giving us free will, God left the decision up to us to go inwards towards the light or outwards toward the darkness. If God did not give us this gift, then we would be mere puppets and he the puppeteer. Such an existence would be unbearable. God's overall plan from when we were stardust until we are consciousness leaves evil and good in the equation. They are both necessary. Contraries are complimentary.

However emergent evolution moves towards the good and the higher. We learn from our mistakes. We rise step by step as if on a ladder, to a higher perspective.

That is the plan of God. Evolution seeks out refinement in order to arrive at what is best for survival. This is what is involved in adaptation of the species and survival of the fittest. It aims at improving, We are now in the noosphere— the era of the mind. The task before us now is to improve metaphysically—to improve mentally. If we renege on this moral and ethical imperative, then as a species the earth will dispose of us.

When we suffer, God suffers along with us. Nazism came about from our own free will, but people could have chosen the opposite path instead. The whole respects the dignity of the parts. God did not create the evolutionary drive to damn humankind, but the whole allows all that is necessary for creativity to live in the parts. Nazism pulled us in the direction of evil, and God necessarily was involved indirectly in the choice since he gave us free will, but we cannot say God chose Nazism; humans chose it in an exercise of free will.

Good and evil exist together, and the clash between them results in either destruction or construction. The trend in evolution is towards construction and refinement, its process towards good. We know this from quantum physics. But construction and refinement and good can come at an awful price. This price, though, even in the extreme evil of Nazism, instructs us. It can teach us that we must never go down this road again. We can learn that war is senseless, although we have yet to do so.

Suffering also teaches that we must become dialogic instead of remaining monologic. When we deduce lessons from evil, we climb another step on the evolutionary ladder. The price of doing so is pain, both spiritual and physical, but luminosity comes out of darkness. We cannot accept privileges without responsibility. Our lot is not entitlement but involvement. Creativity is consequent upon pain. A mother cannot have a baby without it. It is an integral part of the evolutionary process.

If ever there was an anti-Nazi hero it was Jesus of Nazareth, not because he was a Jew but because he was human and suffered terribly for his convictions. He took the road less travelled towards refinement and good. In our evolutionary push, evil and good do not exist in duality. They are a part of each other, just as light and dark are in each other. It is hypocritical to brag about courage when we have no reason to feel cowardly. Faith is hollow if it has not been carved out of doubt. The price of harmony is chaos. Freedom is best appreciated when we have been incarcerated. The tree becomes more lush with fruit when it has first been pruned. It is from the negative and the destructive that creativity unfolds.

Every experience in life is made possible by its opposite. Contraries are complementary. There is only unity. This is the primary law of nature. This is the law of evolution. It cannot be changed. We will not know what light means unless we first know darkness. It is pointless to relate to a baby in its mother's womb the glory of springtime, for the baby has no reference to understand it. This is the way of evolution. It only slowly unfolds its secrets. We cannot impose our sense of time upon it. This may seem to our anthropological mindset un-understandable. We sometimes cannot reconcile suffering with the idea of a benevolent God. But who can understand the emergence of *Homo sapiens* from stardust? Perhaps greater surprises are in store for us on our evolutionary journey.

If we do not accept this primordial law of nature, we will become neurotic. Who are we to tell the cabbage seed that it must grow into an apple tree? It is far better to accept than to contest the inevitable. It is the only way we will find peace. We have to learn to surrender or else we will bemoan the results, and that will only make us more miserable. Nothing natural will change direction This is what nature has given us. It is up to us to like it or lump it.

Nature is the synthesizer and there is no way to short-circuit it. Pain and sorrow are part of our evolutionary journey. We live with infinite departure. Nature is adventure. Newness never arises out of staleness. Emergence requires the clash of opposites. Maurya, the old woman in John Synge's play *Riders to the Sea*, having already lost seven sons at sea and now confronted by the death of her last surviving son, has this to say in her final soliloquy: "Bartley will have a fine coffin out of the white boards and a deep grave surely. What more can we want than that? No man at all can be living forever and we must be satisfied."

† † †

SEPTEMBER 11

Synchronicity and telepathy may be two surprises that nature still has in store for us. At the exact moment when the planes were crashing into the Twin Towers in New York City, Fr Pat was sitting at his desk writing about the Taliban in Afghanistan.

The secretary from the parish broke his concentration when she came over the. "Did you hear the news?" she asked.

"No," Fr Pat said. "What happened?"

"Turn on your TV," she answered. He did so and watched in shock as the Twin Towers tumbled down.

The bodies of eleven parishioners were burnt away on that awful day, and the most powerful nation on earth went into mourning, traumatized by the horror of the incident.

More poignantly yet, for Fr Pat, the body of his niece was also consumed in the conflagration. All the priests at St Judes' went out to minister to the families of the bereaved. It was a soul-wrenching job. Most of the parishioner who had been lost were young men, and they left their wives and children in confusion.

As Fr Pat spoke to them, the horror of the event hadn't seemed to have sunk in yet. They responded to it with silence. Most noticeably, Fr Pat heard none of these families talk of revenge. Out on the streets people had a very different response. Young men especially drove around madly shouting, "Kill the bastards! Kill every fucking one of them!" They hung huge American flags from their SUV windows, and flags appeared everywhere else, too: on civic buildings, highway overpasses, in store windows, and from every home. The whole nation had been terrorized and wanted to show it by their flag-waving, a symbol of their need to come together as a community. They did this instinctually as though they were elephants crowding around a baby to protect it.

Fr Pat did not approach the catastrophe with politics. In his heart he believed that the nationalistic fervour exercised in the flag-waving was a thing of the past. "The only flag worth waving now is the planetary one," he thought. All nations are one. We are our brothers' and sisters' keepers. Quantum physics and Jesus had taught us this.

The attack on the Twin Towers triggered a primordial call to protect and defend. If this meant attack and the need for revenge, then so be it. This was the prevailing mindset.

For his sermon the following Sunday, Fr Pat looked into his own convictions and hammered out an honest response to the attack. He felt this event had to be interconnected and infused with the story of Jesus. Rather than responding with nationalism, as secular society had, he felt called to add a spiritual dimension to this and all things political. His sermon became an invitation to consider the message of Jesus and apply it to the terror. The time had come to be counter-cultural just like Jesus of Nazareth. He wrote these words:

At a time like this, when we all feel traumatized by recent events, it is understandable if we allow our anger to boil over. But we must take care in how we do so. I as a follower of Jesus cannot justify violence of any kind. In a land which is used to instant gratification, perhaps for the first time in our lives we are confronted by a problem which will take time to be resolved to our satisfaction. If our response is to nuke those who did this, as proposed by one of our parishioners, then we had better be careful because in nuking our enemy, we trigger still another reaction, and our choice may come back to haunt us, perhaps by ending humanity altogether. Guns can be pointed in both directions. Often it is the same war weapons which we produce in our own factories that are later used against us.

We may be the most powerful nation on earth, but might does not make right. It is the least threatening nation that is the most powerful. Strength comes from compassion and negotiation much more than violence. It is often the most handicapped people who teach us how to appreciate the gift of life. We cannot but be impressed by their courage to carry on despite the obstacles. Yet we complain about minor disturbances. We want instant solutions for our small inconveniences. Our mechanistic commodity-driven culture has manipulated us to believe that money and might can solve all our problems. We have lost the sense of what is moral. The greatest nation in the world is the most forgiving one. 'Father forgive them, for they do not know what they do'

If our objective is to kill the enemy, we fail miserably as human beings. We fail because quantum physics tells us we are but a part of a whole, an island joined as one to the mainland. All life is interrelated and interconnected, quantum physics tells us, and this interconnection is so profound that the flapping of a butterfly's wings can add to a storm on the other side of the ocean.

In regard to interconnection Thoreau said, "Am I not partly leaves and vegetable mould myself?"

Each part is dependent on the others. We need the fruits of the earth to survive. All living things are in the enterprise of life, not separately, but as one. The cosmos is one. We are all brothers and sisters. We are all in one another. As Meister Eckhart remarks, "The eye with which I see God is the same eye with which God sees me." When the particle goes into consciousness, the metaphysical takes over. Quantum physics teaches that we are one another. All that lives is related. When we kill one another, we kill ourselves. This is a far different story to the one we are used to hearing, but if this world is to improve, We must internalize that Forgiveness and love are the only catalyst for real and lasting change in this world. This message was given to us two thousand years ago, terribly though we have not begun to live it yet.

> If only we had the will to do it, all the bombs and bullets
> in our world
> would in one day be changed into bread and butterballs.

Nationalism is passé. Wrapping ourselves in our national flags is unhealthy for us. The only flag worth waving is the planetary one. From now on, should people ask, "What is your nationality?", Instead of saying "I am American" or German or Italian or English or Irish, just say, "I am quantum." And should they ask you if you are Christian, say "I am a Jesuit."

Jesus was the best of us. He taught and lived in a quantum way. He was a truly integrated man. His prayer was that "they all may be one. The Father and I are in one another. We are all one. Our divisions come from our selfishness. In a country which makes the ego primary, there is little room for that consciousness, which is our future. Whether we like the flow or not, this is the course which nature takes.

Our brains are matter whereas our minds are consciousness. When we kill, we become unconscious. We choose the brain instead of the mind. Nuking and killing is not an option. We must be enlightened enough to realize this, but we do not seem to have reached this plateau yet, for our minds still focus on retaliation, nationalism, and vengeance.

To kill is to be anti-emergent; it is to be anti-future. If we want a better life for our children, then we must first stop our killing. Violence only begets more violence. It is a vicious virus. In killing Bin Laden, we will create ten more leaders to replace him. War is easy and peace difficult.

Is there a better way? Of course there is. We as a Christian people must surely know this. We are only paying lip service to our core belief system if we live as Americans instead of Christians. We need a more global perspective. The central figure in the whole Christian story is Jesus of Nazareth. Rather than *lex talionis*, an eye for an eye and a tooth for a tooth, Jesus proposes that we turn the other cheek. If we have a fight with a neighbour and come to church to light a candle or put flowers on the altar, then Jesus tells us to go back home and reconcile with that neighbour before coming back to church to pray. How many times must we do this? Seventy times? No, seventy times seventy times, Jesus says. "Blessed are the merciful: for they shall obtain mercy . . . . Blessed are the peacemakers: for they shall be called children of God."

A sentimental song which was popular some years ago said that "love means you never have to say you're sorry", but love means the exact opposite:

Love begs for forgiveness. Forgiveness is such a small word, but it can move mountains of hatred in the human heart. Let's start trying it. We may find the peace we seek and deserve through its practice.

Many among us shout about our right to carry arms and call pacifists weaklings, claiming they are out of touch with the real world. But who are the real weaklings? It takes a lot of moral courage to resist violence. Its strength drips down slowly whereas a gun can end a man's life in a second. Construction takes a much longer than destruction. A nation which is hell-bent on retaliation is in line with neither the teachings of Jesus nor quantum physics.

Some people claim that the teachings of Jesus of Nazareth have no practical application to our modern world, that they are but the dreams of a half-mystical Jewish poet. Men laugh at him. They think of him as too feminine because he tells us to "look at the birds of the air" and to "consider the lilies of the field". Real men don't talk like that! But then look at what Martin Luther King did for his people in the name of the mystical nonviolent Jesus and under whose inspiration he claimed, "We now have guided missiles but misguided men." Look at what Ghandi did through nonviolence for his people in India. He accepted Jesus not as God but his brother. "An eye for an eyes makes us all blind," he said. Look at what Mother Theresa has accomplished in the name of Jesus in the slums of Calcutta. Jesus of Nazareth was totally contradictory: he turned all the plans of a society intoxicated with power and violence upside down. "Blessed are the meek: for they shall inherit the earth." Jesus was surely a living paradox! "We gain by losing", "We receive by giving away", he taught us. Perhaps it is time for us who profess to be his followers to overcome our urge for revenge and retaliation. We too can live the Jesus way. Let us begin today.

As Fr Pat preached, congregants walked out on him. He knew he had disturbed many parishioners who were very good people. He knew Jesus of Nazareth disturbed the comfortable and brought comfort to the disturbed, but he had sought advice about this homily before delivering it. Two of his best friends told him that despite the disturbance it would cause, it was his duty as a Christian minister to deliver it. Finally, he reasoned, "This is a moment to confront hostility. If I run from it, I am a coward. As a true follower of Jesus, I must stand up and give witness to unpopular views. Faithfulness to one's own integrity is the only way to bring peace to one's own mind."

After mass, the phones in the rectory kept ringing. People called to say that they were very disappointed with him. Some told him that he should go back to where he came from. Some left the mass without saying anything, obviously moved to contemplation. Others gently remarked that since he was born overseas, he didn't fully understand the American perspective.

One woman said, "I came to church to say my prayers, not to be disturbed."

Another woman said, "I don't know much about this quantum stuff, but if it's against America, then I'm against it."

A man even threatened violence against him.

"Look, Father," another man said, "I read the Bible every day, and never once have I seen the word *quantum* in there anywhere. If it's not in the Bible, then it's not worth listening to. I don't know what you learned in your seminary training, but if it's not part of God's word, then I don't want to hear it."

Still another man reminded him that the Pope forbade priests to speak about politics from the altar. "Did you not learn your lesson from the Pope's suppression of liberation theology in South America?" he asked.

"We are traumatized enough. You don't have to add salt to our wounds," a woman said.

Fr Pat felt traumatized himself, not only by the collapse of the Twin Towers but now, even more intensely, by the parishioners' reactions to his sermon. A few parishioners did agree with him, congratulating him and saying it was great to hear something relevant preached from the altar.

"That took a lot of courage, Fr Pat," one man said. "We need to have truth spoken to us, and I thank you for that."

Monsignor received many calls requesting that Fr Pat be removed from the parish. Through Fr Pat's diminishment, the Pastor was jet-propelled to the highest echelons of holiness. This money-hungry man was now promoted to the level of sainthood by the parishioners. He listened to every parishioner's complaint against Fr Pat assiduously. Yes, indeed, he did consider Fr Pat a heretic, he told them. Almost overnight, Monsignor's reputation as being distant and uninvolved was forgotten. Now he was viewed as a very caring and compassionate man.

At his own masses the following Sunday, Monsignor denounced Fr Pat publicly from the altar.

"I've never had so many complaints in my whole priestly ministry as I did concerning Fr Pat," he said. "I promise you, my dear parishioners, that I am still available to listen to you and help you during these traumatic times. Jesus said, 'Come to me all you who labour and are overburdened; I will refresh you.' God knows we need refreshment at this time. To refresh is the vocation of a true priest, and with all my heart, I hope to fulfil that vocation by serving you."

Miss Prado was so proud of her pastor. Finally someone was listening to her.

"In our discussions," Fr Pat said at the next meeting of the New Basaleans, "we have dismissed as unacceptable both the fundamental dogma of the Church and its equally nefarious materialist counterpart. We've determined that the search of the human mind and heart for meaning can only be answered through an awakening to the light of the spirit which lies within each of us. This is the only way to full integration. We are doomed to be spiritual. We are hardwired for God.

Sooner or later, we must wake up to our own mystery. To recognize and assimilate the ideas that 'My me is God,' as St Catherine said, and 'The eye with which I see God is the same with which God sees me,' as Meister Eckhart said, we must travel to a deeper way of seeing and knowing. We enter into the realm of inscrutability, becoming our own scripture, and this is the first of all principles in natural spirituality. To enter the realm of the inscrutable involves risk and surrender. Objective proof is not necessary. The wisdom of insecurity must be increased. Agnosticism can be the very seed which will one day sprout into the blossom of credulity. Let these words of wisdom inform this week's lecture:

> I am alone on the surface
> of a turning planet. What
> to do but, like Michelangelo's Adam
> put my hand out into unknown space
> hoping for the reciprocating touch?
> (R. S. Thomas)

"The most beautiful and profound emotion that we can experience is the sensation of the mystical. It is the power of all true science" (Einstein).

For his next meeting Fr Pat had prepared the following lecture:

THE UNQUENCHABLE LONGING

We begin our mystical journey in the midst of the ordinary. We find our infinity through our finiteness. All are one when we see with a mystical eye. The most extraordinary way is the most ordinary one

Patrick Kavanagh said it best "God is in the bits and pieces of everyday, a kiss here and a laugh again, and sometimes tears, a pearl necklace round the neck of poverty.

Oscar Wilde put it this way: "Mystery is in the seen, not the unseen.

Once we surrender to the great awakening, all aspects of life take on a new colouring. Everything has meaning and connection. We become integrated human beings. We possess a new zest for life. We become excited and enthusiastic about living, We are no longer involved in trivial pursuits. Unimportant nothings no longer get our attention. Matter no longer reigns supreme. The inscrutability of the mystical sets us free, not by explanation but through experience. The inscrutability of the mind shocks us into astonishment at the silent happenings of our ordinary lives. We take notice of events which we previously took for granted and cloak them in divinity. We begin to wonder at the flight of birds and the swimming of fish in the sea. We begin see the miracle of our own body. As Marcel Proust said, "The real voyage of discovery consists not in seeking new lands but in seeing with new eyes." The wonders of nature are the most powerful evidence for a hidden mystical core. The Big Bang had the mind of humans in mind from the beginning.

How astonishing! William Wordsworth said it well when he wrote, "Whose dwelling is the light of setting suns, and the round ocean and the living air, and the blue sky, and in the mind of man; a motion and a spirit, that impels . . . and rolls through all things."

Our story began fifteen billion years ago in the explosion that was the Big Bang. In a millionth millionth of a second, a speck became a million million times bigger. Eleven billion years later, our planet spun into an independent satellite in the solar system. It took our planet another billion years to cool down, and just about a half billion years later, the predecessors of *Homo sapiens* roamed the central plains of Africa.

For 95 per cent of our cosmos' existence, there was no human presence. Mechanistic science manipulates us into declaring that *Homo sapiens* has a monopoly on all of the wisdom in the universe. This system sees the cosmos only as conquerable territory. It has turned the universe into real estate, where through its dictatorship all life becomes either murdered or tortured in compliance with its rules. Deep down though our collective unconsciousness tells us that if we do not seek a more spiritual approach, the earth will dismiss us.

How astonishing to think that our genome has continued to express itself so diversely and beautifully since the beginning. The amount of genetic information contained in the nucleus of every cell is staggering. "It would take forty-three volumes the size of an enormous dictionary filling a shelf twelve feet long to list the information carried on the double helix," Christopher Wills said. The double helix packs more than 100 trillion times as much information by volume than the most sophisticated computer. The human brain, weighing just three pounds, can outprocess the most sophisticated computer on earth a trillion times over. Do these insights not signify the presence of some great non-local Intelligence?

We feel hungry, and by some inscrutable transformation, the food we eat turns into flesh and blood. The healthy functioning human machine works in silence with little help from its owner. We take it all for granted and scarcely notice it unless we are in pain. We become aware of the air that oxygenates our lungs by its absence more than its availability. We never take time to contemplate the marvellous precise alchemy of the air we breathe. Should there be 1 per cent more oxygen, our earth would incinerate. Should there be 1 per cent less, the human race would asphyxiate.

We open our eyes and see a world of blended colour. Our sight arises effortlessly when we wish to view an object of beauty. We behold it as though doing so is a right. We never think of how inscrutable the process is. Effortlessly, the baby in the human womb makes the most staggering journey of all. It begins as a single cell and multiplies itself 75 trillion times. That single cell carried half of the father's and the mother's genetic code into every other cell it multiplied, realizing its final expression in the form of a baby. Its DNA, wrapped into forty-six chromosomes, when unravelled, would be 196 million miles long—the equivalent distance of two round trips to Mars. Inscrutably, as that single cell multiplies, it creates undifferentiated stem cells that then specialize and go off on a journey of efficiency and harmony to make a heart or a nose or a lung or a kidney until, in an astonishing accomplishment, they combine into a being of staggering magnificence. We delight in the preciousness of a baby's appearance. We have no words capable of describing it; our silence is its expression. Before we were born, our brain cells multiplied explosively, at the rate of 250,000 cells a minute, making a staggering 50,000 connections to our eyes every minute.

Our kidneys sweep all impurities from our blood and dispose of them in our urine. They perform their critical work silently and effortlessly.

Walk into any hospital and notice all the machinery necessary to perform dialysis and we cannot but be amazed that all this is accomplished daily, minute by minute, in a pair of machines each no bigger than two stacked Brussel sprouts.

There are thirteen hundred nerve endings in our fingertips to assist us in our touching. Our tongue, our nose, and our lips have even more nerve endings. Our bones manufacture a billion blood cells every day, silently and effortlessly. Our ears can discriminate between three hundred thousand different sounds, and our eyes between eight million different colours. Our brain is the greatest of all realities. It processes about one hundred million bits of data every second. If mechanistic science can tolerate admiration for the workings of a motor car, then how much more astonished should we be by the machinery in the human body?

Going within a single cell, Noam Chomsky tells us, "The automated factory of the cell carries out almost as many unique functions as all the manufacturing activities of man on earth . . . But with one capacity not equalled in any of our most advanced machines . . . It is capable of replicating its entire structure within a matter of a few hours, and yet this remarkable piece of machinery that possesses the capacity to construct every living thing that has ever existed is several thousand million million million times smaller than the smallest piece of functional machinery ever constructed by man."

The human body contains approximately five litres of blood, and the heart is capable of pumping this blood through all the myriad veins and arteries in the entire body. This organ is so powerful that in defiance of gravity, it can pump its cargo six feet and more in the air. It is very efficient. It can work for a lifetime opening and closing its valves two thousand time every hour.

"Men go abroad to wonder at the height of mountains and the huge waves of the sea, at the long courses of the rivers and the vast compass of the ocean, at the circular motion of the stars, and they pass by themselves without wondering," St Augustine said.

To think reasonably is the goal of mechanistic science. It will not allow us to think mystically. If we are sensitive at all, we cannot but wonder mystically! We are doomed to be spiritual. But Western materialistic culture does not tolerate this type of enlightenment. But we must choose it when confronted by so much mystery and wonder. We must have the courage to be. We have had too much having and not enough being. To be integrated there must be balance. Recognize the bee but also be conscious of the sweet taste of the honey and be grateful.

We can learn from the UN Environmental Sabbath Prayer:

"Great Spirit, give us hearts to understand never to take from creation's beauty more than we give. Never to destroy wantonly for the furtherance of greed. Never to deny to give our hands for the building of earth's beauty. Never to take from her what we cannot use. Give us hearts to understand that to destroy earth's music is to create confusion. That to wreck her appearance is to blind us to beauty. That to callously pollute her fragrance is to make a house of stench. That as we care for her she will care for us. Amen."

We also learn this from Wilfred Pelletier and Ted Poole:

"Wherever you are is home and the earth is paradise. Whenever you set your feet in holy land, you don't live off it like a parasite, you live in it and it in you, or you don't survive. And this is the only worship of God there is."

Life is a gift given graciously. If we believe this, then each moment becomes an exercise in authentic integrated living. We view our lives with new eyes and a different way of seeing.

How can we stand in awe at the migration of birds or the camouflage of fish or insects without wondering where such intelligence comes from?

Ibn al'Arabi said, "God sleeps in the stones, dreams in the plants, stirs in the animals, and awakens in humanity."

When we live with an expanded consciousness, love and compassion erupts from within us. When we feel the sacred and the numinous in all living things, we will embrace the oneness of our togetherness and interdependency. Then mother earth shall be proud of her progeny. When our grasp exceeds our reach, as it does in mechanistic consumerism we retard the evolutionary push. If we refuse to integrate immanence with transcendence, then we as an experiment will perish. When we live in an integrated way, the rush of chemicals from the Big Bang will ignite us. Our dust shall mammalize us and beautiful, unpolluted air will rush in to oxygenate us. We shall be given the intelligence to fly even higher. We shall look on our earth with tenderness and we shall value her as a child treasures its mother. We shall stand in awe of everything and we shall be consciously swept into a mystical no-thing-ness and no-place-ness. And we shall sing and dance forever.

† † †

UNTIL WE MEET AGAIN

Fr Pat heard some rumours from various priests within the diocese that the Bishop had been diagnosed with cancer. His heart skipped a beat. He had much respect for the Bishop; he was a rarity. He had kept a very low profile, and his name was scarcely known on the National Council of Bishops or in the media. He showed no interest in business management or in political manoeuvring, and the diocesan newspaper didn't give him much publicity, for it concerned itself more with issues of global and national importance than with trivia. There was little evidence from any quarter that the Bishop was interested in self-promotion. Fr Pat would miss him terribly should anything interfere with his leadership, He called the chancery office and made an appointment with Fr Larry to see the Bishop for ten o'clock on Thursday morning.

It had been a while since Fr Pat had last seen the Bishop, and in the interim, the Bishop's physical appearance hadn't changed very much, although he did seem more serene.

"How are you, Bishop?" Fr Pat enquired as he sat in the office.

"I'm taking things a day at a time. I'll soon retire, you know. I'm glad you made this appointment," the Bishop said. "I was going to call you anyway; I just haven't found the time with all the fuss surrounding my retirement."

"I understand," Fr Pat said. "I'll miss your leadership terribly. You're a good man."

"Thanks, Father. I've tried to be faithful to that inner voice you've been talking about. Miss Prado still sends me those tapes every week. She's very impatient, but she's consistent."

"You've been doing an exceptional job. I hear you read a lot of poetry and literature.

I try myself to encourage the priests of the diocese to read more. You've heard me say so at our clergy meetings. I happen to think our best theology comes out of literature. We should put the bible back on the shelf and read more of the world's great literature. I can see these fundamentalist preachers coming after me now. What a desert we live in!. The Egyptian Fathers lived in a far different desert though. Theirs was all green and ours is all sand. Remember they told us to be non judgmental. I try my best to follow their rule. It's difficult but it's the only way to sacralize authority. If hierarchy is ever to become whole-archy, then we have to be humble enough to realize that all authority comes from God." The Bishop paused.

"There's something terribly wrong with the hierarchy today," Fr Pat said. "Over 40 million Catholics have left the American Church already, and I'm sure there are more doing so in Europe. That must be sending a message to the Vatican, but they don't seem to be listening."

"You're right," the Bishop said. "Theirs is a voice far greater than that of the Roman magisterium. We called it *sensus fidelium* in the old days, the voice of the faithful. True authority empowers people. It does not walk on them or step over them. Thinking in the Roman Church has always been linear. Perhaps in the middle ages such thinking was tolerable, but it isn't today. All the findings of modern science and the accumulation of other new information changes one's perspective. As a Church or indeed as a society we must think laterally or else become irrelevant.

"I've been reading the essays you sent me and listening to Miss Prado's tapes. In most respects, I agree with you fully. The old myths sustain us no longer. People have had a lot of facts pumped in to them which were claimed to be true but they haven't withstood the test of time. The faithful no longer obey like trained dolphins. The great pity is that the Church refuses to keep pace. It remains much too smug and rigid. Mechanistic materialism in the meantime has run far ahead with its alluring consumerism, using its brain but denying its more mindful consequences.

. The Church offers immortality at the cost of mortality while materialism offers mortality at the cost of immortality. Neither approach is holistic or integrative enough to give us balance. Therein lies the root cause of all our modern confusion. Personally, I think that the voice of the faithful and the voice of the hierarchy are now in deadly combat with each other. In the end, the spirit of God will triumph in the people, as they've looked to their inner light while the hierarchy lusting for the maintenance of its own authority hasn't even begun to contemplate a world devoid of power and contol. Truth is always triumphant in the end."

"You are a remarkable, man" Fr Pat said. "Of course, I would say that, wouldn't I? You think as I do. I still say it's remarkable, though, because of your position of authority. You astound me. You sound more like a missionary nun in a poor foreign country living her compassionate witness with the poor of the earth. Scarcely valued for her heroic witness until some secular media brings her story to the world's attention. Only then does the Church step in to own and value her, dumping much of the glory on its own management. You sound more like a protester than a protector of the status quo. What has made you so different?"

"Well," the Bishop said thoughtfully, "as I've said before, the death of my sister and her family in that awful automobile accident was the most teachable moment in my life. After an experience like that, you dump all your trivial questions into the sewer. Our lives are but a puff in terms of eternity. Ambition, power and control only serve the ego, and accumulation is only about heaping. Competition involves destruction. I want none of that anymore. I honestly believe a lot of my fellow bishops are good men, and I think all priests start off their ministry with the best of intentions. All humans are basically good, until society co-opts them. None of us would put a family member in front of a firing squad, but evil creeps in slowly, and then like flies we get caught one day in a cobweb of sticky issues. We either go on in the confusion and become more entrapped or else we see that to preserve our integrity, we must choose to be different. We must think like Jesus and live more outside the box.

My sister's death drove me into a deeper spirituality. I'd had my suspicions for quite a long time that our Church is ruled by politics more than spirituality, and it took me time to honestly confront the disturbing questions that haunted me. I try to keep Jesus as the crook on which I hang my conscience. I always ask myself, what would he do in this situation?

I'm older now and there's not much more that I can do except be compassionate. As I loosen the dogmatic noose from around my throat, I feel I'm walking with the rest of struggling humanity. Had I realized what I know now the I would never have become a priest. I am grateful, though, that at least I have learned compassion. That's all that matters.

If I were to continue as a bishop, I would have to become a shepherd known more for his gentleness and compassion than for the authority given to him. As I'm sure you've already heard, I've been diagnosed with cancer. I don't know how much longer I'll live. I'm leaving it in God's hands, but the doctors say I must send Rome my resignation. When I couple my own pain from cancer with the loss of my beautiful sister and her family, it all seems overwhelming sometimes, but the greatest problem with suffering is that we hold on to it far too long. The human mind has a magnificent capacity to turn pain into something more sustaining. Just as food and drink are changed into flesh and blood, pain and suffering can be also changed into a deeper reality merely because we long for it.

There has to be a resolution; that's the way of nature. Surely there exists beyond us a justification for our search. I believe some great Intelligence stands behind our astonishing cosmos and that my suffering is preparing me for a deeper saturation into the mystical. Suffering when used constructively is the gestation period for deeper consciousness."

Fr Pat left the Bishop's office with tears in his eyes. The meeting had given him an empowering affirmation. In his prior conflicts with the hierarchy, he had always felt lonely and dissonant, and he wondered if he would ever meet a kindred spirit like the Bishop again. The Bishop treated him as an equal not just because he agreed with Fr Pat's theology but also because the Bishop approached him with dignity and respect. They had never said a rosary together or performed a liturgy, but their conversation, in a way, was a prayer. There was no formula or predetermined dogmatic theology involved. Both he and the Bishop were lively and enthused. Their conversations followed no drab routine or dead mumbling; of the psalms, their shared perspective animated both of them.

"This is what prayer should be," Fr Pat thought. "Not these deadly dull dogmatic encapsulations that ensure creedal control."

He hadn't fully realized the importance of his growing respect for the Bishop until recently. "We find God through one another," he mused.

Some weeks later, Fr Pat was invited to share his thoughts on prayer with a group of parishioners from the local Episcopalian church, and he based his talk on his experience with the Bishop. It saddened him to think that he didn't have the same freedom to give such a talk in his own parish. The New Basaleans, of course, provided him freedom, but the church in general, and especially Monsignor and Miss Prado, would never be so tolerant. The Episcopal church was far more dialogic and curious.

PRAYER

"Prayer must come from the depths of the human experience," Fr Pat began his talk. "It has to be cried out from each individual heart in aspiration and sometimes desperation, but rarely can such feeling be expressed through the manipulation of a formulated creedal prayer."

He paused and looked at his notes. The rest of his speech read:

"Most of the prayers we say in Roman Catholicism are ecclesial, devised for the sake of control and power. The Book of Common Prayer is very beautiful, and it derives its power from poetry. Of course, the Roman Church has its own tradition in prayer, and like in yours, it is this art that speaks to us. Prayer is essentially a cry of the heart. Real prayer is much more personal than it is creedal.. Authentic prayer occurs when we approach God and seek attention. Our prayer should be as individual and original as we are. Our best prayer is our own.

Many people ask, does God listen or even care about our prayers? I say yes unequivocally because of what quantum physics teaches me, that the whole is greater than the sum of its parts. We are the parts related to the whole. If enough of us join our individual prayers together our outcry will have enough energy to create a storm on the other side of our world.

We believe in God, so we have already moved into the realm of the beyond. We would not be here in this Church if we had not already decided that something more than matter exists. Prayer is a connection between the parts and the whole It makes us holy and whole-istic. If anyone asks you, "To what Christian denomination do you belong?" Just answer, "Quantum."

To get back to the question of whether God listens to our prayer. The answer is, of course God listens, just as surely as we listen to ourselves. Prayer is the parts listening to the whole and the whole to the parts. So intensely are we bound together that God cannot *not* listen. There is no telling how powerful the bond truly is. It is so inscrutable that we are not capable of describing it.

Quantum physics suggests that our individual small prayers have as much effect on our wholeness as a butterfly's wings help impact a hurricane on the other side of the ocean. Quantum physics teaches that all happenings have an effect on all other happenings. They are one and the same because the cosmos is one. Put all our flapping wings together and we become a hurricane. Prayer uses our energy for good; therefore, each individual prayer contributes to the good of the universe. Never cease praying. If we join all our prayers together then our energy will turn life into a theophany.

The trouble with our Western culture is that both systems supposedly dedicated to promoting our happiness have lied to us, one telling us that there is no God and the other manipulating the facts to control what is mystical about us. Both systems are idolatrous if not diabolical. Creedal prayer rarely involves the human heart. Most often it does not speak to the many problems facing modern society. Instead, individual and community prayer should be topical, reflecting our bewilderment. We need cries of the human heart and less creedal prayer to heighten our spirituality. Prayer is necessarily attitudinal. Creedal prayer steals our ability to talk conversationally with God.

Creedal prayer bores us to tears. It does not concern itself with contemporary issues, and it doesn't excite or involve our heart in any relevant way., Creedal prayer suits the cry of the established church for the continuation of its own power and control. It does not allow the human heart to really cry. Instead of the parts embracing the whole—God—we make a mockery of our own spiritual integrity. Creedal prayer is the prayer of an institution which is much more interested in it own preservation than our communal or individual cries of reverence or petition.

. When our prayer is purely creedal, we solidify established religion in a way that the Intelligence behind our evolution never intended.

Until very recently in Church history, the Church formulated prayer to be monological rather than dialogical. It prostituted the purpose of prayer to accomplish its own ends. It put most of the food in its own cart, leaving little to feed the spiritual hunger stamped by nature on the individual human psyche. But God is much more interested in the spontaneous cries of struggling humanity than in the synthetic offerings of organized religion. The medicine the Church prescribes is not an antidote but a placebo. Our personal prayer should never be predicated on creedal prayer. When we pray in this way, we keep our individual energy from soaring into consciousness.

True prayer should make us fall to our knees in utter astonishment before the all-encompassing Energy which soaks our being. The recognition that our finiteness is enveloped in infinity feeds our spiritual hunger and gives us purpose. We taste paradise and we want more of it. The vastness, the elegance, and the majesty of the natural world predisposes our minds to see all creation in a revelatory way. Before such elegance and majesty, we cannot but fall into silence. Our silence and awe is often our best formulation of authentic prayer.

There are intimations of God everywhere. There is good in this life; it is far more revelatory than evil. And even evil, when seen metaphysically, can be a stepping stone to embracing a higher reality. God's energy is in the whirlwind. It encompasses all that is natural in our human world, evil and good.

God is like a good baker, infusing leavening into the dough. No matter the ingredients, it is the whole with the parts that makes the masterpiece. And may God be praised as the great baker.

God loves a stuttering heart, for it shows humility. Our stammering is our prayer. God is more interested in our attempts than our successes. We are all stutterers, inadequate before the face of God. There is no way to create tidy formulations to describe the incomprehensible non-local Intelligence.

We cannot computerize divinity God cannot be reduced to the tiny dimension of the human brain We cannot but stand humbly before divinity and give thanks for the privilege of participating in the journey.

Authentic prayer must involve the heart as well as the head. Life is a continuum from the here and now into the hereafter. In the formalized creedal prayer of the Church, we give all our attention to the hereafter to the detriment of the here and now. We jump into transcendence without connecting it to immanence. Instead, we must pray for the courage to play our own part in the construction of the beautiful and the destruction of evil in this world. Beyond that there is only acceptance. Leave the rest to divinity. Harmony will come out of chaos. God shall prevail, and all our crooked roads shall be made straight.

Without even realizing it, we say our most pleasing prayers in the cosy environment of our ordinary homes. Kitchens precede churches. There is no merit in running off to worship in a church unless we have first lived our prayers at home. Washing the breakfast dishes can be the contributing note from a piano or a flute in the musical masterpiece of appreciation. Even the smallest note of all is necessary. The greatest prayer of all is when we make the ordinary holy. Rosaries of glory are more often said in kitchens than in churches. Limits are the truest commandments in the expanding life of a child. Attendance and guidance to ones offspring may be tiring. But this is the the stuff of prayer. God listens when divinity's work in the here and now is dutifully completed.

Love is like a tug of war; it involves a lot of pulling and at times there must also be letting go. There must be space for individuality and indivituation in every home. Balance is the true prayer of a parent. If this prayer is not first attended to in the home, then society at large will suffer the consequences.

Authentic prayer is more often modelled and performed than said. Its natural environment is the home. Home is the cornerstone, for as the family is, so society will be. Home is the first school. In order for parents to teach, they must find guidance from the wisdom of the ages and also from their own inner light. It is in listening to what is deepest about ourselves that we say our best prayers. The same tug of war pulls us all. The same experience is within each one of us. We all, even atheists, live with existential angst. By nature we are doomed to be spiritual. We are strong wired for God. Even atheists, whether they express it or not are still filled with existential angst. There is no escape from it.

Nelson Mandela said in his inaugural speech,
"You are a child of God. Your playing small does not serve the world. There is nothing enlightened about shrinking so that other people will shrink, insecure, around you. We were born to make manifest the glory of God that is within us. It's not just in some of us. It's in everyone. And as we let our own light shine, we unconsciously give other people the opportunity to do the same. As we are liberated from our own fear, our experience automatically liberates others."

It is our innate capacity for mystery and beauty, for harmony and order, that sustains us and animates us. By tapping into the universal source of all our energy, we write our own biography. A book cannot be fully understood or appreciated until all its pages are collated in a continuous connection to make up the story. Heaven starts when we start to live quantumly.

A NEW BISHOP FROM ROME

Not long after his speech to the Episcopalians, Fr Pat received the sad news that his beloved friend the Bishop had died. Even though he believed with every fibre in his mind that death is but a transformation from body into consciousness, he still cried. The Bishop would forever live in his memory.

Two months afterwards, all kinds of rumours ran through the diocese about who would replace him. Finally it was confirmed that the new bishop was coming directly from Rome. His reputation preceded him: he was even more conservative than the Pope. Fr Pat felt his days of acceptance and toleration were at an end. Monsignor and Miss Prado spoke of the new Bishop's appointment as inspired by the Holy Ghost.

Soon after his arrival in the diocese, the new Bishop appointed four young priests as pastors to some very rich parishes. Fr Pat knew each of the priests personally, but as he expected, even though he was more senior, he was passed over. He didn't care anymore. His prayer was his courage to let go.

He despised the politics of the hierarchy. He had always dreamed of creating a new paradigm, with his photography and poetry. He felt such an approach would awaken people to a deeper reality. "God is found in the ordinary" had become the central theme of his creative expressions. He wanted people to see laterally instead of linearly.

That year, St Jude's Church was chosen as the venue for the annual Christmas party for all the priests in the diocese. The new Bishop attended, as was his duty. He was a tall, handsome man with all the airs of a prince. He dressed impeccably, bedecked with his golden pectoral cross and matching engraved golden ring. He looked imposing in his Italian-crafted red cassock. During the cocktail hour, the Vatican's new appointee mingled with his priests. Even though Fr Pat tried to welcome him, the Bishop seemed oblivious to him, sidestepping his outstretched hand and responding to the call of another priest. Fr Pat's old insecurity around authority figures flashed back. He thought the Bishop had deliberately ignored him, and he wondered if Monsignor had already spoken to him.

His insecurity was further heightened when the Bishop sought out an equally tall and handsome young priest. Their conversation became very animated, and they laughed loudly. The Bishop patted the young priest's back and said, "I wish I had a hundred like you in my diocese."

The new appointee from Rome knew nothing about the young man's spirituality or priestly ministry! Even more ironic was that Fr Pat had been the young priest's spiritual advisor. He knew that the young man had fallen in love with a beautiful young woman and soon would be leaving priesthood to marry her.

Fr Pat expected a call from the Bishop at any moment. The tension between himself, Monsignor and Miss Prado had been growing daily. It could not continue to build.

"The Bishop would like to see you as soon as possible," the new secretary said over the phone.

He sounded young, but Fr Pat had never heard of him.

"His Excellency is very busy, as you can well imagine," the young secretary continued, "but he's interviewing every priest in the diocese so that that he can know them personally. Would ten o'clock on Thursday morning suit you?"

"Of course," Fr Pat said. If he had something else scheduled, he would have had to change to suit the new Bishop anyway.

"Okay. Thanks, Father." The phone went dead.

Fr Pat wore his Roman collar to the meeting that Thursday. When he put it on, he suddenly remembered that he had once told a priest friend that he would never wear it again. "Never say never," his friend had said.

As he was leaving, the parish secretary, who usually saw him in lay attire, said, "My God! What's the big occasion?"

"I only rented it for the day," Fr Pat replied.

When he arrived at the chancery, the offices were whirring with activity. To see it one would think the occupants' work involved questions of cosmic importance. The Bishop's new secretary was young, as Fr Pat had inferred from his voice, and certainly handsome. He wondered if the new Bishop had a thing for young handsome men.

The secretary introduced himself as Tom "Please, sit here in the waiting room," he said.

It was the very same room in which Fr Pat had waited for his saintly bishop friend. He missed his friend's reassurance and support, and an awful loneliness crept through him. The waiting room had been refurnished and decorated, but despite the new veneer, he felt the old Bishop's presence in it.

"His Excellency has a horrendous schedule, and he's delayed," Fr Tom said as he approached Fr Pat. "Would you like a cup of coffee?"

Fr Pat refused politely, and after Fr Tom retreated to his office, Fr Pat looked around at the various offices surrounding the inner sanctum of the new Bishop's quarters. Priests and their secretaries working in individual offices were terribly preoccupied with the serious exercise of the management of the diocese. The inner sanctum had an uncanny quiet and no-nonsense air about it. Throughout, everyone gave off an air of efficiency and determination, businesslike in all aspects.

"My God," Fr Pat thought to himself. "This whole business approach is a monstrosity. How has the tattered peasant from Nazareth come to this? Instead of Aramaic, he now speaks computerese. What would Jesus himself say about what religion has done to him? Leadership born from a compassionate heart accomplishes more in one day than the whole technical wizardry of the world can accomplish in a lifetime. All the computers in the world are absolutely useless if they're not backed by a motivated mind and gentle heart.

Machines alone can never ease an unhappy mind or cure a wounded body, but the compassionate mind behind the machine can give integration, and that's the only goal worth pursuing both technologically and religiously."

Fr Pat wondered if the men and women employed in the inner sanctum of the diocese did their work merely for sustenance or whether they were motivated by compassion. How much more glorious the functioning of a diocese would be if its sole objective was compassion. Without this component, integration was impossible.

"Why has the message of Jesus become so complicated that it now needs all these offices to deliver it?" Fr Pat thought further. "Why does the simple message, 'Do unto others as you would have them do unto you,' need all these computers to deliver it? As we grow ever more spiritually starved, our computers grow louder and stronger to obscure our cries of hunger. Surely, among all the governments and the churches of the world, there must be the will for integration. When we live quantumly, we come together as an integrated whole, individually and as a society."

As he thought, Fr Pat sat and waited, sat and waited. At least four times Fr Tom had said, "The Bishop will be with you in a moment." He lost himself in reverie to give him a reprieve from his anxiety, and he was glad of it. He marvelled at the power of the mind. How fantastic was its ability to transport a person from the here and now into another realm, totally obliterating the reality of space and time. His body remained in the Bishop's inner sanctum, but his consciousness was elsewhere.

"Is this what death is like?" he wondered. The body stayed on earth but consciousness lived on in another dimension. He made a point to remember this analogy for his next sermon.

Fr Tom came over yet again to announce a delay. "I know we scarcely know each other," he said, "But I know your pastor, Monsignor Murphy, very well indeed. I hear he has to use a walking stick now. That dog of his is a menace. Murphy tripped over the dog, someone said, is that true? He shouldn't be allowed to lie on the altar while the holy sacrifice of the mass is being said."

"I don't know why Monsignor uses a cane," Fr Pat answered disinterestedly, thinking "You're inflated with a sense of your new importance."

The secretary prattled on but Fr Pat didn't listen, allowing his mind to go into another sphere again.

"Yeah, secretarial posturing, that's what I'll call it," he thought. "He knows quite well why I'm here, and he has to know I'm tense, but he goes on with his silly little game of pretence. Look at his French cuffs and his sterling silver shirt studs—there's alliteration for you. Hmm, expensive aftershave lotion. Polo, Obsession . . . some such stuff.

"Doesn't he know I'm anxious? How could he know, he's one of the Bishop's boys, manicured and handsome. He does what he's told. Obedience is easy when it's in your favour to practise it. Has he ever asked a serious question? He hasn't had enough pain yet.

"I don't want to talk about Monsignor Murphy's dog. It's irrelevant. Look cheerful and pretend you're interested in this nonsense. That's how priests with upward mobility on their minds occupy their time. He's handsome, all right . . . the Bishop sure likes to surround himself with young handsome men. It makes him and the diocese look alive and vibrant. Image is all-important . . . 'Miss Bish', that's what Fr John Mahoney called Fr Tom. Who does he think he's fooling? But he's young. I shouldn't be judgmental. At least he's enthusiastic. He isn't fat or indolent yet. This display of importance annoys me, though. It makes me want to vomit. I have to give him time to grow, I suppose. I hope the game doesn't consume him. If he continues as part of the Bishop's inner circle, time will change his nickname. 'Mr Monopoly on Answers to Issues of Moral Complexity. Mr Authority on the Ins and Outs of Holy Matrimony . . . that's what they'll call him."

Absorbed in thought, Fr Pat hadn't even noticed that Fr Tom had long since gone back to his office, but the intrusion of his voice brought him back to reality.

"Fr Pat, please follow me. The Bishop will see you now."

The inner office had been redecorated to suit His Excellency's taste. Fr Pat silently walked across the spongy plush carpet to shake the Bishop's hand.

The Bishop came forward from behind his desk and, in a ceremonial but inviting manner, said, "I believe you are Fr Patrick Malone, is that correct?"

"Members of the parish call me Fr Pat."

"Please sit down," the Bishop said.

Fr Pat sat in the appointed chair as the Bishop moved back behind his desk to take his seat. He had decorated the huge room impeccably. A Waterford crystal chandelier hung over his desk and vases of beautiful cut flowers seemed to be everywhere. Pictures of the Bishop and the Pope, the Bishop alone, and the Pope alone, peppered the walls. Most prominent of all was the coat of arms, which proclaimed, "Amor Et Veritas", "Love and Truth".

Just as he had at the Christmas party, the Bishop displayed a distinguished and imposing demeanour.

He could see Fr Pat was very nervous, but to defray his anxiety, the interview started with an innocuous question.

"What have you to say about the recession?" The Bishop asked.

"These are tough times" Fr Pat answered, but I am convinced that as Pitrim Sorokin suggests civilization is like the swing of a pendulum. We go very farin one direction and then we recognize we are on the verge of destruction, so we swing back to a safer territory.

We need both God and mammon for survival. There has to be balance. We have swung too far in favour of mammon at present I think.

If we are wise we can learn a lot through deprivation."

The Bishop looked surprised. He was not accustomed to a priest speaking on this level.

"What do you mean?" the bishop asked
"Well as Benjamin Franklin said" 'Suffering instructs'

"You sound masochistic" The Bishop answered

"How can you as a follower of Jesus say that?" Fr Pat asked in an emboldened way.

The statement from the Bishop indicated that he was not a man of depth.

As ever, Fr Pat felt he was confronted by a man who was selected to become the new bishop for managerial rather than spiritual reasons.

"Tell me more" the Bishop said, as he looked at his watch.

"A recession can be like a purification" Fr Pat said. We can learn a lot from it. It can teach us to be more discriminatory about what is important in life.

It can teach us that Metaphysical values are more important than physical ones. There's too much stuff already and too little sensitivity or care. It's what Patrick Kavanagh said—"Through a chink too wide there comes in no wonder" We have to steal back the newness in every stale thing."

Without saying a word, The Bishop picked up a folder and some tape recordings from his desk. He flipped through the pages of the folder and then stopped and studied a particular page. Fr Pat suspected this was his personal file. The diocese kept such a file on every priest. Like a penny catechism, it told the whole truth of the priest's moral character, as definite as a dogma.

Finally, the Bishop flung the report on the desk and said, "Interesting . . . very interesting indeed."

"What is so interesting?" Fr Pat asked.

"I understand you've been serving as a priest in my diocese for the past thirty-five years? Is that so?"

"Yes, it is," Fr Pat said.

"During that time, you have had . . . what shall I say? . . . your ups and downs with us."

"Well, Your Excellency," Fr Pat responded, "I have had my ups and down with previous bishops."

"Fr Malone, a bishop in any diocese of the Church appears on the same line in the apostolic tradition going all the way back to St Peter. How you ministered as a priest under any previous bishop of the diocese continues into my jurisdiction."

"I understand," Fr Pat said.

"I am a little curious, though. In your records, I see a . . . change of behaviour about four or five years ago. Does that mean you've become more amenable and obedient to Our Holy Mother the Church's teachings? I am given to understand from your profile that with the two bishops who preceded our last bishop you behaved rather poorly."

"You are correct that I had my problems with previous bishops," Fr Pat answered.

"But I do not see any negative remarks about your behaviour under the leadership of my predecessor, Bishop O'Reilly. As matter of a fact, he drew a rather glowing portrait of you. It would seem you're rather like a chameleon."

"What do you mean, Bishop? Is there a problem?"

"Fr Malone, you are an intelligent man and you understand quite well what I mean. How can heresy under two bishops become orthodoxy under the next?"

"Bishop O'Reilly could better answer that question than I could. I have never been given the position to decide what is truth and what is not truth. Only the bishops have that privilege in our Church, as you well know. I have the authority only to make decisions on my own behalf, and I do not intend anything else. Two previous Bishops in this diocese have considered me heretical and one has not. I suppose now you must decide for yourself which view you agree with."

"My problem is that this discrepancy confuses me. I do not know you, but I need as many priests in this diocese as I can possibly lay my hands upon," the Bishop said.

"Yes," Fr Pat said. A great confidence surged through him. "particularly tall handsome ones."

The Bishop furrowed his brow. "What do you mean by that?"

"Never mind. Please, continue on." All his anxiety had disappeared. He felt the joy of abandonment. He didn't care any longer what the Church thought about him.

The Bishop composed himself and pressed on. "My problem is that with the shortage of priests, I need every man I can possibly keep to command a post, but what is even more necessary is that every priest must speak the truth as Christ passed it on to the apostles and, naturally, to every consecrated Bishop in the world. We all must speak with one voice. If a priest cannot do this, then he will be dismissed."

"That's your decision to make, Bishop."

"Well, damn it, Fr Malone!" the Bishop said, raising his voice in frustration. Can't you see the dilemma I'm in? I don't know anything about you but what your file and those bloody tapes over there tell me. So I ask you, do you believe in Jesus Christ, Fr Malone and what's this Cosmic Christ thing?"

"I believe in Jesus but not Christ."

"What's the difference? Surely they are the same consubstantially."

The Bishop said dismissively.

"No, they are not," Fr Pat quickly retorted. "You as a bishop surely know that. The authorities in Rome created the split and made their own conclusion dogma. You must know very well at Nicea The Church turned Jesus into what it wanted him to be. Rather than allowing him to speak for himself, the Church spoke for him."

"I think you've been reading the wrong books, Father. You should be more discriminating. I wish the index of forbidden books still existed." The Bishop stood up and rubbed his temples. "Fr Malone, you are a stubborn man. Why did you become a priest?"

"I became a priest to preach the Good News," Fr Pat answered.

The Bishop looked at him intensely and said, "Yes, indeed. The world . . . this country is in an awful mess. We have strayed terribly. We have gone miserably wrong. The days of the Roman circus have returned. All the depravity and the filth, it's rampant. We have to pull back. This psychobabble, this terrible liberalism has brought us to the brink. The media is to blame. And you know what, Fr Malone? Decent people are finally saying, 'Enough is enough. We want values. Let's get back to basics. We need a moral compass. We want someone to show us the way.' Decent people are crying out against decadence, and they admire the Catholic Church for its unchanging qualities. Our church has never veered from the truth. We preach the same message. We remain the same yesterday, today, and forever. People are disillusioned by all this confusion and babble. People want us, they need us. They are telling us to take up the gauntlet and bring the sanity of the gospel message back into our materialistic world.

You would be surprised at the number of influential Jews I've met at different functions who've told me that they look to the Catholic Church for basic values and direction. They admire our courage and consistency. Whims of fancy and fads all blow away, but we're still here. The gates of hell shall not prevail against us. After two thousand years, we are still in the driver's seat. We hold on, no matter the cost.

Fr Malone, do you realize how blessed we are? Do you realize what an honour it is to be a part of the vanguard? You have been given a special calling. I'm asking you today, do you pledge your fidelity to that calling and to me as your bishop?"

"I believe, Bishop, that we receive many calls, and what we make of them depends on who the interpreter is. It's my belief that there are as many approaches to God as there are individuals. Each of us must be guided by our own inner light."

"That's utter nonsense. That's Gnostic heresy. What do you mean by that rubbish?"

"Well, to be precise," Fr Pat said, "No one, not an institution or anyone else, has a monopoly on the truth. We are all gropers in the same whole of eternity. We are all questioning sojourners confronted by mystery. The God of Christians is a surprising God. The minute we define God, we lose him. The God of Christians is unimaginable. All we can do, finite creatures that we are, is make odd stabs in the dark. God is an experience more than a concept. God is an inscrutable great Intelligence. The very name of God is unspeakable. My God is boylike, wild and free. I don't know which hidey-hole he'll jump out of next."

The Bishop looked frustrated, but his service to the Holy See had clearly refined his diplomatic tactics. He took a moment to cool down and collect himself. He looked at the file again and cleared his throat. "Fr Malone, there are some disturbing notes in this report. It says here that you believe in evolution?"

"Yes, Bishop, I do. Life is dynamic, not static. It offers us new disclosures every day. That's why it's so exciting. I believe we are in progress and the best is yet to be. Life is a blessing, not a curse."

"But, Father, Scripture distinctly says that God directly created the world and Adam and Eve. How does your theory of evolution fit into the Bible account?"

"Oh, for God's sake, Bishop, that kind of thinking makes religion sound childish. Evolution is a fact. It's just that the theory ends with the brain and not the mind. It doesn't go far enough. But if you want to talk about the story of Adam and Eve, we can. Genesis tells us that they only had two sons, Cain and Abel. So, are we now to believe that the whole human race came from the seed of two men? Or to take that a little further, suppose Adam and Even had one daughter. Are we supposed to believe that the human race came from an incestual relationship? Scripture is not scientific history."

The Bishop looked at the file and changed the subject. "I see from this file that you're an advocate for women priests. If Christ wanted women priests, then why didn't he make any of them apostles?"

"Perhaps because of cultural difficulties," Fr Pat answered quickly. "Rebel that he was, though, he probably had at least one that we haven't been told about. Mary Magdalene, for example. She seemed to follow him everywhere. But if he did have a few women apostles, our patriarchal church would have soon covered their story up. It's scandalous that half the human race has no representative in the Vatican."

The Bishop turned over another page in the profile., seemingly oblivious to what Fr Pat had just said, "They tell me you have a taste for photography and poetry."

"I do. We are in an era of pre-evangelization. We have lost the ability to see beyond the obvious. But poetry is the language of the human spirit. We need metaphor much more than myth, and poetry implies much more than its words can say. That's why I've devoted so much of my ministry to promoting a lateral rather than a linear way."

"Poetry," the Bishop sneered. "It's never accomplished one practical thing. The world today needs the message of Christ preached to it in plain language. Not some dididlee-di stuff. The world has enough Donald Duck and Mickey Mouse. That's what is wrong with the Church. We have allowed too much of the modern world's crap to enter our parishes. We should stand apart and be counter-cultural." The Bishop smiled.

He placed the folder on the desk and looked Fr Pat straight in the eye. The atmosphere was now dripping with false sincerity. Then, as though he were making Fr Pat privy to some great secret, the Bishop said very gently, "You know, Fr Malone, when I was a young man, I was a very promising concert pianist. So I understand what you're trying to tell me about the value of poetry. Music is the best poetry of all. Provided, of course, it is elevated to its highest expression. Only classical music can achieve this. Anyhow, my music was a passion. I played with various orchestras and quartets. I received rave reviews. My music took me to some of the great concert halls in Europe and America. I rubbed shoulders with kings and presidents.

But you know what, Fr Malone? Something was missing in my life. I wasn't satisfied. Here, I had reached the pinnacle of success—I had love affairs with beautiful women, the world was on my plate—but something was missing. A voice called and told me to give up my glamorous ways and become a priest. I spoke with an old nun who had taught me in grammar school. She confirmed that she always thought I had been called to the priesthood.

She told me, 'Give up your glamorous lifestyle. Forget the piano and follow in the footsteps of Jesus Christ.' I remember her words to this day. And you know what? The old nun was right. When we're only concerned with self-seeking, we remain unhappy and unfulfilled. It nearly killed me to withdraw from my addiction to music, and make no mistake about it, that precisely is what it was. But I did it! And even though it hasn't been easy, I've never regretted that choice. I've kept my hand to the plough and never looked back. I'm happy to do the Lord's work.

I am telling you in fact I'm ordering you to do as I did. Get back into the vineyard of the Lord. Do his work. Stick to the truth of his message as the Church proclaims it. You may think you're gifted as a poet or a photographer, but my God, how can you compare that to the gift of your priesthood? Your hobbies are but peripheral. They are not central. They are but a fleeting distraction when compared to your true vocation to spread the message of Jesus. Of course, I understand how difficult it would be to forsake this multi-media thing, but I did it and so can you. I need you to work full-time as a parish priest. The day of fads and novelty in the Church are over. I see a greater priority for your ministry than the gimmickry stuff you love."

"But, Bishop, what about Jesus' admonition, 'Do not hide your talents under a bushel basket'?"

The Bishop angrily blurted out, "Look, Fr Malone, real men don't write poetry!"

Fr Pat didn't let this ruffle him. "What a sad commentary, Bishop. So many bishops in our church have lost the memory of their mystical roots. Your remark is heresy to my ears. You have secularized poetry." Fr Pat looked around, and his eyes rested on a picture of John Paul II. "Doesn't the Pope write poetry?"

"Oh, come on, Fr Malone. Surely you're not comparing yourself to the Pope."

"Please don't syllogistically dismiss me, "Fr Pat responded.

The Bishop seemed not to understand what Fr Pat meant. His tone became more intense. "Look, Father, I'm going to be frank with you. We've had too much experimentation in the Church. It's time to for you to settle down. You've been doing your own thing and getting away with murder for far too long. I see now that you are exactly as they tell me you are."

"Who are 'they', Bishop? Monsignor and Miss Prado?"

"Yes, and many more like them. Some of your fellow priests, who shall remain nameless, say you shirk your duties as a parish priest to go all over the diocese with your audiovisual programmes. Your passions are your camera and your tape recorder. You give more attention to your avocation than you do to your ministerial vocation. I forbid you to continue in this way. These diversions can no longer consume you. They tell me you're obsessive about this type of ministry, and it must stop."

"Bishop, don't you think it's better to be passionate about something which awakens people to a deeper reality than to spend life in lethargy? People in power are often shielded from the truth, so let me tell you, a lot of your priests are jaded. The spark of life has gone out of them. To numb their ennui, they go on cruises and eat dinners in the finest restaurants and spend every moment they can on the golf course. Now *that* is the reality you should be addressing."

"I assure you, I will face those issues eventually directly with those priests in their personal interviews. But right now I am interviewing you. You are the centre of my attention now."

The Bishop looked at the file once more and breathed deeply. "They tell me that the only agenda you follow is your own. "Why do you continue to preach in Protestant churches? Surely your primary ministry should be to the members of the Catholic community."

"To be honest," Fr Pat said, "I don't do it because I believe in the centrality of their meta-myths. Their core beliefs are as intellectually insulting as those of Catholicism. Having said that, however, I am convinced that the Protestant tradition is more open to honest enquiry. It is not as threatening or as dogmatic as the Roman Church. It is more tolerant of imagination and curiosity."

"I don't quite follow, Fr Malone," the Bishop said. "Give me an example."

"Well," Fr Pat said, thinking for a moment. "I believe that the human mind is the greatest achievement of God's creative genius. Through our intelligence, we can enter into the lofty halls of transcendence. We are the most blessed of all creatures on this planet. The gift of our intelligence carries with it the responsibility to use it sensibly and rationally. But the Roman Church, through its dogmatism, asks me to prostitute this gift by suspending my intelligence in favour of a stopgap theology which makes no sense and is, in fact, quite stupid and childish—"

"I did not ask for a lecture," the Bishop said, furiously. "I asked for an example."

"Well, just look at the difference between the Catholic and Protestant approach to the Virgin Mary."

"Continue," the Bishop said.

"The Catholic Church has deified Mary. Call Protestant churches what you will, but they rightfully argue that Mary is not a goddess. In many respects, Roman Catholicism has replaced Jesus with Mary. Perhaps this is mere tokenism from a patriarchy which in every other respect is anti-woman. Regardless, Mary's importance throughout the ages and into our own day is simply unreasonable. Through some insufferable theological concoction, the Roman Church has declared Mary to be the eschatological icon. But no matter how many dogmas the Church declares about Mary, it still remains impossible for any human woman to be God's mother. How can The All have a mother? To have a mother means having an antecedent, a before a before was possible. Mother of God is an oxymoron. Our anthropocentrism has clouded our intelligence. Were we to accept Mary as the mother of God, then we would have had to accept that she existed before the Big Bang. She would have had to exist outside of the dust from which we all evolved incrementally."

"Fr Malone." The Bishop stopped him. "You talk in circles. This is the chatter of a tormented soul. I hope you never preach that convoluted stuff from any pulpit in the diocese. Quite frankly, I do not know how to handle you. I know prayer can work wonders, so perhaps you should go on retreat for a month to the Trappist monastery in Spencer. I will talk to the personnel board and determine what we can arrange for you. Perhaps it will give you a new perspective.

"In the meantime, though, I ask you to keep a low profile. Your ministry has to be in keeping with the mission of the Church. It's time for a change. I have been appointed Bishop of this diocese, and I must be assured that your preaching is orthodox and that it furthers the mission of Catholicism. I have been entrusted with this mission and I intend to fulfil it. I urge you to get on with the work of the Church and forget about your audiovisual presentations."

"But, Bishop, I have lived my life inclusively, not exclusively. You judge me unfairly."

The Bishop ignored this protest. "When you come back from your rest at the monastery, I'll appoint you as a full-time assistant priest to one of the parishes in the diocese. The personnel board will decide which one. Of course, we will take into account your psychological profile and match you up with a compatible pastor."

"That's very kind of you, but I know my limits. I can't survive in most of these rectories. If you tried one yourself, you'd find that they're hellholes."

"Fr Malone, for too long you've been living in an ivory tower. It's time you came down to earth and got your hands dirty in the everyday affairs of parish life like every other priest in the diocese. We are entering a new phase of Church history, and we must steer the Church back to its previous status as a flourishing institution. Liberal priests like you have had your honeymoon. It's time to face the real world."

"Just what do you think I've been doing for all these years, Bishop? Sitting alone in a loft writing saccharine, sentimental lines of poetry, bereft of life? Art is born out of conflict. My writing would not be worth a damn if I didn't first identify with all the joys and fears of struggling human beings. I've baptized more babies, counselled more people, mourned at more wakes, married more couples, cried with and laughed with and listened to more people's problems than even the Pope could count."

"Ah, what am I to do with you? You're only looking at the small picture. I have the needs of a whole diocese to attend to."

"Bishop, I can meet no needs if you'll have me violate my integrity. I cannot allow you to destroy the God within me."

"Tell me then, Fr Malone. What do you propose I do?"

"Make me a pastor."

"That is a possibility," the Bishop said, "but first you'd have to subject yourself to the tutelage of a pastor I choose. This profile's portrait of you is far from good. You'd have to first prove yourself through obedience and faithfulness to orthodoxy as every pastor before you has done. But there is an apprenticeship in the diocese which must be served. I could put you in it, and after three years of service under that pastor's watchful eye, if the report we receive is satisfactory, then I promise to make you a pastor. I could see you situated quite nicely in the inner-city parish of Sacred Heart. The responsibility rests with you, Fr Malone. You must prove your worth as every pastor before you has done. Only men of integrity and outstanding holiness can be appointed pastors."

"Oh yeah," Fr Pat blurted out, "that's why you make pastors out of embezzlers and paedophiles."

The Bishop started. He looked horror stricken. Fr Pat knew far too much. "If that's your attitude, then why don't you leave?"

"Funny, Bishop. That is precisely the same question enlightened Catholics everywhere are saying about most of the bishops in the Church. I have much more seniority than any of the young guys you have already appointed to the richest parishes in the diocese. You already dismissed me before this meeting because you deem me unorthodox."

"Oh, come on. You're not seriously comparing yourself to those four outstanding young men who earned their badges of honour through sheer hard work in the diocese?"

"You lie. I know two of those men personally. One of them was a chaplain in the army for the past five years, but the army dismissed him because he propositioned two young blonde soldier boys. You know about his history better than I do, and yet you still appointed him."

"Who told you this?" the Bishop asked, shocked.

"Do you want me to go on, Bishop? I can remind you of the history of the other three men."

"Absolutely not!"

"Yes, you're right. Let's not pull priests' names into the muck."

The Bishop looking at his watch and said, "Fr Malone, I am very late. I must go." He got up and led Fr Pat towards the door. Putting his hand on Fr Pat's shoulder, he said paternalistically, "Think about what I said. Talk it over with your spiritual director. Report back to me in two weeks."

Fr Pat already knew he could never enter that office again.

† † †

"You are a priest forever according to the order of Melchizedek." So Fr Pat had been told on his ordination day. He had believed it in the beginning because untested love comes easily. But now, how could anyone say anything was forever? His mind wandered in prayer . . . .

Don't stay. Don't even say the word *forever*. It's not a human word. Human and forever do not mix; they are totally opposite. They are diametrically opposed. Nothing remains. Hopkins said it best:

> Sorrow's springs are the same
> Nor mouth had, no nor mind, expressed
> What heart heard of, ghost guessed:
> It is the blight man was born for,
> It is Margaret you mourn for.

Isn't that what faith is all about? Learning how to walk a tightrope with no safety net, totally vulnerable and frightened and full of dread, taking a step, an inch at a time, until you come to the truth at the other end? How could you leave? You belong. You're needed. You've wanted this since you were a boy. It's in your blood. One cannot stop being what one is forever. Drape yourself in any other cloth and you will still be a cassocked man. Even if you leave, you will still belong. If you walk out, you are lost, you are nowhere.

Nice commitment. You run out when the going gets tough. Love is sacrifice. Die on your cross. I can't leave; I must stay. Love means forever . . . But human and forever don't mix. Yes they do; it's metaphysical. You believe, don't you? Sometimes I have my doubts. I don't know. I'm an agnostic— that is the only legitimate human stance.

Oh, God, I do believe. If I did not believe, the boy inside of me would die . . . Christmas is a great story. I'm a Christmas freak—I'm like a child. Often I've known a presence which cannot be explained.

God, I don't know your name. Are you in the first call of the bird in the morning? Sometimes I hear a whisper through the grass and I love the way someone paints sideways the light in the fields in the evening . . .

Stay. Rise above the system. The world aches and there is work to be done. But how can I continue when I'm not orthodox? I do not believe in body ascensions and assumptions or the virgin birth. They're not for real. How can I suspend my intelligence? I suspect everything that is out of the ordinary. Nature is the yardstick, that's what I think. But what is deepest about the human experience cannot be measured . . . Oh, God, you have to understand that I suspect everything which suspends the law of nature. Mystery is in the seen.

I've yet to meet a man who cannot make mistakes. Ex cathedra be damned. That's politics. I've yet to see a baby who has not been fathered by a man. It's meta-myth; I don't take it literally. This world needs poetry to sustain it. Myth is not untrue—it's just a deeper truth. There's enough work to be done whether Mary's hymen was broken or not, and as for the Pope, let him have his fix. It helps him feel important and secure.

How can I stay? The system is driving me mad. Even biology knows that a refuge for well-being is not advantageous for living organisms. Change and adaptability are the real tools for growth and survival. I must sail on troubled waters. I must take a risk—"the blind leap", a Danish philosopher called it.

Fr Pat did not see the Bishop again. Instead he packed up his belongings and jetted back to Ireland a reverse exile. The valley at the bottom of the Slieve Bloom Mountains always brought comfort to him with its beauty. It provided him with sustenance and the necessary courage to carry on. Even though he was broken and shaken by the whole ordeal, in the deepest recesses of his soul, he knew leaving the diocese to come here had been the right choice. He would miss his American friends desperately, especially his beloved New Basaleans, but he had had enough mental suffering. He didn't want his heart to turn to a stone. He wrote to the Bishop:

Dear Bishop Hogan

After much soul searching and personal turmoil, I have set forth on the only road left open to me. I do so with a heavy heart. It has been a painful experience to set myself adrift from the haven which has been my home for the past forty years. I entered the minor seminary when I was only eleven years old, and since then, I have lived my life according to spiritual considerations. Now that I have returned home to Ireland, distance has provided me with perspective.

In retrospect, I think too much precious time and energy was used up negatively during our momentous meeting. Now that I have had time to reflect on that ill-fated meeting, I think our time together might have been more profitably spent discussing a vision for the Church in the twenty-first century. Instead, you constantly attacked, leaving me with no option but to defend my integrity. I fully realize you work out of a hierarchical model whereas mine is secular-dialogic, but your points were little more than a litany of negatives about my ministry.

The testimony you accepted in respect to my character was little less than an assassination. It is unfortunate that you hold me and my work in such low esteem, but it is my honest opinion that your obvious prejudice stems from your poor performance as an investigator. In respect to my ministry within the diocese, to say nothing of my work in the Church as a whole, you have been misinformed. Perhaps you might have received a better assessment of my priestly ministry by interviewing the lay people of the parishes in which I served. Had you made such enquiries, I know you would have heard that I have been a priest constantly concerned with the spiritual hungers of the people I served.

It is my opinion that we canonize mediocrity rather than creativity in the Church, and the priest who stands apart is always suspect. In a church which refuses a new perspective, a nicely behaved zombie is a far more acceptable minister than a priest with a spark of originality. I no longer flatter myself by thinking that I am anything more than a speck among the myriad considerations you are faced with in the administration of the diocese, but Bishop, your speck is my world, my truth, my life. I cannot allow you violate it.

Deeper than the call of one's bishop is the call of one's conscience, and I must obey mine. Priests are called first and foremost to proclaim the Good News, to recall people back to their divine possibilities, their original ground. Priests should communicate the Good News with some passion, some enthusiasm. Passion for the witness of the historical Jesus along with his mandate that we not hide our light under a bushel basket has been the foundation for my priestly ministry. But you failed to recognize my zeal. I have no option, insecure and frightened though I am, but to journey into an uncertain future. I walk on troubled waters. I would not be a man of courage if I violated my own truth. It is for this reason that I must inform you, Bishop, that I make my choice for life. To allow the institutional Church suffocate my spirit would only spell death. That option is intolerable to me.

Sincerely yours in Christ,
Patrick Malone

The Ireland Fr Pat came back to was a totally different place than the Ireland he had left forty years earlier. It had become a wealthy modern country. He was amazed at its economic success. But like the rest of Europe God figured little in the concerns of his homeland. New houses dotted the landscape and the stores were full of every sort of food, clothing, and gadgetry. Concomitant with this miraculous economic growth was an evident decline in religious faithfulness. The Catholic Church had been racked by all kinds of scandal, and this people, who had once been subjugated to the power and control of religion, had become vociferous in their condemnation of it. The Catholic Church had been dethroned, cast to the sidelines. The people now saw it as a curtailer or a hindrance for justice and development more than a moderate force for them. Church attendance had plummeted and the seminaries were almost empty. Young well-educated people had dismissed religion as nonsense.

Nonetheless, there were a few good, practicing Catholics left in the country, and Fr Pat's much younger brother was among them. He had married late in life and was determined that his children would be raised as good Catholics. His brother loved the tradition of the Church and obeyed its laws without question. Even all the terrible scandals broadcast in the media every day had not shaken his conviction in the Catholic Church or its establishment by Jesus Christ. Not even the devil himself would prevail against it. Fr Pat's brother still went to confession once a week and brought his wife and his children along with him. At Sunday mass, he towed his whole family up to the front pew and disciplined his children to be respectful and attentive to every word the priest said.

His faith was in no way ostentatious. It came out of conviction. The more sacrilegious and profane Ireland became, the more he was determined to fight its monstrous crudeness and vulgarity. He was a man of prayer, and his prayer was creedal. He felt that the family which prays together stays together. Saying the rosary together as a family was compulsory. His lovely wife agreed that he had the right as a father to lead his family.

Fr Pat adored his brother's three beautiful little innocent children and loved them as though they had come from his own seed. They were precious to him. He loved their innocence, and he played childish games with them, the better to bring out their innocent expression. He showed them holes in big oak trees and was so convincing in his stories that they became the homes of fairies. The stories became so real to the children that they actually believed they had seen and spoken with the fairies.

"Oh, Mammy, you should have seen them!" the eldest said. "They were very small but the gold buckles on their shoes were as big as the moon, and the sun was shining on them and I was nearly blinded by the light.

"Their clothes were simply gorgeous," the middle child said, "with feathers like a cock pheasant's hanging off them. And they had furniture made of red mushrooms with white dots on them, and I think there were seven of them . . . No, that's the story of the seven dwarfs. I'm sorry, Mammy, I made a mistake. But anyways, they were magical!"

Fr Pat's nephews and niece looked like Hummel figurines, as though their faces had been brushed with peach paint and their eyes coloured with Mediterranean blue. Their golden hair would have made the setting sun envious. Fr Pat decided to photograph them in the fields of natural wonder which were plentiful in the Slieve Bloom valley. As they played pretend, he tried to photograph them without their awareness. He caught a snap of his niece crying as a big tear ran down her cheek. Her water of sorrow had been caused by a fight with her older brother, but she claimed her uncle had pricked her with a pin when Fr Pat showed the picture to her parents.

He brought his camera when he took his nephews and niece on an expedition in the Slieve Bloom Mountains not long after that. On the way, his eldest nephew, who was sitting in the front seat, looked up at him and innocently said, "Uncle Paddy, are you a priest?"

Fr Pat was taken aback with the question. "Yes, I am. Why do you ask?"

"Well, my daddy said to Mammy that if you're a priest, you're a *quare* one."

Fr Pat laughed hysterically.

Some weeks later, an American friend came to visit, and Fr Pat decided to drive him back to the airport for his flight back home. They had scarcely started their journey when the car decided it would go no farther. Fr Pat and his friend tried everything to start the engine. With sweat pouring out of them, they pushed the car up hill and downhill to give it a running start, but it was dead. Fr Pat was alarmed that his friend would miss his flight, so in desperation, Fr Pat parked the car by the roadside and, taking his friend's suitcases with him, walked to his brother's home, which, thankfully, was close by. He pleaded to borrow his brother's car, and his brother agreed on the condition that he return it by eight o'clock the next morning, as his family had to fulfil their Sunday obligation, and they didn't want to be late for mass. Fr Pat swore on a stack of Bibles that he'd return the car on time.

As it turned out, though, his friend's flight was delayed overnight because of mechanical failure. Fr Pat stayed overnight at the airport with his friend to keep him company, but the plane didn't leave until noon on Sunday. A confrontation with his brother loomed ever larger as Fr Pat drove the car back. His reputation as less than a good Catholic priest in his brother's eyes would now be further enhanced because Fr Pat had broken his promise.

Fr Pat loved his brother and knew he was a moral, principled man. He wouldn't hurt an animal, much less another human being. In his relationship with his wife and family, he always measured a dollop of compassion into his commandments. He worked hard as a farmer every day in stewardship of the land afforded to him. He worked in silence and learned to distinguish the songs of the birds. He considered rain showers a blessing instead of a curse. In every way, he appeared to be an integrated man, and Fr Pat admired him greatly. But they still had a brotherly rivalry, especially when it came to religious vision. His brother's approach was blind obedience to the Church, and this registered as oppression to Fr Pat. If one were to judge the book by the cover, Fr Pat's brother would indeed appear to have chosen the better path on his way to with God, but blind obedience was easy when one was sure of the answer. What was Fr Pat to do when he thought of life as a question more than an answer?

In the end, Fr Pat accepted that they each had to follow their own bliss. Fr Pat could never compromise the intelligence which God had given him. He was happy that his brother and his family were achieving happiness in their own way, and Fr Pat ultimately concluded that this peaceful man was truly guided by his own inner light accessible to everyone and not the one imposed on him by organized religion's brainwashing. Inner light always wins out when consciousness enteres in.

Even though he was very late, Fr Pat had a smile on his face when he entered his brother's home to let him know he was back with the car. His brother's wife and family were sitting around the kitchen table sharing a meal. No one said a word as Fr Pat entered the kitchen, and his brother's wife and children glued their eyes on him as if an atomic bomb was about to fall on his head.

"I'm sorry, Brother," Fr Pat said still grinning.

"You're sorry," his brother said flatly. "Well, you have a right to be. If I was man enough, I'd give you a right kick on your arse."

Fr Pat feigned innocence. "Why, brother? Everything that's broken psychologically can be mended with the right attitude."

"There you go again with your auld codology and your fancy big words. You should have stayed over where you came from. All you do is embarrass me and my family. You made a show of us in front of the neighbours."

Fr Pat got down on his knees and pleaded, "Oh, my dear brother, pray tell, how did I do that?"

"Get up, ya auld eejit. You're making a mockery of something serious."

Fr Pat got up and, serious now, said, "How did I embarrass you in front of the neighbours?"

"The whole lot of us had to chug like hell on the tractor to get to Sunday mass. All the neighbours were laughing at me revving up the engine."

"Well, why didn't you leave earlier?"

"I waited till the last minute for you."

"I'm sorry, brother."

"Saying sorry isn't enough."

"But what else can I do?" Fr Pat said sincerely.

"You made us so late that we didn't get to mass until after the Gospel. And you should know, Reverend Father, that when the Gospel is over, it's too late to go in. Because of you, we are now all in the state of mortal sin."

Fr Pat burst out laughing. When he caught his breath, he said, "Oh, that's all right." He gave the sign of the cross over his brother's head. "I absolve you in the name of the Father, and—"

"You can keep your bloody absolution," his brother said. It's not worth a damn. It's worse than a curse."

With that, the rest of the family joined Fr Pat in laughter.

Fr Pat turned around and faced Alba. The valley of the Slieve Bloom Mountains resonated with mystery. He was sure his link to an ancient spirituality would free him.

A voice much older than Rome's had caught his ear. It involved him passionately as it oozed with the wildness and the wet. He felt at home. Here, the children still spoke with a pretend microphone, and wise old men played melodeons.

"The prospect is great," Fr Pat thought. "I propose remoulding and mending. Stones cry out for the secret of an ancient mortar. I rage against the sores and the scars of Rome's defacement. In the name of civility, stupidity has denuded the past. I will attempt to glue the orgiastic sheela na gigs around Alba's ancient monastery doors again. I will join the old monks on Skellig rocks and sing earth-linked psalms. The Celts' God dances in the midst of the ordinary.

"What fuss and what energy we exert with misplaced passion on promises bereft of substance. We have given our souls away. Anxious for ecstasy, we reduce God to gadgetry and misplace his sacred presence with a lie. But in spite of all, the grand Designer weaves his cloth with precise and meticulous care. Silently, he is always here behind the footfalls of busy men. Buds burst into blossom. They are signs of God's beauty and benediction. This ordinary world which we take for granted, this green ground which we trample on, is the very place where God the artificer displays his wares. This edifice called earth, this holy cathedral of the everyday world, is filled with streams of mystical light more glorious than the stained glass windows of any church. These trees like spires pierce heaven with full-blown passion. Theirs is a grand Hosanna. All earth and all sky is sacred. Clouds, as if in a hurry to some emergency meeting, gather to proclaim God's holy name. Each drop of rain is his assurance that the earth shall not die parched. Faithfulness is God's hallmark and green is the colour of his care.

Acres of bounty hang heavy their yellow heads, fat, full with nourishing food. Some signs of God's love come stamped in green, some are red, and some are yellow. Together, they are providently provided in a bowl as round as the world. Sometimes in the whispers God spells his name across the evening sky, and sometimes, too, in the birth of the young morning when stillness speaks. God walks near and can be heard breathing beside an animal bedded down in the recently alerted summer grass. Marvellous fabrics of seeming inconsequence are woven with such fine thread that they cannot be seen or appreciated by the vulgar busy eye . . .

But the immortal God does speak and laugh and sing. He hangs his gems on the face of seemingly inconsequential things. The ultimate God comes to us in common statements. He is close at hand in the unspectacular things we fail to see. All earth is sacred, and heaven starts where the foot falls. All colour like an alarm begs for attention and asks humanity to praise divinity.

Each leaf of green grass which carpets the fields is munched into the miracle of sacred milk. Each leaf on a tree born new out of winter's defeat blessedly supplies holy oxygen to address our needs. Each kernel of corn, and there are billions of them, is but a sigh of concern from the provident God's haggard hand. Streams, too, pour out their songs of praise. Water is their string and rock is their bow., Eggs laid simply in a nest become a speckled heaven brought low.

Heaven can be touched in the tangible. The transcendent is in the immanent just an inch or so above the head of busy men. All roads, no matter how dusty, no matter how small, lead to the mountaintop where the immortal God waits and lives. Replete is this world with a spiritual radiance bursting forth, suffused with a sublime and passionate presence. God is a burning issue. This is a holy place, and Yahweh still speaks in fiery speech.

If this world were more sane and radically in tune, we, with the wide-eyed wonder of children, would with imagination intact, stand in pure untamed astonishment at the sumptuous display which the immortal God spreads out before our eyes. See God walking everywhere in the midst of the ordinary. Crave not theophanies, for flames burst forth from the burning bush everywhere. Often times He is the unseen shepherd in the meadow where sheep feast. Lift the eye beyond the obvious heaven is here. Do not crush the reed with your footfall for there in the commonplace on this holy ground lies a silver sea of wealth. Unnoticed blades of grass drip with dew. Ah, Artist God, how could we doubt you?"

Fr Pat's experience that day prompted him to write an essay

CELTIC SPIRITUALITY

Dotted around the Atlantic Coast of Ireland, many remote islands can be seen when one gazes out from the mainland. It was on islands such as these and in remote places on the mainland that the Irish monks built their monasteries and hermitages. Celtic spirituality was the first European un-Romanized Christianity in human history and the only non-imperial Christianity in Europe. It developed without the socio political baggage of the Greco-Roman world.

Augustine played an important role in the building of a church very involved with dogmatism and authority. Like a huge multinational corporation, it sought to centralize control with its binding pronouncements made all over the Christian world. Celtic spirituality refused this model, Stating that the spark of divinity within each person must be the guiding light for humankind's spiritual development.

Augustine, however, as the great protagonist of central authority, insisted that Christians believe that we are all conceived in sin. He maintained that original sin had so corrupted human nature that our species had been hopelessly tainted with pride and selfishness. Like Adam and Eve, we, their progeny, were consumed with our own ego. We needed redemption to save us from ourselves. This could only be accomplished by the grace of God. This theology prevailed in the Roman Church all through the ages.

On the other hand, the Celtic Church stressed that immanence was the road we must follow into transcendence. This world was not a valley of tears; immanence was not inferior. This world was holy. God invaded the eroticism of our lovemaking; human procreation was Godlike and linked essentially to the divine. The line between the supernatural and the natural was thin.

Pelagius, a Celtic monk, disagreed with Augustine, insisting that children are born innocent, untainted by sin, and that sin only takes place because of each person's decision to commit it. Celtic spirituality insists that authority rests within ourselves and not in some outside force. Pelagius wrote:

> You will realize that doctrines are the inventions of the human mind, as it tries to penetrate the mind of God. You will also realize that Scripture itself is the work of the human mind, recording the example and teaching of Jesus. It is not what you believe that matters, it is how you respond with your heart and your actions. It is not believing in Christ that matters, but becoming like him.

He was condemned by the Roman Church as a heretic in AD 418.

The Celtic Church gathered to worship as close to nature as possible, mostly outdoors. They met in small communities and performed unique ceremonies that reflected their own inner guidance and indigenous experience. Kenneth Clark, in his series *Western Civilization*, wrote, "It is hard to believe that for quite a long time Western Christianity survived by clinging to places like Skellig Michael—a pinnacle of rock eighteen miles from the Irish Coast, rising seven hundred feet out of the sea."

The Roman Empire never reached Ireland, and as a consequence, Celtic Christianity developed unencumbered and free from centralized Roman authority. Patriarchy and hierarchy played no part in the early Celtic monasteries. Community, like everything else in Celtic Christianity, was based on the idea of the circle. The abbot, considered but a link in a chain, took his place in the circle to serve the community with his gifts whether as farmer or scribe. The Celtic Church never developed a centralized authority. It never held councils or synods.

Celtic spirituality was pluriform by nature. It was tolerant of diversity. Unlike their counterparts on the mainland of Europe, where the Church had become centralized and dogmatic, the monasteries of the Irish Church remained autonomous, each with its own abbot or abbess and its own distinct expression of Christianity. Celtic spirituality was not dogmatic. Surprisingly, its Christian inspiration did not come from Western Europe at all. Instead, Celtic Christianity was the outermost ripple in the monastic movement of the Coptic Church, and the Desert Fathers of Egypt and the Coptic Byzantine spiritually of the East stamped themselves on the asceticism of Celtic spirituality. It received the other great mark of its dynamism from the pagan Druidic cults of the Celts. Instead of rejecting the prevailing pagan culture, the Irish monks blessed and baptized it with the heartbeat of Christianity, colouring Druidic animism with a Christian perspective. Before embracing Christianity, the Celts worshiped many gods in Ireland, including Lugh, the god of light; Aengus Og, the god of youth; and Lir, the god of the sea. They fused these gods into the general Trinitarian approach.

We know of these two foundational influences on Celtic spirituality mainly from the art which the early Irish monks bequeathed to Western civilization. If we look carefully at the panels carved on some of the high crosses, we find representations of Eastern saints from the Egyptian desert.

Above the central carving of the crucified Christ on Muiredach's Cross in Monasterboice, the main house-cap panel shows two figures: St Anthony and St Paul of the Egyptian desert. A raven, who had only recently brought crusts of bread to Anthony in the desert, now brings a whole loaf to Paul, feeding both hermits. Similarly, on the High Cross of Moone, carvings of cichlids, Egyptian mouthbrooder fish, illustrate the Parable of the Loaves and Fishes. The Muiredach Cross also depicts St Michael holding a scale of justice, a carving probably influenced by the Egyptian Book of the Dead. Perhaps the greatest influence from the East can be seen in the gloriously illuminated manuscripts created in the Celtic scriptoriums. These books look almost Byzantine.

Celtic spirituality also found influence in its pre-Christian pagan heritage, never repudiating. Celtic Christianity evolved from a people who were not afraid to fuse the old with the new. The dolmens and various other monuments around which people gathered around to pray, were the architectural precursors to the high crosses, the round towers, the oratories, and the beehive huts.

The greatest of these monuments is Newgrange, a building five hundred years older than the oldest pyramid. At the entrance to this tomb lies a great rock inscribed with spirals. These spirals are indecipherable, but it has been suggested that they represent the seamless flow of the seasons from spring into winter and around back to spring again. Passage graves such as we see at Newgrange may not have been tombs at all, as no bones have been found in any of them. Their original purpose is shrouded in mystery. It is most often suggested that the Newgrange monument was built to capture the solstice of the winter sun, thereby giving valuable information to an agrarian society regarding the planting of the spring crops.

Looked at from the air, this site is swollen in a huge mound much like a womb, pregnant with life. This has suggested to scholars that these tombs were fertility chambers rather than mortuaries. The ancient Celts had a close affinity to the subterranean and the sensual. They were very much in touch with the dark, moist, fertile soil. For the greater part of two thousand years, the pagan Celts were neither puritanical nor dualistic, listening closely to the earth's cycles of fertility. They looked upon the earth and sexuality as generous blessings. They considered their holy wells to be openings into the womb of Mother Earth and the winter solstice to be the cosmic penetration and fertilization of the sun, thus connecting life on earth to the cosmos.

The spirals such as those at Newgrange inspired the early Celtic monks to incorporate this motif into their artwork to represent God's endlessness. We see this motif on the high crosses, in the illuminated manuscripts, and in the megalithic tombs or passage graves. At all of these sites there also exists an interplay between life and death, light and dark—a tension between opposites. This theme was later to become central to Celtic Christian spirituality. The early Irish monks repudiated duality and built their theology around the subterranean and the penumbral. They believed the seen is the surface of the unseen. A great oak tree is a manifestation of strength and glory, but its life and majestic limbs find their source in darkness, in the death of an acorn. Celtic spirituality, capitalizing on the symbols of light and dark, asks, "Who are we to deny the future wisdom of the seed?"

Celtic spirituality knows there is life in death and light in dark; there is no separation between the two. We live interdependently. What is deepest about us is subterranean. Spirituality is our potency. The oak tree's nourishment comes from both the light and the dark. Its leaves trap the sun's energy and its root system feeds underground, combining to create a full blossoming aboveground. We hold both light and dark, joy and pain, bravery and cowardice, life and death, all in the palm of our hand at the same time. Our moments of pain beget new birth. Our moments of humiliation are often our most redemptive ones. Possibilities are stressed by their opposite. We cannot be holy without temptation. We cannot have faith without doubt. All opposites are from the same reality. Bondage creates the urge for freedom.

Celtic spirituality, inspired by its observances at pagan sites like Newgrange, brought the wisdom of the light and the dark to bear on Christianity, only suggesting, never defining. "It is and it isn't" is its unequivocal answer. It leaves much to the imagination. It leaves much unsaid or half said. It passes over the discursive and the abstract. It allows the shadow its secrets.

Celtic spirituality dwells in the mystery of the ordinary. St Columbanus, a great European teacher, said, "If you want to know God, then first get to know His creation." Patrick Kavanagh, a contemporary Irish poet steeped in this tradition, writes what any mystical Celtic monk might have written a thousand years ago: "That beautiful, beautiful, beautiful God | Was breathing His love by a cut-away bog"; "God is in the bits and pieces of Everyday— | A kiss here and a laugh again, and sometimes tears, | A pearl necklace round the neck of poverty." For the early Irish monks, creation revealed God. Beauty raised one's consciousness. Everything pointed beyond itself to the Creator. God penetrates and consecrates the temporal. Ordinary life bespeaks what lies beyond. God breaks through in the ordinary and the familiar. Immanence and transcendence are joined together, Celtic spirituality insists. If we cut ourselves off from the earth, we become impoverished. That is why animals and the whole natural world figure so greatly in the Celtic Christian vision. If we exclude the Giver, then we become enslaved to the material.

Celtic Christianity is an outdoor Christianity. It stresses the inner friendship between heaven and earth, the underworld and overworld, the visible and invisible. The Celtic monk on his journey toward God went from immanence into transcendence. This is the opposite approach of the rest of Western religion. The Celtic monk insists that nature is holy and sacred, there for our careful use and nurture. For the early Celtic monks there was only a thin line between reality and the ineffable, between earth and heaven. Like their pagan ancestors, the Celtic monks believed in thin times and thin places, intersections between the spiritual world and the physical world.

Celtic spirituality is very much a down-to-earth spirituality. Any moment, any work can be a time or place to encounter God. Earth are joined together. Immanence is transcendent and transcendence is in immanence. The great Gothic tradition of Europe, where cathedral spires pierce the sky to signify transcendence, found no expression in Celtic spirituality. The everyday, ordinary world of nature was its cathedral.

Since God could not be defined—explanation is anathema to the Celtic mind—God is the incommunicable thirst for the incomprehensible. Silence and awe are the only answer. Early Celtic spirituality became swollen to the point of bursting with a spirit of curiosity and imagination. Nothing human was forbidden to this spirit of curiosity. Celtic monks wondered and wandered childlike, always full of astonishment. For them, heaven was but an inch and a half above the head of a man. They lamented, "What a pity to be surrounded by heaven and to take no notice of it."

Not only did the pagan megalithic tombs, with their symbolism of light and dark, life and death, impact greatly on the psyche of the early Irish monks, but so did pagan feasts, and monks incorporated them into the Christian calendar. Lughnasa, which honoured the god of the harvest, became a Christian feast of thanksgiving. Samhain, the feast of the dead and the underworld, became the Christian feast of Halloween. According to Celtic paganism, the dead go no place; they are still here, though in shadow form.

Celtic pagan symbols such as cromlechs and other megalithic stones became the inspiration for the round tower, an architectural form unique to early Irish monasteries. These towers, measuring some seven hundred feet tall, served as belfries and as places of refuge for sacred vessels and manuscripts during times of invasion and plunder. The entrance door was some ten feet off the ground and accessible only by a ladder. Once the monks had entered the tower, they pulled the ladder up after them. They then protected themselves and their sacred treasures by dropping rocks on the heads of the invaders as they climbed up their own ladders one at a time.

These early Celtic monks came from an educated class of Irish society. In "green martyrdom", they sought out a solitary asceticism modelled on the lifestyle of the monks in the Egyptian desert. In jagged outcroppings in the sea and in lonely green valleys they carved out their creation-centred spirituality. These monks saw all life as sacred. Even the smallest reed was interconnected to something greater, for all creation reflected God's magnificence. All being was interconnected and interrelated.

When wood and wattles were not plentiful, these monks built stone beehive huts and oratories to live and worship in. Since early Celtic spirituality was essentially an outdoor spirituality, the hermit's beehive oratory was primitive and small. Smallness was one of the hallmarks of Celtic spirituality. God, for the Celtic monk, lived in common statements. A little oratory served as a rood screen, much like the iconostasis of the Eastern Church. In these places, the consecration of the Eucharist was also kept shrouded in mystery. The clashing of light and dark, shadow and substance, became incorporated in the beehive oratories. An outstanding example of this appears in the Gallarus beehive oratory. To enter these small oratories, the monks bowed their bodies and bent their heads in total reverence.

In Celtic spirituality, the without and the within are joined as one. Balance finds its roots in imbalance. The behind is before and the before behind. Christ is with me, Christ is before me, Christ is behind me, Christ is beneath me, Christ is above me, Christ is in me. Christ when I lie down, Christ when I rise. Christ in every eye that sees me, Christ in every ear that hears me.

The ancient Celts' lives were inextricably entwined with the flow of the seasons. Water, wind, fire, the earth itself were primal to them. These sacred gifts reflected God's beneficence. Elsewhere in Europe, the Christian Church was fulminating against the natural world; nature was for exploitation. Not so for the early Celtic monks.

There is no plant in the ground but it is full of his virtue, there is no form on the strand but is full of his blessings. There is no bird on the wing nor star in the sky, there is nothing beneath but proclaims his goodness.

"Why, Morvan, sleepest thou not upon a feather quilt? Why sleepest thou abroad on a straw floor?"

"Kind sir, I have a hut in the wood. Only my Lord knows it. An ash tree closes in on one side and a hazel tree on the other. The size of my hut is small but not too small. The sun shines sideways through the open door. On its gable a she bird sings a sweet song in her black coat. A tree of apples of great beauty hangs plump for me. Fair white birds fly in from the sea. The sound of the wind is all around me. Couple-coloured skies, river falls, the cry of the swan. God is here with me.

The hermit monks lived in harmony with the natural world. They befriended the earth and nurtured it with love and respect. They lived on fruits and berries, trout, salmon, and the produce of their gardens. On the jagged rocks of the Atlantic where they built their hermitages, they lived on fish, seaweed, and seabirds' eggs. A poet tells us:

O Son of the living God, I desire a hidden hut in the wilderness for my home, a narrow little blue and silver stream beside it and a clear pool for the washing away of sin through the grace of the Holy Ghost. A lovely wood close about it on every side and a tree to nurse the birds with all sorts of voices and to hide them. With its shelter looking south for heat and a stream through its land and good fertile soil suitable for all plants. Enough of clothing and food from the king of fair fame. And to be sitting for a while and praying to God in every place. The woodland thicket overtops me. The bird sings on a

choir loft above my lined little booklet. The bird talks
to me. Truly may the Lord protect me. Well do I write
under the forest wood.

Since the early Irish monks came from the educated
class, word of their learning and spirituality began to spread,
and soon pilgrims sought them out. As more and more pilgrims
arrived, cities such as Glendalough and Clonmacnoise sprouted
up. Over time, these monastic cities became university cities,
and thousands of eager students from all over Europe flocked
to them. Like the monks, the students also lived in daub huts.
The physical conditions may have been primitive, but the
quality of education made up for it. These universities were
Christian in the best sense of the word. As The Venerable
Bede noted: "All these the Irish willingly received and saw to
it to supply them with food day by day and without cost and
books for their studies and teaching free of charge." Curiosity,
imagination, and an unquenchable thirst for learning were now
the hallmarks of Celtic spirituality. The monks specialized in
both religious and secular knowledge. They kept both Greek
and Latin literature alive during one of the darkest periods in
European history. They tirelessly copied all this literature in
their scriptoriums, and this priceless knowledge might have
been lost were it not for this effort.

Perhaps to relieve the boredom of constantly copying,
a monk once wrote on one of the scripts: "One day, someone
will say the hand that wrote this is no more." This monk from
the ninth century gives us an insight into his playfulness. On
the margin of a commentary from Virgil, the monk wrote this
delightful poem:

> I and Pangur Ban my cat
> 'Tis a like task we are at:
> Hunting mice is his delight,
> Hunting words I sit all night.
> 'Gainst the wall he sets his eye
> Full and fierce and sharp and sly;
> 'Gainst the wall of knowledge I

All my little wisdom try.

. . .

So in peace our task we ply,
Pangur Ban, my cat, and I

Many beautiful manuscripts rarely equalled in their genius also had their births in these Celtic scriptoriums. The books of Kells and Durrow are probably the most exquisite the world has seen. One can behold playfulness and imagination running through every page of them. Faithful to the pagan Celts' respect for nature, these great Christian manuscripts depicted animals and plants as interconnected. They take on an inscrutable, mystical overtone. They riff on circularity. Like God, the books tell us, there is no beginning and no end. These great works present no straight lines, telling us there are no straight answers, only curved ones. Nothing is final. All is circular. The intricacies of the penumbral and the shadow run rampant in life.

Of all the artefacts which the Celtic imagination has given us, none is more universally recognized Than the Celtic cross. The high crosses are books written in stone. Biblical passages were turned into carved panels by stonemason monks. The depiction of the last judgment carved in the tenth century on Muiredach's Cross at Monasterboice is a masterpiece. On one side of the cross, we see Christ in a flowing robe holding a cross and a flowering bough, which symbolizes the Resurrection. This is the Resurrected Christ of Glory. To Christ's right stand a piper and a harpist leading a parade of the elect, all facing Christ. On the left we see the damned driven away by devils, one armed with a fork and the other kicking the rejected into the fires of hell.

The opposite face of Muiredach's Cross shows the scene of the crucifixion. It seem gruesome. The carved man on the right thrusts a lance into the side of Christ, while the man on the left offers Christ a sponge steeped in vinegar. It is a scene of intense suffering. Yet if we look more closely, we notice that the arms and hands of Christ are huge, totally disproportionate to the rest of the body. If we were to look at this in a contemporary way with the eyes of a quantum evolutionist, this beautiful panel carved over ten centuries ago tells us, "Yes, there is darkness and death in our midst; we must not deny it. Crucifixion and suffering are very real. But the outstretched arm of the Christ tell us that God is not finished with us yet. Harmony will come out of chaos." Goodness and love in this world are far more revelatory than death and Chaos. In the end, God's compassion wins out when we accept matter as a flow into consciousness.

In Muiredach's Cross, we see the non-dualistic Celtic approach to life. The stone carver monk held the human experience of good and evil, death and life together in tension and balance. On one side of the high cross, the Christ of Glory is dressed in a long tunic; on the other side the crucified Christ is almost naked. This is a symbol of contradiction, telling us that out of the ashes of suffering comes new life. The circle of the Celtic cross represents the great 0 of creation. The interplay of light shining through the circle but obscured by the cross represents the tension between light and dark, joining them in one reality, showing us that we cannot have one without the other, that life is a continuum. This approach to reality is not Western. It came from Egypt. Irish Celtic Spirituality is non-imperial. It is based on the circle, not the straight line.

The powerful Roman Church, Aristotelian and dualistic to its core, was not prepared to tolerate this Eastern mentality in monasticism. When the Irish Celtic monks brought their learning to the continent of Europe, they paid little regard to Rome's imperialism, setting up monasteries without even consulting with the local bishop, much less Rome. One monk quipped, "If to Rome you want to go, know that you will not find him there unless you already carry him in your own heart." Rome's intolerance of Celtic spirituality increased in the cause of centrality and control. The rule of St Benedict became the norm for the West and Celtic spirituality faded away.

Most of us today live our lives in concrete and asphalt cities. All our bodily needs are adequately met by our supermarket chains and shopping malls. We have adapted to this life of convenience, and we rarely connect our food to the natural world. We see everything objectively with materialistic eyes used only for functional purposes. We rarely connect subjectively to appreciate the gifts which the natural world gives us for our sustenance. We are out of tune with the world of nature. We pay more attention to our toiletries and our lavatories than to the effortless functioning of our incredible bodies. If only our world paid more attention to the marvellous interconnection and interpenetration of all things natural, then indeed our prayers would be truly spiritual. Our kitchens are our centres for real prayer, much more than our churches. We think of ourselves as sophisticated and enlightened people, and we may think the Celtic way of prayer is quaint. It arose from an agrarian culture, so we may find it unsuitable for our more complicated machine-driven world. But the Celtic monks used their imaginations to adapt and embrace a pagan culture totally different from their own without destroying it. No matter where we live today, whether it be in a city or the country, if we are to become truly spiritual, then we, too, must use our imaginations and can make our prayers contemporary.

Nothing has changed in our ontological make-up since the Big Bang. We are all stardust. Our perspective may change, but our nature has not. We must recognize the common heritage of our stardust and formulate our prayers with a contemporary perspective. No matter where we live, we can invite the great non-local Intelligence into our homes and ask for guidance and assistance in the ordinary chores of our ordinary lives.

Even though we may be removed from the world of nature, still we carry with us our bodies, which proclaim the crowning achievement of God's creative glory. Just to be conscious of the magnificence of our own machine can be a wonderful prayer. Sometimes, also, we can say a beautiful wordless prayer if through our conscious connectedness to the vegetables we prepare to eat at our dinner tables.

Celtic spirituality can still teach us much about the human prospect. It centres on individual potential rather than the religion of a corporation. It calls for attentiveness and awareness. It makes each individual his or her own mediator between God and the world. It asks that we baptize the ordinary. If we accomplish our smallest task with mindfulness, then that is a prayer. Even when taking a shower or washing the dishes, we can be mindful that without water we would soon die, so water is a blessing. Water is inside us, making up 70 per cent of our bodies. Do we take it too much for granted? Are we good stewards of its preciousness? Perhaps only people in drought-parched lands know how to appreciate the beneficence of water. Their rain dance is a prayer. We can do without oil, but never water.

Haughty centres of power and control, whether they be political or religious, are not God's favourite places. The great non-local Intelligence cannot be pleased when considered a mere afterthought. The Western way of prayer is too strong on petition and too weak on reverence. The European Constitution never mentions the living God's name, but if our planet is to survive, then it must integrate spirituality with materiality. Science must be balanced with prayer. Our world will continue and prevail only through the incremental reintroduction of spirituality into all human affairs. This will come primarily from our individual mindfulness which in turn will embrace the whole planet.

A CELTIC PRAYER

The curtain of night hangs across the sky once more, having accomplished another flawless mission to turn away from the sun. We travel a million miles a day, yet I do not even sense a creak as the planet makes its flight. Who put the nuts and bolts into our planets wings? What mind, what energy keeps its engines running? We live out life's preciousness in a fragile eco-ship of interrelatedness and interdependence. Our consciousness has been cast in a forge of precise temperature. Its hammering has been exactly calculated for our begetting. With a quadrillionth of a one per cent margin of error, our planet made an astounding soft landing. Elements combined, and we were born out of the hot embers of stars. You have created us from stardust, O Lord of the flow.

What a journey we've been on! We have come a long way from molten lava to Jesus of Nazareth and Mozart. Elaborate planning down to the smallest of details is now evident in our genesis story. Sister Venus, too close to the sun, would boil our bodies into vapour. Brother Mars, distant and cold, would turn our hearts into stone. The moon, whose precise features look like mountains of snow from where I stand, invite me to take an astounding sleigh ride into wonder. The silver saucer in the sky, impudent daughter of the sun, determines the waves of our seas, flowing in and out. Without the precise pull of the moon's gravity, the seas of the earth would stand stagnant, causing consciousness to collapse.

O great secret, non-local Intelligence, Cosmic Tree, God, whatever we call you, it is never enough. There is no prayer sufficient to bless you, yet I feel compelled to praise you. Hail to you, Sacred Centre, Engine of Energy, King of all Life-making! Be my eye that integrates me. Be my voice which calls praise in my enthusiasm for you. May the moon of all moons who comes through the vapour of the clouds shine on me and every one of us upon the earth, suspended as we are in mortal fragility.

Fair God, you are the outside, greater than any of us, and yet you have knitted us together with the stitches of your care. We find you inside of us, near and accessible. How incredible that you, the King of the universe, should want to live in the humble abode of our humanity! You are the all, the underjacket of the sun, the overcoat of all the stars, the totality of the galaxies.

The heartbeat that pumps the sun's energy is the same heartbeat which pumps energy in me. I hold a candle in my hand as a mediator between night and morn, and like the candlelight, I too must learn the secret of life's inconclusive shadows. I rejoice in this little light. I crave not the big beam which destroys mystery. Far better you avoid full disclosure, for it would make you too small for a future-emergent imagination. May I project you more than I reject you. You are as real to me as insubstantial love and laughter. You are as inscrutable as our singing or crying. I grow to know it is in the deprivation of definition that I find you.

Deliver me from the drudgery of empirical science, which denies you as the all-encompassing Intelligence. How stupid of men to admire the painting but not the artist. You are the God of divine hiddeness. I have no choice but to surrender. You are the God of consciousness. You live beyond the revelation of the atom smasher. You are the only Expert!

You live in the land where opposites clash. There is disturbance and suffering involved in the churning of the child, but through your entanglement with the human story, harmony comes out of chaos. Streams must lower themselves from a more lofty height in their urgency to reach the sea. Sour milk is the base but butter the top. Fragile life becomes numinous through a slit in stone wall. I sense you on the thin edge. The cascade of green leaves on a tree come out to play because of subterranean prodigiousness. All life is penumbrally rooted.

And so on the morrow, in my own small routine, I will begin my day in the name of your hidden inscrutability. Overcoat of the whole universe, cast your careful eye in my direction. Be with me in my sleeping and in my waking. The planet moves on its axis, and what seemed the west to my un-awakened eye has now become the east. You possess a pulley unknown to humans. O Great Enterpriser, I worship the effortlessness of your engineering genius. While I have slept, unconscious, you watched over me in my bedroom to serve me a morning menu. I must be up and on my way. It is a new day for churning yellow butter. Universal Shepherd, ever thanks to you that the gentle light of another morning has invaded my sleeping room. I arise with the energy through which you engender me. O Great Secret, I bless you. Even now as I am covering my body with the yarn spun from the sheep in our yellow meadow, I ask you to keep me so completely warm that every corpuscle of my blood, red and white, will rush, exercised with your inbred presence. I splash my face with the water of the Great Well-giver. With a palmful of your condensation, I wash myself. Refreshing, sacred water, stuff of life. I praise you, God, for your generous overflowing. Blessed water, main ingredient in my cup of morning tea, main ingredient in me. I splash my face with my God's provident love When I splash my face with you.

Beyond the window of my bedroom, a tapestry of pink and golden thread has been hatching in the maternity room of the sky, slowly at first, with only a suggestion of future glory, but then like a hen's egg, the sun splashes out on the lower roof of the eastern sky. A young love cannot be impeded. Earth becomes a green paradise through the miracle of photosynthesis. The natural world basks in the baking of new nourishment. Cattle in the midst of a young morning appear as though they are walking on water like Jesus coming over the lake.

O God, bless unto me each thing my eyes see this day. O God, bless each odour which catches on the hair filtering my nostrils. Bless also each sound which whispers through the hills and valleys of my ears. Bless, O God, the voluptuous tastes which kiss my tongue. You are the music in the notes of my song. I bless you as the Creator of all that comes my way.

Make me aflamed with kindness to share the bread of my bakery and the butter of my churn with any stranger who comes begging. May I see Christ in everyone. My neighbour, my foe, my friend, to my kindred all, may I enkindle them. Come and eat breakfast with my kindred, Lord. Feel comfortable with us. Be thou our unseen Guest in our eating and our drinking. May we be the outward sign of your invisibleness.

As we are linked to you for our nurture, so may we be linked to the cow for her milk and her butter and the whole food chain for our sustenance. Fair wheat, with your golden head, you blow in our morning bread. Three seasons of ripples are in your baked appearance: A sowing, a growing, and harvest. We are married to your seed. We are shaken by the same wind that first fire-fed you. Seed feeds seed. We return as fertilizer to some future seed. Who am I to deny your wisdom? All that is is the genesis for what will be, synergistically. O Great Yeast, your implosion seeds explosion. You are the swell of the future. You are ahead of before. Give us, O God of the morning meal, nourishment for our bodies, which frame our souls.

You unite us, God. You untangle our knots and knit us together in an integrated way. You are our primary purpose; all else is secondary. Lord, be with us by night and be with us by day. May we hear you in the whistle of the kitchen kettle. Be with us in our lying down and in our getting up, in our speech, in our walk, in our work. Bless the farmer who milks the cows, which give us cream and butter. Bless, O God, each teat. Bless, O God, each finger. Bless thee each drop that falls into our buckets.

Sacred. giving animals, through thick of dark, Through light of day, through rain and sun, faithfully carry on and provide us with blessings which we take too much for granted. When was the last time I thanked a cow for its milk? Or stood and praised a tree for its generous flow of oxygen?

The wide stretch of the awakened sun has turned the morning into day. It laughs through the half door with searching fingers which invite us to go forth and energize what has been given to us. We must be on our way. Be with us, Lord, in everything we do this day. Be in the bread we bake, be in our knitting and darning, be in our spouse, our children, and in our lovemaking.

There is not a plant in the ground but you are in the underground of it. There is no fish in the sea that sees without your eyes. There is no bird in the sky that flies without you navigation. Nothing lives without your authority. Nothing exists beneath the sun that does not reflect your beauty. You alone address the irresistible ache in the human heart for completion. Pain and ugliness surround us daily. It is only you who can convert chaos into harmony. So far we are your greatest expression on the evolutionary tree. Give us the courage to climb one step higher, to discover more your glory. True prayer is a pleasure. It is a circle. Our beginning is our end and our end is but another beginning. We make a step only to discover you are already here, not around us or above us or under us but inside of us. Our greatest prayer is the inward one. We thank you, Lord. We remain a mystery. Our greatest discovery is you inside each one of us. When we discover this, harmony and peace will reign on our planet. We blow the candle out. Good night.

ABOUT THE BOOK

Religionless Spirituality claims that neither religion nor materialistic science satisfies the ache of the human heart for meaning or significance. We have experienced wonderful progress through the advances of science. Unfortunately, our achievements in many respects have become our atrocities.

Since the Enlightenment, mechanistic science has insisted that it is only through reason that we can objectively prove anything, thereby excluding all subjective experience. This is the predominant paradigm by which capitalism and materialism prevail. Modern society has almost completely adopted this model. Because of this near total embrace, the environment of the human habitat is becoming more and more threatened. Through this model we infer that infinite growth can fit into a finite world. The ego is catered to as a consequence, but our spirit grows ever more impoverished. What use is verification by the human eye if the subjective experience of sight is excluded? Science explains but tells us nothing of experience. We need a spirit of transcendence, something that lies beyond matter, to explain the human construct.

This is where spirituality enters. Religion, for its own ends, has politicized spirituality and co-opted for power and control. Individually, spirituality calls us to reclaim the birthright of God's divinity alive within each of us. True spirituality calls us to look to the power within. True spirituality belongs to each individual. We must adopt a new paradigm, decontaminate ourselves from organized religion, and see our own individual divinity.

ABOUT THE AUTHOR

Patrick Mooney was born in County Laois in Ireland. He was ordained a priest at the Catholic University of America, and he subsequently devoted his vocation not only to ministering in a parish hospital and school but also to the art of writing and photography. Convinced that the Church needed a new form of stained glass windows to awaken its members to the glory and magnificence of ordinary life, he devoted much of his energy to the development of audiovisual meditation programmes on topics such as family life, child-parent relationships, poverty, the environment, the liturgical feasts of Christmas and Easter, the third world, sacramental theology, and Celtic spirituality. Most of these programmes are now available on Mooney's website, SpiritualSpring.com. He is the author of *Praise to the Lord of the Morning*, published by Notre Dame University Press, and his other written work has been published by Paulist Press, Alpha Corporation, and Twenty-Third Publications.

Mooney is presently involved in retreat work based on the theology of Celtic spirituality in his native Ireland.

Made in United States
North Haven, CT
14 August 2025

71694834R00166